HIKING AND BIKING PERU'S
INCA TRAILS

About the Author

Will 'KB' Janecek grew up in the US on a small lake in Minnesota, where he learned his love of the outdoors from his father. After a narrow and daring escape from an office cubicle, he rediscovered his passion for adventure activities. His pursuit of high-altitude mountain biking and trekking led him first to Colorado and then Europe and Africa, before finally settling in Ollantaytambo, Peru where he runs a small hotel and adventure tour guide business (www.kbperu.com). In his spare time, he enjoys drinking coffee, listening to music, and high-altitude mountain biking and trekking (preferably all three simultaneously).

HIKING AND BIKING PERU'S INCA TRAILS

by KB (Will) Janecek

CICERONE

2 POLICE SQUARE, MILNTHORPE, CUMBRIA LA7 7PY
www.cicerone.co.uk

© Will Janecek 2013
First edition 2013
ISBN: 978 1 85284 631 2

Printed in China on behalf of Latitude Press Ltd.
A catalogue record for this book is available from the British Library.
All photographs are by the author unless otherwise stated.

lovelljohns.com   Base mapping by Lovell Johns

Route mapping by Clare Crooke

Dedication

To John McKinney for introducing me to the mountains; my brother Charles for spending twenty years with me playing in them; and to Colleen Elizabeth Faye for reminding me just how precious it all really is.

Advice to Readers

While every effort is made by our authors to ensure the accuracy of guidebooks as they go to print, changes can occur during the lifetime of an edition. If we know of any, there will be an Updates tab on this book's page on the Cicerone website (www.cicerone.co.uk), so please check before planning your trip. We also advise that you check information about such things as transport, accommodation and shops locally. Even rights of way can be altered over time. We are always grateful for information about any discrepancies between a guidebook and the facts on the ground, sent by email to info@cicerone.co.uk or by post to Cicerone, 2 Police Square, Milnthorpe LA7 7PY, United Kingdom.

Front cover: A herd of llamas near Ausangate (Routes 39 and 40)

CONTENTS

WARNING

All mountain activities contain an element of danger, with a risk of personal injury or death. Treks described in this guidebook are no exception. Under normal conditions, wandering the trails of the Sacred Valley will be neither more nor less hazardous than walking among big mountains anywhere in the world, but trekking involves physically demanding exercise in a challenging landscape, where caution is advised and a degree of stamina is often required, and it should be undertaken only by those with a full and proper understanding of the risks involved, and with the training and experience to evaluate them. Trekkers should be properly equipped for the routes undertaken. The effects of altitude and the potential for altitude sickness (AMS) or worse, and how to deal with it, should be understood before you go trekking.

While every care and effort has been taken in the preparation of this guide, the user should be aware that conditions can be highly variable and change rapidly. Rockfall, landslide and crumbling paths can alter the character of the route, and the presence of snow and the possibility of avalanche must be carefully considered, for these can materially affect the seriousness of a trek.

Readers are warned that trekkers sometimes die of hypothermia or acute mountain sickness; others simply lose their balance and fall from the trail due to a momentary loss of concentration. Since there is no organised mountain rescue service in the Sacred Valley, such as exists in some mountain regions of Europe and the US, if an accident occurs self-help may be the only option. Note too, that where it is possible to summon a rescue helicopter, the cost of doing so is very high and guarantee of payment essential. Make sure your insurance includes such costs, and carry a credit card with sufficient funds to back its use for the initial call-out.

Everyone trekking in the Sacred Valley should assume responsibility for their own safety and look to the needs of those with them. This includes especially members of a trek crew, as well as fellow trekkers.

Therefore, except for any liability which cannot be excluded by law, neither Cicerone Press nor the author accepts liability for damage of any nature (including damage to property, personal injury or death) arising directly or indirectly from information given in this guide.

Acknowledgments

There are two groups of people without whom this book simply would not have been possible. The first group is those good folk at Cicerone Press. I used to wonder why there were accolades in every book for its editors and other literary professionals, but now I can see why. Watching them take my manuscript and turn it into a definitive adventure book for the Sacred Valley of Peru was a true pleasure. Thanks to Jonathan for believing in the project and to map creator Clare Crooke, who was more than any other person responsible for bringing it to press.

The second group of people that made this book possible are some of the people I have shared an adventure with in the mountains. There are too many to list here, but each one taught me something during the journey. Those who made a particular impression were: my brother Charles Janecek, Matt Ryan, Justin Kleiter, Dan Walsh, Rob Dehoff, Manny Duerson, Jose Manuel Ortiz, Robert Visina, Farnham and Dee St. John, Chet Jarvis, Chris Korn, Cory Ctvrtnik, Chad and Alaya Sexton, Jason Deflorin, Carl Fluhri, Johnny Mac, my sister Betsy and her family, my sister Tracy and her family, Steve Koehler, my father Bill, Alistair Mathew, Sarah Baldwin, Quinn Filla, Chris Phillippi, Mike Masteller, Joe Kaplan, the Martin family, Yoshi, Graham Hannegan, Lluc and Chrissy, Alejandro Puente Emeril and Tio Raul, Richard and Raul Cobos, Smith Nguyen, Pepe Lopez, Daisy Jung, Dustin and Mikey, Clyde Thomas, Alex and Joshue Tehran Guzman, the Cobos brothers at Hostal Sixpac and Leoncio and Agara. Thinking of every one of you brings a smile – and a memory of getting lost somewhere! Thank you all.

Map Key

━━━━━	paved road	**Ⓑ**	bridge
┅ ┅ ┅ ┅	2wd track	⓪	archaeological site
═══════	4wd track	◑	Incan steps
··············	footpath	🛆	camp
▪▪▪▪▪▪▪▪	railway	⤬	pass
━━━━━	route	⏟	steps
────────	river	⛪	church
⬭	lake	•	place
	glacier	■	building
⊙	village	←	direction arrow
	town	←	route direction
▲	peak	●	waterfall

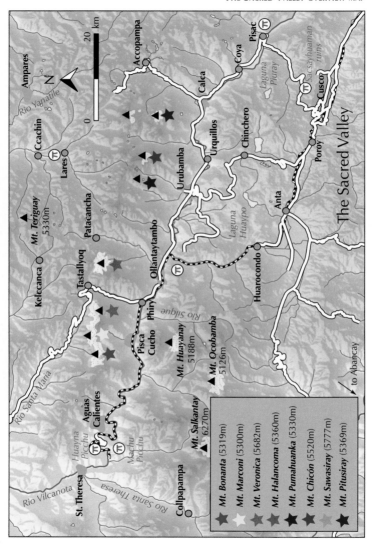

THE SACRED VALLEY overview map

9

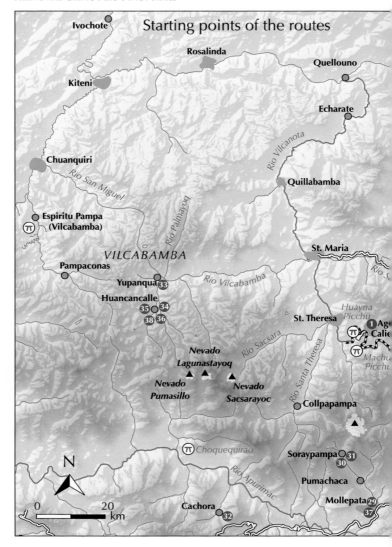

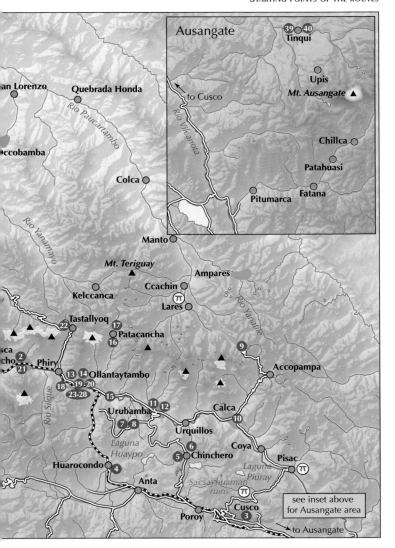

Ausangate

39 ○ 40
Tinqui

to Cusco

Upis ○

Mt. Ausangate ▲

Chillca ○

Patahuasi

Pitumarca ○   Fatana ○

Rio Vilcanota

see inset above
for Ausangate area

→ to Ausangate

an Lorenzo ○   Quebrada Honda ○

Rio Paucartambo

ccobamba ●

Colca ○

Rio Yanamayo

Manto ○

Mt. Teriguay ▲

Ampares ▲

Ccachin ○
π
Lares ○

Kelccanca ○

Rio Yanatile

Tastallyoq ○   22   17
                16 Patacancha ▲

sca
cho   2   Phiry
      21

13 14 Ollantaytambo
18
19·20
23-28   15   11 12
        Urubamba   Calca
      7 8   10
              Urquillos

Accopampa ○

9

Rio Sique

Laguna
Huaypo

5 6 Chinchero

Coya ○   Pisac ○
                        π
Laguna
Piuray

Huarocondo ○   4

Anta ●

Sacsayhuaman
ruins
π

Poroy ○   Cusco
        3

11

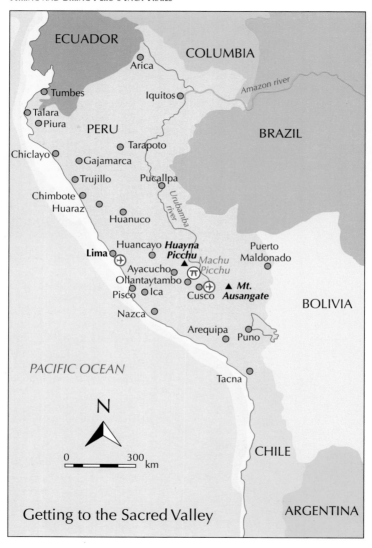

ECUADOR

COLUMBIA

Arica

Iquitos

Amazon river

Tumbes

Talara
Piura

PERU

BRAZIL

Tarapoto

Chiclayo

Gajamarca

Trujillo

Pucallpa

Urubamba river

Chimbote
Huaraz

Huanuco

Huancayo   *Huayna*
Picchu

Puerto
Maldonado

Lima   ⊕

Machu
Picchu

Ayacucho   π

Ollantaytambo

Pisco   Ica   ⊕   ▲ *Mt.*
Ausangate

Nazca   Cusco

BOLIVIA

Arequipa

PACIFIC OCEAN   Puno

N

Tacna

0   300 km

Getting to the Sacred Valley

CHILE

ARGENTINA

FOREWORD

For 30 years, I've wandered the coastal deserts, eastern jungles and high country of the Andean world, finding fabulous scenery, wonderful people, unstudied history and adventure at every turn. There's no place on earth with more to offer the imaginative traveller, whether on foot or mountain bike, and nowhere is this more true than in the old Inca heartland, surrounding their once-great imperial capital at Cusco, Peru. The nearby Sacred Valley of the Río Vilcanota, the Inca Trail to Machu Picchu and the 'lost' province of Vilcabamba have long provided some of the finest trekking in the world.

Now, my old friend and fellow explorer, Will (KB) Janecek, a veteran with years of experience travelling these routes by both foot and pedal has produced a guide to many of these spectacular trails. This guide, with its clear, simple route descriptions and handy, reader-friendly maps, opens up a vast, historic region to anyone with a fit body, proper gear and an adventurous spirit. Thanks to KB, all of us can enjoy memorable biking and trekking experiences once limited to the fortunate few.

Of the hordes of tourists that annually visit Cusco, the Sacred Valley, Machu Picchu and the Inca Trail, surprisingly few people get off the beaten track and into the back-country opened up by this guidebook. An especially rare treat awaits those who venture out into the still remote province of Vilcabamba (Espiritu Pampa – Route 38). Once the Incas' last stronghold when their world came apart in the face of the Spanish Conquest, it remains seldom visited and free of the increasingly pervasive influence of the outside world. Here among soaring 6,000m, ice-draped peaks, the intrepid visitor will find several hundred kilometers of intact Inca roads leading to fascinating ruins only recently cut from the tropical cloud forest. The few local residents continue to live on farms and in villages preserving much of the ancient flavor of the Andean highlands, while offering friendly, comfortable services to visitors. Recent years have also seen the introduction of many kilometers of rustic new roads offering ideal conditions for mountain bike trips.

Wherever you decide to go in this fascinating region, and whether you travel on foot or on tyres, this guidebook will be an invaluable companion. You just need to get out there and go!

Vince Lee

Architect, explorer and archaeologist and author of
Forgotten Vilcabamba: Final Stronghold of the Incas

Crossing the river near Kelccanca (Route 17)

INTRODUCTION

Climbing down a ridgeline of Mt. Veronica with Ollantaytambo in the background (Route 21)

Peru... Even the name sounds exotic, and this incredible country certainly won't disappoint. With its majestic snow-capped peaks, Incan ruins, roaring rivers and Amazon jungle resorts, Peru seems to be a country created for adventure lovers.

Peru is a country of extremes: it has the driest desert, longest river and biggest snakes, and the geography is no exception. The eastern slope of the Peruvian Andes is one of the most dramatic and biologically diverse places on the planet, dropping from over 6000m (20,000ft) of altitude to just 200m above sea level, all in less than a few hundred kilometres. This dramatic drop in elevation produces a wide range of constantly changing climactic and vegetative zones, and one can often hike from the base of a glacier down to the jungle in just a day or two. The beautiful terrain, combined with the countless number of Inca archaeological sites along the way, are just two reasons why the trekking and mountain biking in Peru are among the best in the world.

THE STORY OF THE INCAS

By most accounts, the highlands around Cusco were occupied up to the time of the Incas by a series of small local tribes, unorganized until sometime after AD600, when the peoples now known as the Huaris, or Waris, thrived. It is believed that the Huari culture was responsible for the style of many of the pre-Incan settlements and forts that still dot the hilltops of the Sacred Valley. At some point, probably early in the 14th century, the Huari culture and peoples declined, and the Incas rose to power and took their place.

Technically, the word 'Inca' refers specifically and exclusively to the highest line of royal rulers and it is not correct to refer to the entire civilization as Inca. However, the name has come to mean just that in modern times and thus the word Inca is used in this guidebook to describe the civilization as a whole.

Because the Incas had no system of writing, much of what we know about their early history is murky and has probably been reshaped many times – first by the Incas themselves, in order to paint a rosier and more glorious picture to their subjects and to the many other empires they conquered. It was then rewritten a second time by the Spanish, who naturally sought to portray themselves and their conquest of Peru in a more sympathetic light.

The Incas' spiritual history of their origins comes in two versions, but both of them involve Lake Titicaca and a white, bearded god known as Viracocha. The more common story is that the first Inca, Manco Capac, left Lake Titicaca with his brothers and sister-wives and travelled to Peru, emerging from the sun itself at a place called Pacaritambo (literally in Quechua 'rest house of tomorrow' but translated as 'house of the dawn'). This temple, located just outside of Ollantaytambo, was one of the most sacred Inca shrines and still exists today, although it is not well known. Every year at the winter solstice the morning's first rays of sunlight shine directly on the same door out of which Manco Capac is said to have emerged from the sun and into their new kingdom.

What was to become one of the world's greatest empires apparently had a rather humble beginning, and seven or eight generations of leaders came and went with little fanfare until the ninth Inca, Viracocha Inca. Around the year AD1438 there was a battle with the neighbouring enemy tribe, the Canchas or Chankas, and the Incas were losing. Viracocha and his firstborn son and heir fled the scene to avoid being captured or killed. A second son stayed behind and, with the reported and convenient assistance of many field stones that turned into warriors, defeated the Chankas and won the battle. His name was Pachacutec or Pachacuti ('he who moves the earth' in Quechua), and although many of his accomplishments may be embellished, he nonetheless remains

The classic shot of Machu Picchu, one of the Seven Wonders of the Modern World

one of South American history's most important and influential figures.

Pachacutec is given the credit for the construction of both Cusco and Machu Picchu, as well as of a great many of the empire's greatest buildings in the Sacred Valley area, such as Sacsayhuaman and Ollantaytambo. Some disagreement exists as to how much was actually built under Pachacutec and how much by his son and successor, Tupac Yupanqui or Topa Inca. What is known is that very early in his reign, in order to survey his new kingdom, Pachacutec travelled to both Lake Titicaca and the Tiahuanaco site in Bolivia, as well as to the Vilcabamba region of Peru. It seems likely that, in creating the architectural style for which the Incas would become famous, he borrowed heavily from the large stonework at Tiahuanaco. Some even believe that during his travels to Vilcabamba he saw the site of Choquequirao (built by an earlier civilization that had come up from the jungle), and combined its mountaintop grandeur with the elaborate stonework of Tiahuanaco to create his own work at Machu Picchu.

In any event, his son Topa Inca without a doubt then embarked on a massive expansion of the Inca empire, reaching as far north as Ecuador and as far south as Chile. His rule was marked by further development of the Inca society and government. They organized labour and began a

17

The trail to Yanama, with the Pumasillo massif in the background
(Routes 34, 35 and 36)

massive campaign of civil works that included waterways, food storehouses and an international network of paved roadways throughout the Andes. Their advanced statehood allowed them to assimilate many of the other civilizations they conquered without ever lifting a weapon. Indeed, it is reported that most Inca conquests were not violent – rather, the Incas would use the inducement of a healthy supply of food, which they were willing to share with their future colony, and they had the wisdom to offer the local chief the opportunity to continue as leader if he offered up his subjects to Incan rule. This was an attractive proposition to the majority of the conquered tribes; the rest were simply defeated in battle by the superior size of a well-fed Inca army, supported by reinforcements moving efficiently via the royal road system.

The empire continued to prosper and flourish, and after Topa Inca's death power was handed to his son Huayna Capac, who oversaw the final expansions of the Incan empire into southern Chile and, finally, to Quito in Ecuador ('Quito' in Spanish literally means 'I quit', as in 'I stop here'). In an ominous foreboding of what was to come, an epidemic tore through all ranks of Inca society and killed off huge numbers. Modern historians believe the disease was smallpox, which had probably migrated down from Mexico and Panama, where Cortés and other

Spanish *conquistadores* had subdued Aztec and local populations through military might. It is probable that, in addition to their military prowess, the Spanish were greatly aided by the devastation wrought upon the locals by the same germs that would soon weaken the Incas.

Huayna Capac himself, as well as his firstborn son and heir, were killed by the sickness, and a dispute over his rightful heir soon plunged the empire into civil war. Already weakened by the smallpox epidemic, Inca society was further weakened by battles between the two opposing sides, Huascar in Cusco and Atahualpa in Ecuador. Atahualpa was reportedly an illegitimate son and heir, being born to an Ecuadorian princess not of Inca royal blood. Eventually, after a prolonged and contentious campaign, Atahualpa defeated and then imprisoned his half-brother Huascar. Huascar was to die in prison of uncertain causes – either murder or smallpox seem the two most likely.

In a very short time, one of history's most powerful empires had slowed to a halt. The double blow of civil war and epidemic had left Inca society severely crippled, and then along came a small group of Spanish conquistadores looking for a country to conquer, preferably one with lots of gold and beautiful women – and they landed in Peru.

Francisco Pizarro and his two brothers had sailed south from Panama and in 1527 had encountered an oceangoing raft occupied by Peruvian fishermen or traders. Setting ashore in Tumbes in northern Peru near the border with Ecuador, they were soon met by representatives of the Inca Atahualpa, who was resting inland at Cajamarca. It was arranged for the Spanish to meet with the Inca, and they travelled to Cajamarca before camping the final night on the outskirts of the Inca city.

By all accounts, the Spanish must have wondered what they had got themselves into, as they were reportedly outnumbered by nearly 10,000 Inca warriors. After spending a no-doubt sleepless night under the watchful campfires of the massive and orderly Inca army, the next morning the Spanish explorers went down to the plaza and waited for several hours. Finally, the Inca Atahualpa arrived amid great pomp and circumstance to the main square of Cajamarca, carried on a litter above the ground by his attendants.

As the story goes, he was met in the plaza by a Spanish priest who offered him a copy of the Bible. The Inca (probably because he didn't know how to read) reputedly threw the Bible to the ground, which was more than enough reason for the Spanish to justify their attack. In such a brief and sudden moment that the story's veracity must perhaps be questioned, the Inca leader was surrounded by Spanish soldiers on horses who stormed the plaza on cue to a prearranged signal. Then followed a brief but furious battle, during which the Inca's bewildered attendants attempted to defend him against both horses and steel swords – neither of which they had ever seen before. It was over in a matter of minutes, and Pizarro seized the Inca, and thus history itself, in his hands.

No one really knows for sure why the Inca warriors waiting just outside the city did not attack the Spanish army and use their superior numbers to overcome them. It is said it was due to direct orders from the Inca himself, who feared for his life and hoped to find a way to save himself. For whatever reason, the Inca army never attacked and Atahualpa was left to negotiate his famous ransom, offering the Spanish enough gold and silver to fill two rooms in exchange for his life.

They quickly agreed and thus began one of the most prolific transfers of wealth of all time, as llama caravans from throughout the kingdom were ordered to proceed to Cajamarca with as many riches as they could muster, and quickly. In less than two months the rooms were filled up to the agreed upon height.

Ironically, Atahualpa had almost certainly sealed the fate of both himself and his people's way of life, because once the Spanish saw the astonishing amount of gold and silver the Incas possessed, the outcome was never in doubt. On the pretence of fearing that Atahualpa was planning an armed escape and rebellion, the Spanish quickly held a mock trial, declared him guilty of treason and sentenced him to death by burning.

A biker overlooking the pass above Tastallyoq (Route 14)

He could, they assured him, avoid being burned (which the Inca believed would prevent him from going on to the afterlife) by declaring allegiance to the Bible, and they promised merely to hang and bury him instead. Atahualpa reportedly then pledged his faith in the Christian word; to the surprise of no-one who has ever studied history, the Spanish hanged him and then burned his body anyway.

And so, with one stroke, the Spanish effectively ended an empire. The Inca society's autocratic style of government meant that it was crippled without its leader, especially when the loss was combined with the damage wrought by the smallpox epidemic and subsequent civil war. The Spanish encountered relatively little resistance as they marched on Cusco and declared it for the Spanish crown in a ceremony on 23 March 1534. Life after the Conquest was by no means peaceful, however, and nearly all of the original conquistadores suffered a violent death at the hands of either Inca revolutionaries or their own jealous countrymen. As they continued their harsh treatment of the local natives, a young Inca royal, who had been set up as a puppet ruler to keep the masses happy, organized a massive rebellion that nearly succeeded in changing history. The story is a fascinating one, all the more so because many of the routes in this book go over the exact same terrain as that travelled by this Inca revolutionary.

The young man's name was Manco Inca, and he would prove himself brave and cunning in his attempts to shake off Spanish control of his people. In the spring of 1536 he organized a massive rebellion and set fire to Cusco in an attempt to kill off the Spanish. The narrow streets of the city were piled high with brush and stones to prevent them escaping on horseback. However, the Spanish managed to fight their way through and up the hill to Sacsayhuaman, from where the Incas were staging their attack. After storming and taking the tower (although Juan Pizarro was killed by an Inca slingshot to the head), the Spanish regained control and put several thousand Incan warriors to the sword. Manco Inca escaped to Ollantaytambo, from where the Spanish tried unsuccessfully a few times to flush him out. Ollantaytambo remains the only place where the Incas defeated the Spanish in battle.

Unfortunately, the thrill of victory would prove to be short-lived: reinforcements were sent from Cusco, and Manco Inca was forced to choose a more defensible location. He chose Vilcabamba, a rugged and remote region to the northwest that had previously been conquered by Pachacutec and that already had an infrastructure of many impressive buildings. The area was ideal, located in the midst of massive mountains that presented very difficult access for an invading army. Nonetheless, the Spanish

The remains of Manco Inca's palace 'Vitcos', in the Vilcabamba (just off Routes 33 to 36 and Route 38)

pursued them relentlessly, following them over the Incan road from Ollantaytambo, over the pass of Abra Malaga and up into the Vilcabamba. The Spanish army advanced on Vilcabamba despite the difficulties of the terrain, and ransacked Manco Inca's palace at Vitcos, attempting but failing to capture him. They did, however, capture his son Titu Cusi. After this defeat Manco Inca was forced to move his rebel base further down into the jungle at Espiritu Pampa. He was assassinated in 1544 at the site of Vitcos by Spanish visitors on a diplomatic mission.

After a weak and ineffectual reign by Sayri Tupac, and then a longer but peaceful period of rule by Titu Cusi, another son of Manco Incas, named Tupac Amaru, took over the helm and began an aggressive campaign against Spanish rule. In April 1572, after Amaru killed a Spanish envoy, the Viceroy Francisco de Toledo declared war and sent out a war party to end the rebellion once and for all. And end it they did – first by capturing Vilcabamba and then by finally capturing the great Inca rebel leader himself. Tupac Amaru, the final hope of the great Inca empire, was executed in the plaza of Cusco, beheaded in front of his subjects, and so ended one of the greatest civilizations the world has ever known.

THE SACRED VALLEY

The 'Sacred Valley of the Incas' is that part of Peru generally defined as the area being bordered by Mount Ausangate to the east, Abancay to the west, and the Urubamba and Apurimac Rivers making up the north and south borders, respectively. Woven throughout this mountainous area are many glaciated peaks over 5000m, connected by numerous Inca roads, many still in excellent condition despite being over 700 years old. Clinging high to the mountainsides in typical Inca fashion, these roads and trails provide superb opportunities for trekking and mountain biking. This is what sets Peru apart from other destinations – the dramatic alpine scenery, combined with the spectacular Inca archaeological sites to be found along the trails. Nearly every route in this book uses an Inca road or visits an Inca ruin – and most do both.

Within this area is, of course, the world-famous archaeological site of Machu Picchu, widely regarded as one of the Seven Wonders of the Modern World. But there are also literally hundreds of other Inca ruins scattered throughout the Valley. Some, like Choquequirao, Vitcos, Pumamarca, Sacsayhuaman, Moray and others are well known and frequented. Yet many more like Pitumarca, Inca Wasi, Inti Punku, Ñaupa Iglesia and others remain relatively unvisited and await only your arrival. Indeed, there are

The mountaintop perch of the well-preserved Incan site of Inca Wasi (Route 33)

23

very few places that can boast of the archaeological richness of the Sacred Valley of Peru.

Most travellers come to the Sacred Valley to visit Machu Picchu and its obligatory sidelights – Sacsayhuaman and the ruins of Cusco, the fortresses/ temples of Pisac and Ollantaytambo, and others. Only recently have people begun to realize that in addition to these sites, there exist treks and bike rides that in most parts of the world would be a country's number one attraction. You can literally start at the edge of a glacier at an altitude of over 4400m and 4hrs later, after biking down an Inca road, be picking a banana at the side of the road!

HISTORY IN THE MAKING

This is a very exciting time in Peru. As this book is being written, hundreds of Inca and pre-Inca sites are being uncovered and restored in the Sacred Valley. Centuries of storms and vegetative growth have covered up these sites – many travellers have walked, biked and driven right past them and not even realized they were there. Sizable Inca ruins are being uncovered and cleaned everywhere, even at Machu Picchu, where in 2010 a major new section of the park was discovered. In early 2013 as this book was going to press, a major tomb was discovered at Machu Picchu that may be that of the Inca Pachacuti himself.

The intricate terracing and integrated stone llamas at Choquequirao (Routes 32, 34 and 37)

The stonework of Pisac, the astonishing terraces of Muscapuquio near Ollantaytambo, the engineering of the steps and terraces of Huayna Picchu, the absurdly sized stones of Sacsayhuaman, the fine stonework in the cave at Ñaupa Iglesia, the stunning 'llamitas' section at Choquequirao – all are expressions of the highest level of human creativity and achievement. These are all sites that can leave even the most jaded traveller speechless. Visitors to the Sacred Valley are inevitably astonished at the number, and majesty, of Inca sites here, all built during less than 150 years of Inca empire rule.

Up until the late 1990s, adventurous souls hiked the Inca Trail with no guide or supervision and camped where they pleased, a far cry from the herds of organized groups today. More than a few of these adventurers dragged their backpacks and sleeping gear past a lone, snoozing nightwatchman and slept in the sacred grounds of Machu Picchu itself. For obvious reasons, this is no longer permitted and nor is it possible. Yet Peru is one of the few destinations that not only retains the raw adventure and fresh discoveries that independent travellers are seeking (and in large doses), but it is getting even better as time passes. Nearly every site in the Sacred Valley has expanded, as local and international researchers continue to uncover buildings on the edges of known sites. These are not small sites with a few tumbledown walls, but rather major architectural and archaeological wonders that would top the list in most countries around the world.

Choquequirao, for example, is known as the 'sister site' to Machu Picchu. More isolated and less visited than Machu Picchu, it has become apparent that its true size and importance have been underestimated until recently. Entire mountainsides around Choquequirao are being cleared of vegetation and debris to reveal Inca works of truly astonishing scope. Much of this work was not uncovered or visible before 2004 or 2005, so only recent visitors get to see the 'real' Choquequirao, a rare and gratifying treat to an adventurous soul trying to find something new in today's shrinking world.

As we move forward through the 21st century, it often seems as though the challenges facing humankind are formidable: increasing scarcity of resources like fresh water and food, deforestation and destruction of our natural habitat, and a sense of having lost control of the very society we have created. All the Spanish chronicles of the Conquest share a common theme of admiration for the civil engineering and societal order of the Inca society the conquistadors found in 1532. If there is any lesson to be taken from the Incas, it should be to remember that virtually anything was possible for a society that had three principal rules: *Ama Llulla* (Don't tell lies), *Ama Sua* (Don't steal), and *Ama Quella* (Don't be lazy).

DON'T MISS...

With so much to see, this list of some of the top attractions in the Cusco and Ollantaytambo area may help you whittle down your options. The Boleto Turistico (tourist ticket), a popular pass sold by the Instituto Nacional de Cultura (INC), allows entrance into most of the Incan sites in the Sacred Valley. This pass can be purchased at any of the sites it includes, such as Sacsayhuaman, Ollantaytambo, Pisac, Tambo Machay and others.

Machu Picchu
For most people the famous 'Lost City of the Incas' is the reason they came to Peru in the first place. Therefore, many travellers arrive with a sense of trepidation, fearing that the site may be too crowded and 'touristy', but it is all a matter of perspective and expectations. It is true there are a lot of visitors each day, but Machu Picchu is a large site and there are plenty of isolated corners where you can find a little privacy. What is more, the park is a sanctuary for an impressive array of plant and animal life. Very few people come away from this architectural, historical and natural wonder with anything less than an overwhelming sense of wonder and awe.

Sacsayhuaman
This fortress sitting on the hill overlooking Cusco from the north is famous for the immense shaped and fitted boulders that served as its foundation and still remain perfectly intact, despite the fortress itself being all but destroyed by the Spanish during the rebuilding of Cusco after the Conquest. Above Sacsayhuaman (or 'sexy woman' as it is more easily pronounced) lie several more Inca sites strung out in a row, all clustered within a few kilometres and easy walking distance.

Pisac
This site anchors the far eastern end of the Sacred Valley (Ollantaytambo marks the western end) and is considered by many to feature some of the finest stonework in the entire Inca empire. Pisac is also known for its craft market, particularly on Sundays and Thursdays when Andean mountain folk from all around the Valley come down to sell their unique wares.

Moray and Salineras de Maras (Salt Mines)
These two unique Inca sites are definitely not to be missed. Moray is a set of natural sunken earth impressions that have been reworked with stone into what some say was an agricultural experimental laboratory in Inca times; others believe its use was more ceremonial.

The Salt Mines of Maras, believed to have been in continuous operation for over a thousand years, are a large number of gravity-fed evaporation pools, fed by a naturally salinated stream, that continue to produce

The carved Incan shrine of Yurac Rumi, or 'white rock' in Huancancalle (just off Routes 33 to 36 and Route 38)

thousands of kilos of table salt every year.

Lares

There are many naturally occurring hot springs in the Sacred Valley area, but these *baños termales* have the advantage of a tropical climate and improved facilities, including an on-site hotel, and the drive up and over the Cordillera Urubamba into Lares is one of the most beautiful in the region. A popular trekking destination.

Vilcabamba

The name is a bit confusing as it can refer to what was thought by Hiram Bingham (the modern-day discoverer of Machu Picchu) to be the final refuge of the Incas, as well as to what is now known to be that final refuge

(now called 'Espiritu Pampa'). It also refers to the general area in which both of these sites are located, and holds many other secrets as well, including the enigmatic White Rock.

EXPLORING BY BIKE OR ON FOOT

It remains a bit of a mystery how, until very recently, Peru has managed to stay off the beaten path of adventure travel. Considering that the Inca Trail to Machu Picchu is one of the most famous hikes in the world, surprisingly little information is available on hiking or biking other routes. Indeed, much of this area has only been mapped in recent years. Until now independent travellers have had to strike out on their own without any

27

real information about how to get to their destination.

This guidebook contains 40 different hiking and biking trails in the Sacred Valley and features maps and routes that until now have not been described in detail. It includes many half- and full-day routes easily done from Cusco or Ollantaytambo, as well as multi-day trips. Peru seems to have become an increasingly popular destination recently and permits for hiking the Inca Trail are difficult to come by in the peak months of June to August, and even its formerly lesser-known sister site, Choquequirao, is becoming more and more crowded every year. Yet, if you are in search of a more 'authentic' or remote Andes experience, take heart. In this guidebook, there are numerous different routes that arrive at Machu Picchu on foot or bicycle via Inca roads and trails (but without the crowds or required permits).

In addition, there are two more routes that end at the start of the Inca Trail, allowing you a few days of solitude and acclimatisation before starting the world-famous trek. Also included are several different ways to reach Choquequirao. Indeed, by combining some of the routes in this book you could easily put together a two- to four-week trek, for example from Cachora to Espiritu Pampa, without ever encountering a single motor vehicle or road.

CENTRES AND BASES

Machu Picchu is best known for its namesake Inca site and the world-famous Inca Trail that reaches it. What

A solitary moment on the Inca Trail (Route 2)

Trekking in the stunning scenery near Chungana, on the route to Choquequirao (Routes 34 and 35)

is perhaps a little less well known is how many alternative routes exist that also reach Machu Picchu, without the need for the high fees, crowds and mandatory guides that hiking the Inca Trail requires. Many of these alternative routes are covered in this book.

Cusco is one of the centres of Inca culture and its largest city, with numerous museums, shops, restaurants and a surprising number of Inca sites. While there are only a handful of trekking or biking routes that leave from Cusco, nearly all travellers end their stay here. This area not only contains the various sites in and around Cusco but is also the departure point for trips into the Ausangate area, the Amazon jungle and several of the routes to the ancient archaeological

sites of Choquequirao and Machu Picchu itself.

Urubamba is a bustling, mid-sized town with a commercial feel. It lies in the heart of the Sacred Valley at the base of the Cordillera Urubamba, a large mountain range dominated by the 5700m glacier Chicón and its tributaries. This range is part of the Continental Divide and separates the Sacred Valley from the descent down into the jungle and the Amazon basin. While not in itself an attractive town, some popular routes to Inca sites and day tours in the region (including the popular route to Moray/Salineras) pass through Urubamba, and it is an important transport centre. There are also a couple of treks that start here, climb up and over the Cordillera Urubamba, and then plunge downward towards the jungle and the popular hot springs village of Lares.

With countless Inca sites within a half-day walk, **Ollantaytambo** lies in a valley at the confluence of two important rivers: the Vilcanota (Urubamba) and the Patacancha. It is gaining a reputation as the Adventure Capital of Peru, and is the best place to base your adventures. From here you can trek or mountain bike to Machu Picchu, Quillabamba, Choquequirao and nearly every other major site in the Sacred Valley. The town itself retains its original layout, Inca architecture and culture, and small village charm. It is also known for the massive and spectacular Inca fortress that looms over the entire town.

The spectacular, high-jungle mountain zone of **Vilcabamba**, choked with vegetation, harboured the Incas during their 40 years of post-conquest life and is rich in history and natural beauty. It contains several major Inca sites, and is now recognized as one of the most important regions in the entire empire. This area used to receive many fewer visitors than the others covered in this book, partly due to the difficulty and time needed to reach it. The road up to Huancancalle has been expanded and improved in recent years, however, and taxis and *collectivos* (shared taxis) from Santa Maria now regularly ply the 3hr white-knuckle ascent up to Vilcabamba. Routes in this guide include the 'lost city' of Manco Inca, Espiritu Pampa,

as well as his palace of Vitcos and the intriguing site of Yurac Rumi, or the White Rock as it is also known.

Dominated by the massive, 6270m, Ausangate, the highest peak in the Cusco area, **Ausangate** is well known for its various outstanding treks. It is a climbing destination as well and several parties a year attain its summit. The views here are some of the most spectacular in all of South America, and the area is dotted with many high lakes fed by glacial runoff, with their characteristic electric blue colour. The proud inhabitants still travel primarily by horseback, checking their llama and sheep herds. There are a few archaeological sites, but not nearly as many as in other areas in the Sacred Valley. There are, however, some excellent hot springs. Access to the Ausangate region, its glaciers and hot springs is usually gained from the small village of Tinqui, which lies on the road to Puerto Maldonado and is a few hours' drive from Cusco.

GETTING THERE

Getting to Peru

Nearly all visitors fly first to the capital Lima, then take a second flight to Cusco. It takes about 6–8hrs to fly to Lima from most cities in the US. Flights from Europe often stop first in Miami but there are direct flights as well – check with local airline carriers. Most but not all international flights arrive in the late evening, requiring an overnight stay in Lima. A typical flight pattern is

An aerial view of Mount Salkantay

to fly into Lima, arriving in the evening, then stay the night and take a short 1hr flight to Cusco the following day.

It is not necessary to apply for an immigration visa in advance. They are usually granted automatically, as you enter the country. The length of this visa is negotiable and runs from 30 to 183 days, the maximum stay allowed. If planning to stay more than 30 days be sure to notify the immigration officer right away and ask for the desired number of days, which is usually not a problem.

When you enter Peru you are entitled to bring several items into the country without taxes or any other remittance, such as a digital camera, laptop and other electronic items. Also included in that list is a bicycle for personal use, and sleeping bags and tents are also exempt.

All incoming baggage is inspected and X-rayed at customs at Lima airport. If any of the equipment is brand new, particularly a bicycle, expect to be questioned. Bicycles in particular are scrutinized carefully, for some reason. In all cases, be sure to maintain a calm demeanour and insist politely that all items in your luggage are for personal use during your trip to Peru. Ultimately, it is unlikely there will be problem – just be aware that they are paying great attention to the matter.

Getting to Cusco by air
Four main airlines serve the Lima–Cusco route: LAN Airlines (www.lan.com), TACA Air (www.taca.com), StarPeru (www.starperu.com) and Peruvian Airlines (www.Peruvianairlines.com). Fares have

31

doubled in recent years, rising to about $120 (€87) each way, or about $250 (€181) for the round trip. These flights should normally be booked in advance, and definitely during the high season from May to September. Buying a ticket to Cusco without advance notice during these months will be very difficult.

When checking in for the flight to Cusco, try to obtain a seat on the left side of the aircraft for spectacular views of the mountain ranges between Lima and Cusco. During the dry season of May to September in particular, the views of the 6000m peaks are spectacular and the route to Cusco goes right through the heart of them.

Cusco airport is small but adequate and is located just a few minutes from the city centre. There are always plenty of taxis waiting to provide transport into Cusco or Ollantaytambo. There are also public buses outside the airport, but these are hardly worth the considerable effort except for the most diehard or budget-conscious traveller. A taxi from the airport to the centre of Cusco (the Plaza de Armas) costs approximately 10–12 soles, or about $4 dollars (€2–€3). Travellers looking to save a few soles can walk outside of the airport and catch any passing taxi into the centre; this will cost approximately 6–7 soles. Transport from the airport to Ollantaytambo can also be easily arranged on the spot as you exit the main terminal: expect to pay around $45 (€35) or 120 soles for the 2hr drive.

Getting to Cusco by land

Another common method for getting to Cusco is by bus or train. There is no train from Lima, but there is one from Puno, and also from Arequipa. There is only one train station in Cusco, the San Pedro Station; from here trains leave for Machu Picchu and arrive from Puno. The station is located just a few blocks southeast of the Plaza de Armas, in the city centre.

Many travellers arrive by bus from Lima, La Paz, or Arequipa and the bus station is located in the southern part of the city, a few kilometres from the city centre and approximately halfway between the airport and the Plaza de Armas. Again, there are plenty of taxis waiting outside the door to take you into the centre of Cusco or to Ollantaytambo.

GETTING AROUND

Cusco

Take a deep breath! The altitude of Cusco is 3360m above sea level, and your body will need time to adjust. Be sure to drink lots of water. Go to the Plaza de Armas and have a coca tea.

Cusco is not a very large city, and most of the activity is centred around the Plaza de Armas. Though in a relatively flat valley nestled between the mountains, its general layout runs slightly uphill from the south up to the northern end, where the Plaza de

The main plaza at Choquequirao (Routes 32, 34 and 37)

Armas is located. North and uphill from the plaza the impressive Inca sites of Sacsayhuaman, Tambo Machay and others are located; beyond lies the road to Pisac, Ollantaytambo and the Sacred Valley. Unless you are travelling to the airport, bus or train station, or perhaps the city market in the middle of the city, the main method of getting around is walking. Nearly all the tourist hotels, restaurants and nightlife are within a 10min walk of the Plaza de Armas.

For locals as well as visitors, the most common method of getting around, besides walking, is private taxi. Generally speaking, taxis are very inexpensive compared to most places in the world – they are also

convenient, and easy to find and use. Nearly every vehicle on the road in Cusco is a taxi, and you rarely have to wait more than a few seconds to flag one down. During daylight hours, the standard fare is 3 soles or about $1 (€0.80). This fare will cover nearly any route in the city, except for the airport, areas further south, or the many Inca sites above the city including Sacsayhuaman and beyond (the fare you will be charged to these sites depends on how good your Spanish and bargaining skills are!). During evening hours, the standard fare rises to 4 or 5 soles.

There is also a public bus system of sorts, although it is really just a motley assortment of old minivans

33

The trail down from Pumamarca is a local's favourite (Route 13)

(or *combis*) passing through the city on the main thoroughfares. Some of them are marked but many are not. Perhaps more confusingly, many of them are marked with route and street names bearing no relation whatsoever to their actual destination, having been pressed into service wherever they are needed. The fares are even cheaper than taxis, from 20 centimos up to 50 centimos depending on the destination, but again they are best taken by only the most frugal or adventurous of travellers.

To travel to destinations beyond Cusco, there are a few bus stations scattered around the city. These 'stations' are more often than not just a street corner where combis and taxis gather, waiting for enough passengers to depart for their destination. Unfortunately, these street corners can and often do change without notification, so it is probably best to ask around before heading out.

Shared taxis, often called collectivos, leave for Ollantaytambo and the Sacred Valley from a street corner known as Pavitos, which is Spanish for 'turkey'. The term 'collectivo' is sometimes used interchangeably for 'combi'; both refer to any vehicle which gathers passengers together to a fixed destination. It may be a full-size bus, a smaller minivan, or a station wagon taxi. The fare to go directly to Ollantaytambo from Cusco is 12 soles. Collectivos also depart for Urubamba from the same location for 10 soles. You must specify your destination or just succumb to the frantic shouting of the drivers looking for passengers to their destination. Collectivos bound for Mollepata and Limatambo/Curahuasi, two popular starting off points for treks to Choquequirao and Machu Picchu via Salkantay, leave from the street just above the San Blas Plaza, called Arco Punku.

Finally, there is a traditional bus station just below the Ovalo Pachacutec, at the lower end of Cusco, that features large, lumbering buses that run to all these destinations for a few soles less than the shared taxis. This method has fallen out of favour even with the locals, as it is much slower and not much cheaper. Ask around for the latest information.

The Sacred Valley
The transport system around the Sacred Valley is by and large fairly convenient, safe and inexpensive. Of course, the further you venture from the beaten path, the more expensive and complicated transport can become. Transport logistics will play a major role in your mountain travels and their success, and it is recommended you pay close attention to these details when planning your trips.

Most transport options require a decision as to which is more important: money or time. If time is more important, then a private taxi should

Classic Incan road architecture at nearly 5000m (Routes 34 to 38)

be hired. Private transport is faster and generally much more comfortable. It also allows the traveller the flexibility to stop for photograph and toilet breaks. Most travellers are surprised how inexpensive private taxis are compared to their home country. The cost varies depending on destination and origination, but 30 soles (about $10 or €7) per half hour is a good general guideline. Private transport can be arranged in all major towns and most of the smaller ones.

A local bus trip is even less expensive than the shared taxis that leave from Pavitos – the bus is crowded and slower (takes about 2hrs 30mins) but costs only 3 soles, and is a great way to experience a different culture. If you've always fancied bouncing around in the back of an open-ended truck jammed with people and animals, there will be many opportunities to do so while travelling around the back roads of Peru!

Hitchhiking is common in the Sacred Valley, although it's not really called that. The locals simply stand at the side of the road if they want a ride, and passing traffic that has space will stop. It is perfectly acceptable for foreign travellers to get around in this manner, too. Price is generally negotiable in these situations. If the route is a common one, there will likely be an accepted standard price (probably very low) and it is rare for the driver to ask a tourist to pay more. Large buses, small taxis, and 'combis' all ply the

roads from dawn to dusk and will usually stop to give a ride. Other types of vehicles such as transport trucks may stop also, and in these cases a price should be agreed upon before accepting the ride.

Generally speaking, it is quite safe for foreign travellers to get about in this way. Reports of safety problems are quite rare, but appropriate caution should always be taken. You can get virtually anywhere in the Sacred Valley and beyond this way, although it may require waiting around for a while – sometimes that might mean all day or even overnight.

WHEN TO GO

The best time to visit Peru is from May to September, particularly if planning a trekking or mountain bike trip. Simply put, during these months it is sunny nearly every day and rarely rains. This is the high season for tourism, so hotels and attractions are naturally more crowded. However, it is probably a small price to pay to be virtually guaranteed splendid weather every day. The rest of year is still quite hospitable, with warm and partly cloudy days mixed in with rain. From December to March is the heavy rain season, when it rains nearly every night and also in the late afternoons.

The mountainous area of the Sacred Valley has its own regional weather patterns and climate, which are very different from the coastal areas. The temperature is varied and changes rapidly. In the winter months of June to September, it is usually around 3–5°C just before sunrise, and the temperature will rise to 25°C in just a few hours. Then again in the evening (or anytime the sun goes behind a cloud) the temperatures drop from 25 down to 5°C. The strength of the high-altitude, tropical sun often makes the temperature seem higher than it is, so extreme caution should be used to protect the skin from the sun. The nights are pretty cold, and during the winter months even more so. Technically, winter and summer seasons are reversed from the northern hemisphere, but in reality here in the Sacred Valley the year is divided into the rainy season and non-rainy season, rather than summer and winter. The Sacred Valley is located at a latitude of just 17 degrees south of the equator, which means that the temperature variance between seasons is not very extreme.

ACCOMMODATION

Lima, Cusco, Pisac, Ollantaytambo, Urubamba and Aguas Calientes offer the full range of accommodation options, from humble hostels (small, family run inns typically with shared bathrooms and cold-water showers), up to three-star hotels and beyond. The Sacred Valley in particular is exploding in growth, with new options popping up every day. Prices

A typical Andean home, with stone walls and a thatched roof

range from as little as $5 to over $100 per night (€3–€73). Outside of these areas, accommodation is rustic and not widely available. Details can be found in the introduction to for each section of this book.

FOOD

Most travellers enjoy the food in the Sacred Valley immensely, perhaps due to its freshness. Local food in general tends to be fairly bland by Western standards; spicy foods can be found but are not common. Typical Andean fare includes staples such as potatoes, chicken and rice, which form the basis for nearly every meal in rural areas. While Peruvian cuisine is gaining international acclaim, particularly *ceviche* (a form of raw fish prepared with lemon juice) and other forms of seafood from the coastal regions, most local fare is pretty basic. In Cusco you can find international food of most types, and pizza restaurants can be found on nearly every corner of the city. Pizza seems to be the most popular tourist offering just as much in Ollantaytambo and Aguas Calientes, but quality international food is much harder to find in these two villages than it is in the city. Of course, no visit to the Sacred Valley would be complete without sampling the ubiquitous *cuy*, or guinea pig. Typically roasted or boiled with the skin still on, this dish is considered a local delicacy and is often consumed at large family gatherings and holidays. It can be found at many tourist restaurants in the area but is rarely served in local restaurants.

Peruvians tend to eat a large and hearty breakfast with soup, chicken and rice being the most common dishes. Every town, large or small, has a local market with fresh, hot food served from 6.00am, at astoundingly low prices. Additionally, street food is common in Cusco, Ollantaytambo and other larger towns, with *choclo* (boiled cobs of giant Andean corn slathered in butter) a real treat.

Not all the food you may be offered will be safe to eat. Partly because hygiene practices are not yet up to Western standards, but also because all areas of the world have different bacterias to which the average traveller's stomach is simply not accustomed, stomach ailments and diarrhoea are common and appropriate cautions should be taken. The old adage of 'peel it, wash it, or boil it' is a wise one to follow. Soups and salads in particular should be approached warily.

HEALTH MATTERS

Before you leave
Many who are travelling to Peru for the first time will wonder how the different diet and high altitude will affect them, and whether there is a risk of malaria. Unfortunately, many travellers do experience health problems when visiting Cusco, but by following the simple guidelines described here,

The trail between Huancancalle and Choquequirao (Routes 34 and 35)

you can significantly reduce your chances of becoming ill.

There are three main factors that, alone or combined, are the cause of most of the health issues experienced by travellers arriving in Cusco: the altitude, the food and the rigours of travel. Most travellers arrive having not slept enough in the preceding days. Whether travelling by plane or by bus, it is a long and gruelling trip that by itself could cause anyone to feel below par. Getting lots of sleep and drinking lots of water in the days before your trip are two of the best preventative steps to take and cannot be overstated.

The altitude in the Sacred Valley, where most travellers spend their time, is generally between 3000 and 3500m. Machu Picchu itself is located at approximately 2400m above sea level. However, many of the trails and roads in this book climb to 4000m and higher. Depending on the altitude of where you live, arriving in Cusco can cause a mild case of *soroche* (altitude sickness), but generally it is not serious and doesn't last more than a few days. Most travellers find that descending to a lower altitude (like Ollantaytambo or Pisac) as soon as they get to Cusco minimizes the effects of the altitude. For example, Ollantaytambo is nearly 500m lower than Cusco and that makes a big difference, especially in the first few days at high altitude. After a day or two at lower elevation, you will be much more adjusted to the altitude and less likely to have problems in Cusco.

There are a few pharmaceutical products available that claim to minimize the effects of the altitude, but reviews are mixed. More common is to chew coca leaf or drink the tea made from its leaves, an age-old remedy for altitude sickness that is very effective. Very few people suffer any real problems after a day or two of acclimatizing, and no special acclimatization programme is necessary. This is true even for people who live at sea level who travel up to high altitudes after even just a few days in the area.

Either Hepatitis A or B is always a possibility when travelling to remote areas that lack the normal hygiene practices of Western countries. However, cases are very rare here. Check with a medical professional about the pros and cons of the hepatitis vaccine. There have been some recent cases of Typhoid fever in the valley, so it is advisable to have a current vaccination. And of course, having an up-to-date tetanus vaccination is a good idea no matter where you live, and it is highly recommended to have this done before travelling to Peru. A tetanus shot provides immunization for 5–7 years; again, check with a doctor.

Malaria is not prevalent in this part of Peru, but if you are travelling on to the Amazon that is not the case and appropriate medicines and precautions should be taken. Current advice is that travel as low as 1000m altitude, which covers all the routes in this book, is not a malaria risk. The Espiritu Pampa and Pongo trips are more high risk for malaria than the other routes, so if planning to travel there, check carefully with health professionals at home as well as locally.

In Peru
The healthcare system in Peru is reasonably adequate in most major towns. In the Sacred Valley there are now various heath clinics specializing in services for foreign travellers. In the Lima, Cusco and Urubamba areas there are modern hospitals and doctors.

However, outside of these areas the remote rural locations have few, if any, medical services. Be advised that many routes in this book are several days from medical attention of any kind. If taking prescription medicines, be sure to bring an adequate supply from home. Consider dividing it into two stashes and putting one in both your day pack and suitcase, in case one of them should be lost or stolen. There are ample pharmacies, called *boticas*, in all but the smallest towns of Peru. In the event of an emergency, note that a prescription is not necessary to buy even the strongest types of medicine, and although the names are in Spanish they are generally easy to translate as they are usually similar.

SAFETY

Many guidebooks warn against rampant crime in Peru but the reality is quite different. Like any city of 9 million inhabitants, Lima has its dangerous neighbourhoods, particularly after dark. However, most travellers rarely venture outside of Miraflores and this area is quite safe. In Cusco violent crime against tourists is very rare and is usually experienced only by inebriated travellers stumbling around dark streets late at night. Muggings or assaults of any kind outside of Cusco and Lima are virtually unheard of. Walking around Ollantaytambo, Urubamba or Pisac alone at any time of the night is quite safe. As in many places in the world, however, bus stations and buses themselves are rife with pickpockets and petty thieves. Keep your wits and belongings about you. Beware of the common tactic of distraction – if someone bumps into you, spills a liquid on you, or stops to ask you a question – guard your belongings. Also, use extreme caution when on an overnight bus and put anything valuable physically on your person, preferably deep inside a pocket. If possible, sleep with your backpack under your feet or it may be gone when you wake up. Otherwise, just practise common sense and you are unlikely to experience any problems while in Peru.

LANGUAGE

The primary language spoken in Peru is Spanish (*español*). It has slightly

Incan steps in the canyon of Urquillos (Route 6)

different pronunciation and grammar rules to European Spanish (*castellano*) but you will be understood perfectly well using either.

English is still not widely spoken, except at the more expensive hotels. The many street touts and hustlers in Cusco speak enough English to do their business; however, outside of Cusco the number of locals who speak English is quite small. Fortunately, the languages share many common words and you can expect the locals to be able to conduct basic tourist transactions in English.

Other languages such as French or German are rarely spoken, except by agencies and hotels specializing in travellers from those countries. In the rural areas and in most of the areas traversed by the routes in this book, virtually no English of any kind is spoken, so if you are travelling independently you should carry a basic Spanish phrasebook.

The other language spoken frequently, especially in the outlying areas, is Quechua, the enduring language of the Incas. In many of the more remote villages contained in this book, Quechua is the primary and often only language spoken. A beautiful and simple dialect, it is well worth the time to learn just a few words of it if planning to travel into the mountains of the Sacred Valley; mastering just a few simple phrases will open doors, literally and figuratively, available to very few foreign travellers.

MONEY

The currency in Peru is the Nuevo Sol, but is referred to as simply 'the sol' (rhymes with 'goal') and the plural form is 'soles' (pronounced 'sol-ees'). At the time of writing a US dollar is worth 2.6 soles and a euro is worth about 3.4 soles. The US dollar is the only foreign currency accepted with any regularity in Peru, although the euro is reasonably easy to exchange in Cusco and, occasionally, in Ollantaytambo. No other currency is easily exchanged, except in Lima and a few banks in Cusco. There are both official and unofficial currency exchanges on nearly every corner in Cusco, as well as in major tourist areas in Lima such as Miraflores. Outside Lima and Cusco it becomes increasingly difficult to exchange US dollars, apart from at a few places in Ollantaytambo, Urubamba and Aguas Calientes (the town of Machu Picchu).

Most tourist businesses in Cusco, Ollantaytambo, Pisac and Aguas Calientes will accept either soles or dollars. Non-tourist businesses, such as small stores, accept only soles. Outside of these areas, all foreign currencies, including the US dollar, are virtually worthless as only Peruvian soles are accepted. You will definitely not be able to buy goods or services in US dollars in the rural and mountain areas described in this book. Fraudulent money changing practices from street corner vendors is uncommon but is not unheard of.

Any storefront advertising currency exchange is generally reputable.

It is recommended to change a reasonably large amount of currency in Lima or Cusco, depending on your travel plans, then supplement it along the way with ATM withdrawals. ATMs are plentiful in Cusco and Urubamba, and there are now a few in both Ollantaytambo and Aguas Calientes. Currently there are no ATMs in the Sacred Valley outside of these areas. Bank charges for withdrawals and conversion to soles can be high; you should check with your bank before leaving home. It is also a very good idea to travel with a minimum of two ATM cards as it is not uncommon to have an ATM machine inexplicably 'eat' a bank card and it generally cannot be retrieved.

Traveller's cheques have become outdated and are not recommended, as converting them can be difficult and time-consuming. A bank debit card is a much better bet. There are several Western Union offices in both Lima and Cusco for emergency transfers.

Although many major hotels and restaurants in Cusco take them, credit cards are not yet widely accepted. This is changing rapidly, with more businesses in outlying areas like Ollantaytambo accepting credit cards.

Finally, it is consistently difficult to change large bills (50 and 100 sole bills) virtually anywhere, even in Cusco. Expect to have to wait while the shop owner or manager runs down the street looking for change. The best policy for this is to try to use a large bill at nearly every transaction to get change as often as possible. Do not expect small businesses to be able to provide this service; travellers are often upset that a vendor cannot change a bill but it is simply the way it is. It is likely to be difficult to change large bills of any kind on the Inca Trail, or nearly any of the small mountain towns encountered while travelling on the routes listed in this guidebook.

COMMUNICATIONS

This is another area where things are changing almost monthly. Communications in Lima and Cusco are quite modern and easy to find. Internet cafés are located on nearly every street corner in both cities, with service being surprisingly fast and inexpensive. Internet costs about 2 soles an hour in Lima, 3 soles an hour in Cusco, and 4 soles an hour in Ollantaytambo and Aguas Calientes (Machu Picchu). Internet service is being brought to even the smallest of mountain towns, although most of it is dial-up and slow. Currently, 'high-speed' internet reaches as far as the town of Urubamba, with Ollantaytambo on the verge of receiving it. Wi-Fi is now common in hotels in Lima, Cusco and even Ollantaytambo, depending on the hotel and its price level. It appears likely it will only become faster and more available as time passes.

To make a telephone call to Peru from another country, the country code for Peru is 51. Telephone service is widely available throughout Peru, and it is relatively easy with the help of a phone card (sold at nearly every neighbourhood corner store) and a landline or public phone. Ask a local for assistance. Otherwise, count on the Sacred Valley mimicking most of the rest of the world in that public payphones are disappearing and being replaced by mobile phones. This is happening rapidly, as mobile telecommunications are being brought to even the remotest areas of Peru, including Machu Picchu and Salkantay. Mobile phone coverage now includes Machu Picchu, Ollantaytambo and many towns in this book, but not so much in the more remote areas. As in other countries, coverage tends to deteriorate further away from centers of population.

The other option if you want to make a telephone call is one sight that may not be familiar: small gatherings of three or four locals on street corners and parks, usually wearing a bright green coloured vest. They are selling phone calls, for people who don't have their own mobile. Simply walk up to them and give them the number you wish to call. The service is convenient and cheap, about 50 centimos per minute for local calls.

Peru does have a postal service with both national and international delivery capability. Look for the blue and red Serpost signs. This service is not recommended, as it is unreliable, but if you are hoping to send a postcard back home it is worth a try. A better bet is to buy the stamp and then wait until you get to Lima airport where there is a mailbox for international deliveries – this will increase the likelihood of the postcard actually arriving at its desired destination. For sending or receiving packages to or from back home, the best bet is DHL, which has offices in Cusco and Lima. There also is a FedEx office in Lima in Miraflores, but currently not in Cusco. Expect this to change too, however.

TREKKING

Hiring help or going it alone

One of the first and biggest decisions to be made is to whether to travel alone or with local assistance. Essentially there are three options: to hire an agency specializing in treks, travel with just a local guide, or to travel alone without any assistance. Each of these options has its advantages and disadvantages, and it is important to understand them, as this decision will have a major impact on your trip. Trekking in the Andes is one of the most amazing experiences life has to offer; however, it also can be quite challenging both physically and logistically.

In general, our recommendation is to do a little research and then hire an agency or guide service. They have the local expertise and knowledge that a traveller from outside the area simply cannot have. The wasted time and frustration they will eliminate is priceless. They know where the hidden hot springs and little ruins are, they know where the best campsites are, they know how to solve the (frequent) transport and logistics issues that arise, they speak both local languages, Spanish and Quechua, and in the end can make sure you have a better experience than trying to go it alone to save a little money. That said, here are the pros and cons of each option and how to go about them.

Hiring an agency or organised tour
This option is certainly ideal for those travelling alone or with just one other person, as the fixed costs (transport to trailhead, guide, etc.) can be shared among more people.

Indeed, for this reason even if two or three people were to book an organized tour it would be less expensive than going it alone. There are many advantages to hiring an adventure tour agency, including the fact their guides and cooks are likely to speak fluent Quechua and Spanish. They also will have a great deal of local knowledge that even travellers who have done their research simply won't have. They will certainly have better contacts for what is often the most difficult part of a multi-day trek in the Andes: the logistics of hiring mules and horses.

Other advantages include the benefit of varied company on long walks, better food (and someone to cook it, serve it and then clean up afterwards!) and probably most importantly, the knowledge of the

A group of trekkers near the pass of Aobamba (Route 31)

*An arriero approaching the pass of
San Juan (Routes 34 and 37)*

guide. They can help immensely with the logistics of where and when to camp, having the right gear ready before you climb/descend in the heat/cold, smoothing out problems with the mule guides (*arrieros*) or campsite hosts, and a variety of often unseen activities, all which will optimize the experience you get.

When taking an organized tour you can expect to have vehicle transportation to and from the trailhead and horses prearranged, camping equipment (tent, pad and sleeping bag) supplied, nightly meals and snacks provided (including the always important early morning hot tea or coffee), and of course local knowledge of both the route and the

culture along the way. For most travellers, these advantages considerably outweigh any cost savings, which are usually negligible anyway.

Hiring a local guide

This is sort of a middle ground solution between hiring an agency and going it alone. Essentially it involves contacting the local people directly, at the village of departure, for their services as a muleteer/guide. It certainly sounds ideal at first: bypassing the middleman to benefit the local people on the ground. However, there are several things to consider. The most important is time, and how much of it you have to spare. One of the things a guide or agency does best is save you the time and headache of organizing the logistics.

If this is your first trip to Peru, that service is much more valuable than it may seem at first. Most of the multi-day trips described in this book leave from small mountain villages, where few services are available. Even in Ollantaytambo, you can rarely expect to show up and acquire horses or mules the same day. These arrieros generally don't have yellow page ads, so to speak; most do not have a phone at all and it is a question of phoning their brother/cousin/neighbour, who will then pass on the message.

Other factors involved in hiring a local guide are the often considerable difficulties in communicating – even if you speak Spanish, most of the mountain arrieros speak more Quechua than Spanish, and have a culture and language all their own. They are wonderful people but are accustomed to doing things a certain way and may not look at things the way you do, which can manifest itself in a variety of ways.

Going it alone

For reasons that usually centre around language and cultural concerns, as well as the practical problem of taking the correct route, the vast majority of visitors to Peru hire a guide for any serious outing. Even people who normally do everything on their own prefer to have someone handle the details while adventure travelling in the Sacred Valley. That said, it is quite possible to go it alone on most routes in this guide and those routes where it is best to use an agency or local guide are indicated.

One thing to remember is that a guide's primary job is not so much finding the trail – surprisingly often that is fairly straightforward. Rather it is the constant problem-solving required to overcome obstacles such as landslides, roadblocks, mutiny among the porter or arriero ranks, vehicle breakdowns, etc. If you are going it alone you should possess a lot of confidence, a good level of mastery in the Spanish language, and excellent improvisation skills. If all three of these traits are found in the leader of the group, there should be no problems at all travelling on your own.

MOUNTAIN BIKING

The mountain biking in the Peruvian Andes is some of the best to be found anywhere in the world. The area features a dizzying mix of high-altitude trails, Inca roads, different cultures, and of course lots of Inca sites. Mountain biking as a sport is still very new in the Sacred Valley. As recently as 2003, there were few, if any, agencies offering mountain bike tours, and quality bikes of any type were very hard to come by. Slowly, though, the word spread that perhaps the best way to enjoy the stunning mountain scenery and Inca sites was on two wheels. Then an international downhill mountain bike race known as the 'Inca

Catching some air near the route to Urquillos (Route 6)

Avalanche' came to Ollantaytambo. Downhill mountain biking refers to a version of the sport that features riding almost exclusively downhill. Full-face helmets and body armour, heavy-duty bikes with long travel suspension both front and back, and riders without fear are the hallmarks of this discipline. Generally too cumbersome to ride uphill, these bikes must be brought up to the top of a mountain before plunging back down at high speeds. Ollantaytambo, Cusco and the areas around them are perfectly suited for this type of mountain biking and the sport soon took off.

Of course, this isn't the only form of mountain biking available – countless dirt roads traverse the countryside, offering the opportunity to experience the culture and beauty of the Andes from the seat of a bicycle to just about anyone: novice, intermediate riders, or experts alike. Now, there are mountain bikes (albeit cheap ones) on nearly every street corner in Cusco and Ollantaytambo, and it has also become a popular way to travel to Aguas Calientes and Machu Picchu itself.

Hiring a bicycle and guide

The sport of mountain biking has grown exponentially in recent years, as locals and travellers alike discover the joys of roaming Inca roads and territories on two wheels. Most visitors choose to hire a bike and guide in Cusco or Ollantaytambo rather than bring their own bike from home. The biking in the Sacred Valley is some of the best in the world, but there is one thing to remember: if renting a bike, be sure to check the quality. Disc brakes are nearly essential in the steep and rocky conditions of nearly all the local rides: if the bike you are offered doesn't have them, you are advised not to use it. Also the bike should be double suspension to cope with the rugged terrain. There are currently only a small handful of agencies in Cusco and Ollantaytambo that offer quality mountain bikes.

Finally, many mountain bikers inquire about the availability of clipless pedals and shoes. These are generally not available in the Sacred Valley. The steep and unforgiving terrain means frequent dismounts and hike-a-bikes, for which the clipless system is not well suited. Wide pedals and flat shoes are the standard equipment used in the Sacred Valley. If you are uncomfortable riding without the clipless system, bring your cleated shoes and pedals from home – they

take up very little space or weight and can quickly and easily be put onto your rental bike.

Although also covered under 'Dangers and Annoyances', another word about the sun and insects. Both are a constant in this environment. For these two reasons, wearing shorts is not recommended. Nearly every route in this book contains a lot of exposure to both sunshine and biting insects. Take a tip from the locals and wear lightweight long trousers. In addition, a wide-brimmed hat to protect from the intense high-altitude sun is a necessity. Insect repellent, which incidentally doesn't seem to work very well here, is available in Cusco and in some smaller towns but it is best to bring it from home. The best protection from both sun and insects

A group of mountain bikers with the Chicón glacier in the background (Route 5)

is lightweight, long-sleeved shirts and trousers.

In Lima and for the most part in Cusco you can buy almost anything you need for travelling. Standard toiletries (shampoo, soap, toothpaste) are readily available virtually anywhere, even in the smaller villages. Female hygiene products are also easy to find. Again, all the essentials can be easily found in Cusco and most smaller towns, but you should bring with you any items not easy replaceable or health-specific, such as prescription medicines or extra contact lenses and solution.

The other important issue is camera equipment and accessories such as film, memory cards and batteries. Most types of camera equipment and especially memory cards can now be readily found in Cusco and sometimes in outlying areas but it is best to bring your own. Pay particular attention to the charging system of your camera. It is best to bring a camera that uses standard AA or AAA batteries as these are readily available. Cameras requiring separate, special charging units can cause problems for two reasons: first, charging units are often forgotten, lost or stolen; and second, not all areas in the region have electricity, and even in the areas that do have it the service is unreliable. Bringing a camera that operates on standard batteries will eliminate this problem.

Otherwise, aside from trekking, camping and biking equipment

Trekking up the trail to the lower camp spot of Veronica (Route 21)

(covered below) there are very few items besides personal effects that need to be brought from home.

Technical gear

Having the necessary gear (as well as not having a lot of unnecessary gear) will go a long way toward making a visit to the mountains more enjoyable. If you are only planning day trips from Cusco or Ollantaytambo, all that is really needed is good footwear and a good shell that will protect you against wind and rain. If planning any overnight trips, the list of necessary items will obviously be longer.

For any hiking, camping or mountain biking excursion, all equipment and gear should be brought along as there is not a great deal available locally and what there is tends to be of low quality. The only place to buy any type of gear is in Cusco. The equipment checklist lists all the items you will need for a trek or bike ride in the Sacred Valley, but of particular importance are the following items.

Backpack

The type of backpack to be brought will depend on how much time you plan to spend on the trail and, even more importantly, whether you are planning to carry all the gear or to hire mules. Do not skimp on quality as you will be relying heavily and often on your backpack, and it is likely to see a fair amount of abuse during the various forms of transport. If travelling on a multiday excursion, it is a good idea to bring two backpacks: a primary pack for all the gear needed during the trip, which is usually carried by the horse or mule, and another smaller but sturdy one for day use, which should be carried on your person at all times to ensure access to needed items. This day pack should be chosen wisely as you will be carrying it every day for long periods. A pack with a large built-in water reservoir is always a good idea, and it should also have a pull out rain cover to protect your pack when hiking in the rain. Be sure that both packs fit well and are tested out before arriving in Peru.

Footwear

One of the most important gear choices will be footwear. Avoid bringing a new pair of shoes or boots that have not yet been 'broken in'. Even casual walking around the uneven cobblestone streets of Cusco and a day visit to Machu Picchu will test the feet – so take the time to ensure your feet will be comfortable and happy. One good pair of shoes should be sufficient for both daily travel and multi-day hikes. A rugged boot with good ankle support is best, with a good breathable material and preferably a Gore-Tex or other type of water repulsion technology. While water will inevitably find its way in eventually if the trip is long and wet enough, waterproofing should go a long way towards ensuring foot comfort.

Footwear of all types inevitably gets wet while travelling in the Andes.

Consider bringing a pair of sandals, as they come in handy from everything to wading a river to lounging around camp. It is a good way to go, as the most important time to have dry feet is at the end of the day.

If you are coming to mountain bike in the Sacred Valley and you normally ride clipless pedals, consider leaving them and the special shoes they require behind (see 'Hiring a bicycle and guide' above).

Rain gear
No matter what the season is, quality rain gear is essential. Most important is a rain jacket or poncho, followed closely by headwear and footwear. Gore-Tex type materials are very popular and with good reason. A quality water-resistant material with the ability to breathe can make all the difference between a pleasant outing and a miserable one. Cheap plastic rain ponchos are available on nearly every corner in the Sacred Valley in the event yours is lost or forgotten; however, cheap is the operative word and they tend to last less than a day or two before falling apart. More durable ponchos are an outstanding way to keep dry. They come in two varieties, rubber PVC-types such as those sold in military surplus and outdoor stores, and the heavy ponchos made of wool that are worn by the locals. The best choice is a one-piece, rubber, PVC-type poncho with a hood. As it is seamless, water simply cannot penetrate, and a good poncho is guaranteed to keep the body dry from the head down to the knees. Otherwise, a good and previously tested quality rain jacket from back home should do the trick. Do not rely on buying one in the Sacred Valley.

The other important part of rain protection is good headwear. There are many types on the market, including some that do double duty in protecting from both rain and sun. A wide-brimmed hat will help keep the rain off the face and body. Hoods that can be added to your rain jacket sometimes work well but the cheaper ones will allow rain to enter at your neck, and run down your back – not a pleasant experience. Finally, if you are travelling during the rainy season and you are heavily averse to hiking while wet, a compact and lightweight umbrella is not out of the question. They may seem or look a little silly in the mountains, but they are virtually guaranteed to keep you dry and are a boon if you wear spectacles.

Clothing
Everything you bring will soon get dirty anyway, so one option to consider is wearing the same hiking clothes every day – quality breathable ones can be easily washed each night at the campsite and will quickly dry out. Another good idea is to bring a comfortable set of cotton clothing to wear each night, and keep it clean and dry for reuse every evening. If you are travelling during the rainy season, it is probable that everything on the

Biking down to Patacancha (Route 22)

body and in the packs will be wet anyway. One item worth its weight in gold after a few days of trekking is a fresh pair of socks every day, so bring plenty extra.

Trousers are a more sensible choice than shorts if hiking or biking in the Sacred Valley, primarily because they offer defence against sun, biting insects and sharp cactus thorns, all of which are present in great quantities here. Many travellers have suffered badly from sunburn, insect bites and scratches on their exposed legs, so consider instead bringing lightweight, sturdy hiking trousers made from breathable material to keep you dry. A popular choice is the type of trousers with lower legs that zip off, leaving a pair of shorts.

Denim jeans are not recommended, as they are heavy and slow to dry. Nights at altitude are cold enough to warrant tights, or long underwear, for the lower body.

Next, select a layer system for the upper body. The layer against the skin is one of the most important, and should be chosen with care. Choose a highly breathable wicking material, never cotton. This is very important, as it is likely to get soaked with sweat and needs to be able to dry quickly. Bring several of these base layers, depending on the length of time you are planning to hike or bike. The next few layers are for warmth, so choose a good fleece top or two. Finally, the outer layer's job is to protect from wind and rain.

53

The bottom line is that you can stay warm, dry and comfortable with just three important items: a long sleeve, breathable inner layer; a warm thick fleece; and a fairly waterproof outer layer. Pay particular attention to their quality and do not forget them when you set out on the trail. In fact, a fleece and a rain poncho should simply be kept stored in your backpack at all times, regardless of the weather.

Hats and gloves

It is a good idea to have at least two hats: a wide-brimmed hat to protect from the intense, high-altitude sun during the days; and a warm knitted hat for keeping warm at nights and other times. A long-fingered pair of gloves will round out your cold protection. Gloves will also come in handy while hiking the routes in this book, as on many of them cacti and other sharp plants seem to be everywhere you put your hand down.

Sleeping bag and tent

A good sleeping bag is another area where you should not skimp; pay careful attention to this detail when packing. Due to the high moisture levels and possibility of rain, a synthetic fibre bag is recommended – down is warmer but fairly useless when wet. A good insulating sleeping pad is essential. Many travellers prefer a Thermarest type inflatable sleeping mat, which are more comfortable – until a leak develops in which case they, too,

are fairly worthless. A thick, foam pad is thus recommended.

Which tent to bring is a personal choice. The main factor to consider is its durability and resistance to weather. Expensive, lightweight alpine tents are great if you are carrying your own gear; however, if you are travelling with horses or mules, where weight is not such a factor, consider bringing a heavier and sturdier model. The trails are often thorny and equipment can get ripped, even inside of the travel bags, so be sure to protect your bag and tent with a thick protective covering if possible. Be wary of tents that require a staking system to be set up, because much of the terrain is rocky. A dome tent is the best bet, as backpacks and other gear can be placed in the corners to help it to retain its shape.

Finally, you might want to consider bringing quality but older gear in the event you really enjoy the company and service of your porters and guides – most do not have this type of gear and it makes a great tip at the end of the trip in lieu of money. In the times of the Incas, quality outerwear was used as currency, as it had much more worth than actual money in the harsh and unforgiving climate of the high Andes. The same is still somewhat true today.

Water filter

A dependable means of filtering or treating water is essential for back-country travel in the Andes. There will be no problem finding a water source on nearly every route in this book, as

One of the many footbridges on the way to Occobamba (Route 23)

there are plenty of fresh glacier water rivers to choose from. The water is usually clear and free of debris. However, virtually all stream water in Peru is faecally contaminated by animals upstream; the water therefore needs to be filtered to eliminate giardia and other micro-contaminants. There are many new types of filters on the market – some of the newer ones work with ultraviolet light and are very small and compact. The standard backpacker filters are lightweight and filter out nearly everything, and the old standby of iodine pills still works if you can stand the bad taste. Be sure to have two different means of filtering water if you are planning to be out more than one night. That way if one of your filters

malfunctions, you still have a back-up system. This is especially important if you are using one of the electronic ultraviolet light types of filters, as they run on batteries which may not always work in the high-altitude cold.

Cooking gear

Several types of cooking gas can be found for purchase in Cusco and Ollantaytambo. The typical butane/propane mix that fuels a backpacker, alpine-type stove comes in canisters; there are two sizes so be sure to get the right one or else risk eating cold noodles. The small, lightweight backpacking stoves that run on compressed gas are the best and most reliable.

EQUIPMENT CHECKLIST

Items considered essential for a multiday trek or bike trip are listed here. Nearly all can be acquired if need be in Cusco or Ollantaytambo, but it is much better to bring them from home as both availability and quality can be spotty.

- Large, correctly fitted backpack if travelling on multiday trip
- Smaller day pack for day use, preferably one with many pockets for storing gear
- Dual-purpose rain jacket/windbreaker
- Warm fleece(s) to wear beneath, or instead of, rain jacket
- Warm knitted cap for cold evenings and mornings, also gloves for the same
- Quality hiking footwear and a quality pair of sandals for wearing around camp or in the rain. The common advice of not bringing footwear that has been previously tested and broken in definitely applies; do not set out on a multiday trek with new footwear
- Lightweight, breathable hiking trousers and long-sleeved shirts for hiking
- Comfortable sleeping-type trousers and cotton shirts for lounging at camp
- Wide-brimmed hat for sun protection – the type that offers protection for the back of the neck is highly recommended. The intensity of the sun cannot be overstated
- Hiking gloves, for protection from sun, cacti and biting insects
- Headtorch with batteries
- Walking poles, many hikers benefit from them
- Sunglasses with quality lenses, preferably polarized
- Waterproof matches and/or lighter
- Quality sunscreen of 30 SPF or higher
- Quality insect repellent
- Lotion and/or lip balm
- Refillable water bottle
- Water filtration system for longer treks
- Swiss Army-type multitool and knife
- All prescribed medicines plus a basic first aid kit with blister protection and pain relievers, antihistamines and antibiotic ointment
- Prescription spectacles and all contact lens solutions that may be needed
- Camera and all extra film, batteries and memory cards, and extra charger
- Pen and paper for communicating, writing journal entries or leaving notes
- A small but complete first aid kit should always be carried on your person

It is always a good idea to bring two stoves in case one of them breaks, and keep them stored in separate packs. Bring extra canisters of gas – they are not available along the trails. Gas canisters can be purchased in Cusco and (although not reliably) in Ollantaytambo. They cannot be found anywhere else.

HAZARDS AND ANNOYANCES

This is probably a good place to mention that you should use caution when asking the locals in the mountains for directions. Their precious inclination to please in any way they can will often result in a positive affirmation – an enthusiastic 'Si!' if you lead your question in any way, such as 'Is there a good place to camp up ahead?' Unless someone in your party speaks Spanish, expect to have a pretty hard time making yourself understood. It is often necessary to use hand gestures and very basic words to communicate. This can prove to be sufficient to communicate the basics, but remember to always view sceptically any answer to your questions that is a 'yes'.

Another warning is that time estimates – 'How much further to the river?' – are likely to be woefully short of reality. If you are travelling without a guide be very wary of relying on time estimates by the locals in the mountains. Part of the reason for their constant underestimation of the time that you will be toiling with your

River crossings are frequent, and often treacherous

pack on your back, is that they have spent their entire lives running around at 4000m, carrying produce and children, and as a result are in amazing physical condition, with a lung capacity that would make most endurance athletes jealous. The other reason? Once, after a particularly brutal and never-ending 5hr climb which we had been promised would take less than 2hrs, we noticed that the local who had been giving us our time estimates didn't even own a watch. So, there's probably something lost in the translation there as well!

Bugs, pests and animals

The most common questions on this subject asked by travellers to Peru relate to snakes and the risk of malaria (from mosquitoes). Regarding malaria, most travel in this book is outside of risk areas but you should check with your doctor for official and expert advice (see Health Matters).

There are some snakes in the mountains of Cusco and a few are mildly poisonous. However, encounters are relatively rare – in more than ten years spent travelling the mountains and high jungle valleys of the Sacred Valley the author has seen only one snake. If you are walking on the trail you will almost certainly make enough noise to scare them off long before they see you. During the hot midday sun, however, snakes often go into a lethargic state while sunning on an open trail and it is possible to surprise one. The best precaution is to use extreme care if you are scrambling around in rocky or grassy hillsides and using your hands for balance. Besides all the cacti, there is a risk of putting your hand on top of an unseen snake. Traditional snakebite advice such as tourniquets or sucking the venom out of the wound is for the most part outdated. Anti-venom kits are available but should only be used by a knowledgeable person, and only after checking them against the type of snake you are likely to encounter in Peru. The best thing to do if someone in your party is bitten by a snake is to calm them, clean and disinfect the wound, and get to the next town. If possible, kill the snake and bring it with you for identification; otherwise have someone write down a complete description of the snake so that if it is poisonous the medical authorities will be able to administer the proper antidote.

There are enough of a variety of poisonous spiders and scorpions that you should use caution. Always check your shoes after a night camping. This common advice is often perceived as a joke but in fact scorpions like to find things warm from your body heat and it is not uncommon to find a scorpion in your shoe or tent. Always use caution when putting your hand into places you can't see, like a backpack that has been open all day in your tent, or a food or dishes bag.

Mosquitoes and biting flies can be quite a problem on many of the treks and bike rides in this book. Everyone seems to have a favourite brand or type of insect repellent, but few of them work very well. Your best protection is trousers, shoes and a lightweight long-sleeve shirt. Do not scratch bug bites as they become easily infected and can take months to heal.

Rabies, though not common, does exist in Peru and is a valid concern. The most likely form of transmission is a dog bite; for this reason, extreme caution is always recommended around dogs, whether in rural areas or in larger cities, as animals are rarely vaccinated here. Avoid being bitten by a dog at all costs, and if bitten seek medical attention immediately. The dog owner should be located and asked for proof of rabies vaccination, and unfortunately the dog may need to be killed and tested for the disease. There is no known cure for rabies. There is a post-bite vaccination that can be administered but it is very painful and carries its own set of risks.

Sightings of large mammals such as pumas or bears or rare but do occur. The author has seen several of both while hiking, usually at dusk. Attacks, however, are virtually unknown.

Cicerone's *Pocket First Aid and Wilderness Medicine* would be a useful addition to your pack for full information on how to deal any medical emergency on the trail.

Hiring mules
A cultural classic, this process has been described at great length by

Blindfolding nervous pack animals while loading up is a common practice

many previous authors and for good reason. It can be an amusing or an exasperating process, depending on your attitude. The main thing to remember is that the actual loading of your gear onto the mules or horses is a time-weathered Andean cultural tradition, none of which you can change or even hasten along. It is typically a long, drawn-out affair akin to a choreographed ballet, with the arriero and his helpers moving things around and constantly tying and re-tying things until finally he will pronounce they are 'listo', or ready.

There are several things to watch for. Once on the trail, you will probably get separated from your arrieros and your gear that they are carrying. Thus you should be careful always to have the extra water, clothing and food/water that you need in your day pack and not packed on the horses. Discuss clearly with your arriero expected meeting and wait times and places, then discuss them again to be sure there are no misunderstandings. Be aware that there are various shortcuts and other footpaths leading from the main trail; even a short detour on the wrong one could be enough time for the rear party to pass the front party without either knowing it and both parties thinking the other is ahead/behind when in fact they are not. This is a very common occurrence so use caution.

Landslides

If travelling over a high pass during the rainy season, there is a real risk of landslides and they also can occur at any time during the year when there is a lot of rain. The road from Calca to Lares and the section of road to Quillabamba, between the pass of Abra Malaga down to Huyro, are particularly prone to landslides between December and April. Use caution and be aware of your surroundings if travelling these routes, especially during or after rain. If you come upon a road closed due to rock or mudslide activity, do not attempt to cross or even get close, even though you may see other tourists or locals doing it. The author has walked across a 20ft section of a slide that seemed to have subsided, only to see the entire section of mountainside collapse minutes later!

Road closures

The most important thing to remember about travelling the roads and highways in the Sacred Valley is that random delays are possible if not probable, and you need to be flexible in your plans. Delays can be caused by police checkpoints, landslides, damaged roads or bridges, broken down vehicles, transport strikes, or a variety of other reasons. It is possible to cross a bridge, only to return two days later to find the bridge completely gone and a work crew milling about. Generally it is not a big concern, but you should try to avoid returning from a long trip the evening before a flight that cannot be missed.

CULTURAL IMPACT

Lima is a big and cosmopolitan city with a culture similar to that of most international cities and the cultural differences encountered there tend to be small. Cusco has a much more unique and local culture, but its status as an international tourism hotspot brings a certain normality that all such spots share. Outside of Cusco, however, you begin to enter a different world. Instead of trying to sell you something, as in Cusco, the locals are more likely to say a brief, polite 'hello' or to ignore you altogether. The people who inhabit the high mountain villages are very friendly, but can also be a bit reserved or shy. A culture centuries old is slowly giving way to the new, yet part of the reason we travel to places like Peru is (or should be) to experience cultures that differ from our own.

The inhabitants of these Andean mountains are wonderful people, very humble yet proud. Self-sufficient, these descendants of the original Incas live a life of abundant simple pleasures that most people in the developed world can only look at with envy. The residents of the high mountains outside of the towns in the Sacred Valley, in particular, have a culture and lifestyle that is generally quite similar to the way their ancestors lived a few hundred years ago or more. Until very recently there was no electricity or indoor plumbing, and most live almost entirely off the land around them, maintaining the family crop fields and tending their livestock. While for the most part they truly enjoy their encounters with travellers from other countries, here are a few suggestions for cultural interactions of mutual respect.

Try to use restraint when taking pictures or video of the local residents. Think how it would feel if you were going about your everyday business back home and someone came up and put a camera in the face of you and your family. Consider putting your camera away and instead truly experience the interactions you are

Wearing traditional clothing is still common in towns like Ollantaytambo

61

Children from the lovely Andean village of Yanama

making. Always ask permission first if you want to take a photo of another person. Even better is to chat with your subjects first for a while before pulling out the camera.

Use discretion in using and displaying your electronic items and other expensive gear. Try to refrain from pulling every gizmo from home out of your backpack. You don't have to hide them, but it doesn't have to all be worn on the belt or constantly be used, either. Realize that a simple digital camera or GPS represents a few months' wages to many of the locals. Please use restraint when giving gifts or flashing large amounts of money. It is a common practice among the locals to ask how much a certain item cost. While honesty is always the best policy, consider first the impact of your words – sometimes there are other ways to answer

a question. Also, try to choose clothing that is fairly modest. For example, sport bras for women or going shirtless for men are not generally acceptable in the mountain culture.

Try to have patience. You almost certainly will be subjected to delays or problems that don't seem to make sense. Getting agitated only lengthens the delay. Time doesn't mean as much here in Peru and unless you speak fluent Spanish you probably won't even be understood anyway. Always leave an extra day when planning a multiday excursion. Instead of wondering why the locals do or don't do things a certain way, better to take a break and enjoy the views. Remember that experiencing a different culture is for most people the very reason they travel in the first place.

You may encounter begging or excessive requests to buy something, most likely in Cusco but possibly in the mountains as well. Regarding the proper response to this, no one person or guidebook can claim to have the correct answer. That said, here is ours: besides encouraging a mentality of receiving something for nothing (which very much goes against a centuries-old Andean culture of sharing and mutual reciprocity of goods and labour), it only serves to reinforce many locals' image that all *gringos* are walking candy and money dispensers. However, many if not most of the children in the Sacred Valley are at some level of malnourishment, and so a reasonable compromise for all is to offer some food when asked for *dulces* (sweets) or a *propina* (tip). While giving them the food (fruits, vegetables and bread are three recommended items), try taking a few minutes to talk with them, asking them their name, or something to help let them see you for what you are: just another person.

Peru seems to be one of the few tourism places where tourists and locals mix with very little friction – please help to try to keep it that way. Say hello and smile when passing someone on the street or trail and try to learn a few words of Spanish and Quechua, as it will really go a long way. They will quickly warm to you and will be eager to share details of their personal lives.

MAPS AND WAYMARKING

The Peruvian government has produced a series of topographic maps of Peru that are fairly accurate. They can be found in various bookstores in Lima and Cusco, at the SAE explores club in Cusco, or online at www. omnimap.com or www.stanfords. co.uk. Even if travelling with a guide it is always a good idea to be self-sufficient, so you should have a map and preferably a compass and know how to use it. Many people do not bring a compass any more and rely on GPS technology. This is understandable but carries its own set of risks. The GPS satellite coverage in the Andes is often patchy and it is not uncommon to lose signal for a few hours, as well as the usual problems with dead batteries or other electronic malfunctions. Remember that batteries usually do not function as well or for as long in the cold temperatures at high altitudes.

When travelling with a group and guide, it is a good idea to know the rough directional plan for the day as well as any major landmarks and stopping points.

Route finding in the Andes can be quite difficult, even with a guidebook. There are virtually no signposts or trail markers of any kind. Another reason is that growth and change are coming so rapidly to the region that roads and houses are springing up overnight and can alter a landmark description. Fortunately, there are usually locals on the trail going about their daily lives and they can point you in the right direction should you become lost.

USING THIS GUIDE

There are 40 different hiking and biking routes described in this guidebook. These include day trips and multi-day trips ranging from 11km to 380km in length. The routes are arranged in six sections. The first describes the tourist trails to Machu Picchu, and contains plenty of useful advice, whether you are visiting the ruins from Agua Calientes or doing the classic Inca Trail. Other sections describe routes around Cusco, Urubamba and Ollantaytambo and further afield, culminating in Ausangate 100km south east of Cusco.

At the beginning of each route an information box gives the start and finish points, distance, estimated time required to complete the route, total ascent, total descent, high point and trail type, along with an indication of the difficulty of the route, whether the trail is suitable for hiking or biking and whether or not you will need an agency or guide to complete it. Trails are described as 'classic Incan road' when they have been restored and cleaned and 'old Incan road' when the road is overgrown and the stones are no longer visible. Where appropriate, in addition to describing the route taken, the route description also suggests suitable campsites, and where to get supplies and hire mules or porters.

There is also a route summary table in Appendix A to help you select the best route for your location, tastes, ability and the time you have at your disposal.

Timings

The time estimates in this guidebook are based on first-hand experience over many years of doing these very routes with different travellers in a wide variety of conditions. Thus, the times given are the average amount of time it takes someone, or a group, to hike or bike that section. These times include short stops for toilet breaks, taking photos and so on but do not include extended breaks or frequent stopping. The very steep terrain here in the Andes means that the amount of time it takes to complete a given route can vary significantly. Note, too, that some routes can take a similar amount of time to complete whether you are on foot or on bike.

Many of the trails in this book travel over very steep terrain in rugged conditions. Take account of trail and weather conditions, as well as the physical condition and state of the trekkers and mountain bikers. Time estimates given are just that, estimates, and will depend on the capabilities and performance of your group. Use caution.

Variant spellings

The Incas had no written language that we know of, and thus the correct spelling of Incan words is a common area of disagreement. For example, sources don't even agree about the correct spelling of the word 'Inca' itself! This is due to the common differences of writing a 'c' as opposed to a 'k' or even sometimes a 'q', so that Inca becomes Inka, Cusco becomes Q'osco, or Patakancha becomes Patacancha. And so it goes with many other Quechuan words. Other examples include spelling 'wasi' instead of 'huasi', turning Wakawasi to Huacahuasi, Ñaupa instead of Ñawpa, and endless other discrepancies. Current maps and books do not seem to reach a consensus. For more information, see the glossary of Spanish and Quechuan words in Appendix B.

Not only are there are often many different spellings of the same place name, it is also not uncommon for a valley or mountain peak to have as many as three or four different names, one or two in both Spanish and Quechua. For example the Vilcanota River that flows through the Sacred Valley is often just called the Urubamba River. Other places have differing names even in Quechua, such as the White Rock near the Vilcabamba routes, which also goes by the name of Yurac Rumi in Quechua but also Ñusta Hispaña. Generally this guidebook uses the original Quechua words, like Rio Vilcanota, when possible, over the more recent Westernized names like Urubamba River. This is done as a small contribution to the movement of continuing the restoration of the Inca and Peruvian culture, via the increased interest in the Quechua language.

Regarding language, there are two Spanish words that the reader should learn that will greatly facilitate travel in the Andean backcountry. The first word most people know anyway, *rio*, which means 'river' in Spanish. The other important word to learn is *abra*, which is Spanish for 'pass', as in a mountain pass. Because these words are so prevalently used by locals and foreign travellers alike, as well as on all the maps, they are used in this book. Thus, the Vilcanota River is called the Rio Vilcanota, and Malaga Pass is referred to as Abra Malaga.

Hiking from Vitcos, former palace of the great Incan leader Manco Inca, in Huancancalle (Routes 33 to 36 and Route 38)

PRACTICALITIES AT A GLANCE

Currency
The currency in Peru is the Nuevo Sol. At the time of press the exchange rate is approximately 3.4 soles for one euro; 2.6 soles for one US dollar; 3.9 for one pound sterling. Both soles and dollars are accepted in most places in Lima and Cusco, as well as most tourist attractions outside of these areas. Otherwise, only soles are accepted. **Other foreign currencies such as the euro and the pound are not widely accepted.** Bring plenty of cash for travelling anywhere in the mountains: bring soles and lots of small bills and coins. ATMs can be found in Cusco, Pisac, Ollantaytambo and Aguas Calientes, although they are often out of service so be prepared.

Visas
Visas are normally granted automatically at time of entry into Peru and are valid for 30 days. However, up to 180 days is usually granted upon request. Carry a photocopy of your passport with you at all times.

Health precautions
Malaria is generally not a concern unless you are travelling below 1000m. Altitude sickness (*soroche*) is common, but usually mild. Get lots of rest and drink plenty of water and/or coca tea. Drinking water must be filtered, boiled, or chemically treated. There are very few communication or health emergency services outside of the main towns. High-altitude sunlight is very strong and appropriate precautions should be taken.

International dialling code
The country dialling code for Peru is 51.

Time zone
Peru is in the same time zone as the Central Time Zone of the United States during their Daylight Saving Time, otherwise it is 1hr ahead. Peru's time zone is 7hrs behind Continental Europe and 5hrs behind the UK (GMT).

Language
Spanish is the dominant language of the region, along with the Inca dialect Quechua, which is still quite prevalent. English is spoken in the more upscale tourist businesses in the Sacred Valley, but seldom spoken elsewhere.

1 TOURIST TRAILS TO MACHU PICCHU

Machu Picchu, with Huayana Picchu in the background (Route 1)

INTRODUCTION

Aguas Calientes is the name of the town below Machu Picchu itself, which lies 6km away by road up a steep lush mountain. If you are doing the Inca Trail, as described in Route 2, you will go directly to Machu Picchu and won't see Aguas Calientes until after the visit. All other visitors, however, will arrive either by train, or by the 'back door' route from Ollantaytambo to St. Theresa then walk the train tracks to Aguas Calientes, described in this book in Route 26.

To get to Aguas Calientes by train, there are two different companies to choose from. PeruRail (www.perurail. com) used to be the only train service, a monopoly which allowed them to raise the price of a basic ticket from $11 (€8) just a few years ago to nearly $120 (€92) today. However, now there is a competing service run by a company called Inca Rail (www.incarail. com) so prices have come down a bit. The train can be taken from either Cusco or Ollantaytambo, but it is more economical to take a taxi or bus from Cusco to Ollantaytambo, and there board the train to Aguas Calientes. The train ride from there takes just under 2hrs and is quite beautiful and passes by several major Inca sites.

Having got to Aguas Calientes, however, travellers frequently find it difficult to get accurate information about how to reach Machu Picchu and how to get around the site, how to get permission for the Huayna Picchu hike, and other questions. Route 1 in this book attempts to answer all those questions.

Route 2 describes the classic Inca Trail to Machu Picchu. Despite being only moderately difficult, the Inca Trail is one of the most rewarding journeys to be found anywhere on the planet. It is Peru in a nutshell – with a wide variety of conditions, terrain and climate in just a few days, as well as a host of impressive Inca sites.

In fact, the Inca Trail is literally covered with Inca buildings, terraces and complexes. And one of the great things for the modern-day traveller is that there is a large amount of Incan construction that has only recently been excavated and documented. This means that a trekker on the Inca Trail today will see things that weren't visible to other travellers just a few years ago, giving the rare experience of something new even in one of the world's most popular trekking areas.

ROUTE 1

Aguas Calientes to Machu Picchu

Start	Aguas Calientes (2040m)
Finish	Machu Picchu (2480m)
Distance	6km; 7km with ascent of Huayana Picchu
Total ascent	440m; 720m with ascent of Huayana Picchu
Total descent	negligible; 280m with ascent of Huayana Picchu
Difficulty	Moderate to strenuous with some exposure on the ridge to Huayana Picchu
Time	2hrs; 4–5hrs with ascent of Huayana Picchu
Trail type	Classic Incan road and engineered trail
High point	2720m
Bike or hike?	hike
Agency/guide?	no

Although you can take the bus up to surely the most famous Incan site in the world, it's more rewarding to hike the trail, which shortcuts the endless switchbacks of the bus route.

If you're prompt enough to get a permit (see below), you can also extend your hike to tackle Huayna Picchu, the iconic pinnacle just behind Machu Picchu itself, on a vertiginous but well protected trail. If not there are three alternative hikes available from Machu Picchu (not described here) and all of them are spectacular. Ask any worker for directions to the hikes known as Inca Bridge, Machu Picchu mountain, or Inti Punku (the 'Sun Gate') the culmination of the Inca Trail.

The Machu Picchu site is big enough to warrant a full day and after 4pm or so the vast majority of the crowds have gone home for the day and there is much more opportunity to walk around alone. The park closes at 6pm and you can return on the last bus of the day to Aguas Calientes, where plenty of hot food and cold beer options can be found.

To walk up to Machu Picchu, follow the road taken by the shuttle buses west along the river for about half an hour to the Puente Ruinas bridge. Cross the bridge. Follow signs to the trail as it begins climbing steeply up the mountain, eventually arriving at the entrance to the ruins. It takes 1–2 hours to reach Machu Picchu from the bridge.

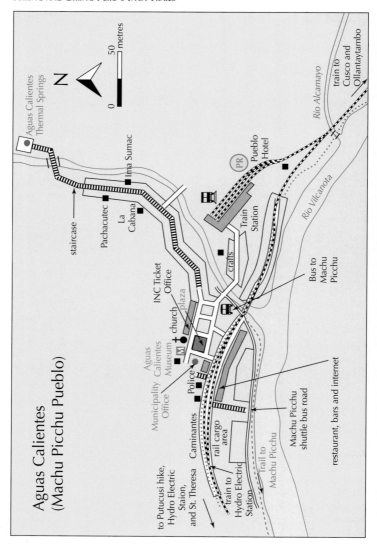

Aguas Calientes
(Machu Picchu Pueblo)

TICKETS AND PERMITS

There are three ways to get an entrance ticket to Machu Picchu, besides those included with hiking the Inca Trail. The first is online at www.MachuPicchu. gob.pe. The second is at the main ticket office in Cusco, currently located on Avenue de la Cultura but liable to move so you may need to ask when you get there. Tickets are also sold in Aguas Calientes at the INC ticket office, which is located just off the main square (see map). The office is open from 5:30am until 9:50pm every day. The cost of a ticket to enter Machu Picchu is 128 soles, half price for students under the age of 26 with a current and valid student ID. The office does not accept credit cards of any kind, nor do they accept US dollars, the euro, or any other kind of foreign currency. Bring exact change, as they rarely seem to have any. You can pick up a free map to the site at the entrance.

If you're planning to climb Huayna Picchu, don't wait to get to Aguas Calientes to buy your Machu Picchu ticket. The Huayna Picchu extension must be purchased in conjunction with your Machu Picchu ticket, and the allotted Huayna Picchu extension tickets are generally sold out several days in advance. The best way to get your tickets is to go to the official website, www.MachuPicchu.gob.pe.

There is a limit of 2000 daily visitors to Machu Picchu. Only 400 will get permission to climb Huayna Picchu – 200 starting at 7am, and a second 200 starting at 10am.

Climbing Huayana Picchu

Huayna Picchu is the mountain just behind Machu Picchu itself. In the Quechua language, *huayana picchu* means 'young mountain' (*machu picchu* means 'old mountain'). It features an incredibly engineered trail hewn out of solid rock that reaches the top of the mountain and accesses the many Incan buildings there.

The hike up to Huayna Picchu and back from Machu Picchu takes 2–3 hrs. Many people believe the engineering accomplishments of this site to be even more impressive than Machu Picchu itself – be sure to look at the massive stone foundations built into the side of sheer cliffs in order to support the mountaintop structures themselves.

Also located on this hike is the trailhead to the shrine known as Temple of the Moon. This is a fairly long hike around the back of Huayna Picchu mountain to a cave

Machu Picchu as seen from Huayana Picchu

and some very fine Incan stonework. The cave itself is very interesting but many people find it not to be worth the 2–3hr roundtrip hike.

SHUTTLE BUSES

There is a modern fleet of buses that leave Aguas Calientes for the 25min drive up to Machu Picchu. The bus station is located just downriver from the train station, across the big blue bridge, and the ticket office is open from 5am to 7pm. Bus tickets can be purchased either one way or round trip. They are also available up at Machu Picchu for the trip back down to Aguas Calientes. Bus tickets cost 45 soles, or $17 (€13) round trip and 23 soles or $9 (€7) each way, children 12 and under pay half price. The first bus up leaves at 5.30am, and they leave every few minutes after that depending on demand. The last one up leaves at 3.30pm and the last one back at about 5.30pm.

ROUTE 2
The Classic Inca Trail

Start	Pisca Cucho (2700m)
Finish	Machu Picchu (2480m)
Distance	46km from Km 82
Total ascent	2200m
Total descent	2400m
Difficulty	Moderate to strenuous, lots of steep stone steps
Time	4 days hiking
Trail type	Classic Incan road
High point	4200m
Bike or hike?	hike
Agency/guide?	required

The name 'The Inca Trail' is perhaps a bit misleading, given that there are hundreds of Inca trails throughout Peru, but that is how this route is known as it is considered to be the most important of them all, going as it does to Machu Picchu. It can be a bit more demanding than the Cusco travel agencies would have you believe, but anyone in reasonable physical condition should be able to manage it. The main concerns are the knees, ankles and heart. All three will take a real beating during this trek, so be sure to get cleared by a doctor if there are any doubts.

It is not possible to do this trek except with an agency, and they should provide a comprehensive list of what to bring and what not to bring. Be certain to pay attention to this list. Like all treks in the Sacred Valley, it is often very hot, but also often very cold. Both heat stroke and hypothermia are possibilities.

The classic Inca Trail hike begins in **Pisca Cucho**, which is on the rail line between Cusco and Aguas Calientes. The rail line is marked with signs indicating the distance from Cusco, and Pisco Cucho is located at Km 82, 12km west of Ollantaytambo. Technically the trek itself begins in **Huayllabamba**, further downriver, and it is possible to use one of the many routes in this book that end in

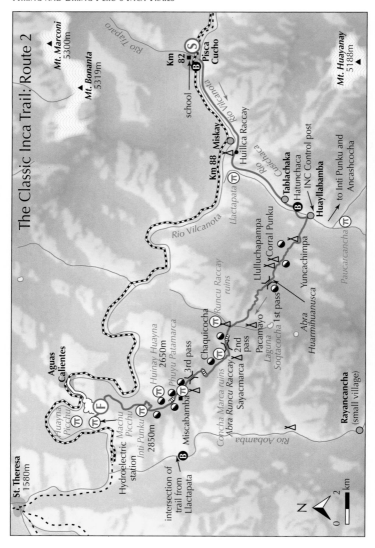

The Classic Inca Trail: Route 2

Huayllabamba as an extension for acclimatization and pleasure purposes. Arrangements would need to be made ahead of time with the agency organizing the trek.

There is an INC control point in Pisca Cucho at the end of the dirt road, at the river. After passing the control point, cross the bridge over the **Vilcanota (Urubamba) River** and go right (west) on the other side, climbing steeply away from the river for a bit before the trail becomes more level. Pass the village of **Miskay** before going down into and then out of a steep ravine to arrive at **Huillca Raccay**.

> **Huillca Raccay** is a fort overlooking the Rio Vilcanota, as well as the Cusichaca river valley which comes down from over Mt. Salkantay. It is believed to pre-date the Incas by quite some time and, catching your breath and looking around, it is easy to see why.

Turn left and begin going south up the Cusichaca valley. The walking is pleasant and the gradient is not very steep. There is a bridge called Hatunchaca ('big bridge' in Quechua) that crosses over to the western side of the river after 1hr of walking, and in another 45mins you will arrive at **Huayllabamba**, which lies at the mouth of the canyon known as Llulluchayoc. The altitude here is 3000m and this canyon is the official entrance to the Inca Trail. Huayllabamba was a very important junction in the Incan empire: continuing upward and straight ahead would bring you to trails back to Ollantaytambo via Paucarcancha and Ancashcocha, or else the trail climbs up and over Salkantay via the pass of Sisaypampa and on to Salkantaypampa, from where there are routes to Machu Picchu, Choquequirao and other important sites. Instead, enter the canyon to the right via the trail and after climbing for about 15mins there is a new **INC control post** where you will be required to register. ▶

After leaving the control post, the trail continues up the left-hand (southwestern) side of the Rio Llulluchayoc for just under 2hrs before arriving at **Yuncachimpa**.

It is a good idea to carry a photocopy of your passport while travelling in Peru, and it will definitely be needed here.

This site is also known as The Forks or sometimes Tres Piedras which means 'three stones'. This is a popular campsite with trekking groups. It's an acceptable choice if arriving late in the day, but otherwise there is a much better choice up ahead. So after a rest, the trail continues climbing up the valley. Fairly quickly the trail enters a sort of enchanted forest, quiet woods with moss hanging off the trees and birds chirping. This is woodland known as 'polylepis', and makes for wonderful walking. Most of these forests have long been cut down, replaced by the faster growing Eucalyptus tree. Enjoy this section – it is one of the most beautiful on the whole Inca Trail. It is also one of the steepest. The path climbs continuously along the river for another 2hrs, passing the lower campsite of **Corral Punku** before finally arriving at **Llulluchapampa**.

Llulluchapampa, 'lazy meadow' in Quechua, is a good place to camp and rest up for the following day's ascent to the highest point of the Inca Trail, Abra Huarmihuanusca ('Dead Woman Pass'), which can be seen from here. The climb up to the pass from Llulluchapampa takes a little less than 2hrs. The vegetation gradually thins out, into the *puna*, or high grasslands, typical at this altitude in the Andean mountains. There is nice stone paving on the ascent up to the pass; it looks Inca but actually was laid by the INC to prevent erosion on this part of the trail. The views are spectacular as you make the final ascent to the pass at 4200m. ◄

From here, the next pass can be seen, with the site of Runcu Raccay just below it, but for now just relax and enjoy this pass and its views – they were well earned!

The next section of the trail is a long, steep descent down to **Pacamayo**. The trail drops over 800m in just under 3km down to the river, and it takes 1–2hrs to get to Pacamayo, the next campsite, which lies at an altitude of 3600m. It is a nice and large campsite, with a little space to move around and a pleasant climate. The next destination is **Runcu Raccay**, which is 1hr and 200m of walking uphill from Pacamayo. This is a smaller site than others along the trail, and probably served as a *tambo*, a strategically located rest area and changeover point for the Inca relay messengers known as *chasquis*.

Trekkers enjoying the sun at Abra Runca Raccay

From Runcu Raccay it takes 1hr to walk the 1km to the next pass. There are a few false summits before arriving at two small lakes on the left; there are suitable sites for camping here, but they are pretty chilly. After one last stretch of steps, the trail arrives at **Abra Runcu Raccay**. At 4000m it is a little lower than the last pass but it is still high altitude, and the sections on both sides of the pass feature outstanding examples of Inca stone stairs. Take a moment to examine them, and ponder how much work must have been involved in making them.

From the pass the trail drops steeply down in classic Inca form, winding its way down for 1hr, with a brief rest in the middle at a *pampa*, or high, flat open space, before arriving at a short side trail to **Sayacmarca**. This is a very interesting site whose exact purpose is not certain; it certainly has a commanding view of the two river valleys it faces and in Quechua the name means 'inaccessible town'. After checking out this impressive site (as well as the nearby Concha Marca) continue down the trail to reach the valley floor.

This next section of trail is what you came to trek the Inca Trail for. It has absolutely superb stretches of **original Inca stonework** among its many elevated walkways in this marshy area. The misty clouds that are so often present only heighten the senses as you walk along this Inca road marvelling at not merely the sheer technical skill of the people who built such things, but also the overall sense of awe and joy that walking on a classic Inca road always provides.

At **Chaquicocha** the trail begins to climb fairly steeply, passing through a pretty cool Inca tunnel before arriving at the third pass. There are now views in all directions, as you continue to develop your appreciation of how the Incas wove their roads and their lives through the very heights of these huge mountains. Inspiring, indeed.

Fifty metres below the pass there is yet another impressive site, this one being **Phuyu Patamarca**, at an altitude of 3610m. It has a series of ritual water fountains cascading down its steep steps and drops, and there is also some very fine Inca stonework here. The name means 'cloud town' in Quechua and it is easy to see why, as it is frequently in the mist or with long streams of white clouds streaming by. There is a campsite here that is used by a lot of tour groups. It is worth spending some time here wandering around, before heading out the west end and back on the trail. Now comes the last of the knee-jarring descents; this one is again on a very fine section of Inca stair work, in fact some of the best on the whole trail.

It takes 3hrs to get from Phuyu Patamarca to **Huinay Huayna**, which is located just downhill from the trekker's hostel. The site is extensive and features more of the ceremonial baths to which you have no doubt become accustomed.

It is interesting to consider the role of things like these **baths** when thinking about what the purpose of the various Inca sites might have been. Archaeologists frequently use the presence of fountains to ascertain that a site had a religious worshiping of water aspect

Incan stonework in the mist

to its purpose. But perhaps it was merely that many of these sites were simply vacation homes for noblemen high in the ranks of Inca society, and much like the reader might have a small water feature in the house that they live in, so did the Incas – only much more elaborate.

The water features and stonework of Huinay Huayna are very impressive indeed. After spending a while checking them out, it is now time for the final stretch into Machu Picchu. The trail leaves from the lower corner of the trekker's hostel and takes a mostly level course for the next 1hr on an Inca stone pathway.

The **final approach** is, again, classic Incan. They always exercised total control over arrivals to their sites; the roads themselves are designed to impart maximum impact on the visitor. There is no getting many little glimpses of a site as you approach, but rather the whole entrance is designed to be an experience, and a profound one at that. Often it will reflect and integrate with the surrounding terrain. The Incas apparently noticed false summits while trekking as much as we do now. They used to their advantage both the unwelcome extra effort and disappointment that results when you realize the destination is still further ahead, and also the heightened suspense and extra enjoyment that comes at the end.

The Incas in their roads seemed to have duplicated the false arrivals that exist naturally in the mountains. Here is the classic example then: as you sense that the end is near there is a steep set of stairs of fine stonework making the final ascent to Machu Picchu. One last time, you must wait a few more minutes to see the goal of the previous four days of walking. One final set of stairs and you arrive at **Inti Punku** and its classic view of Machu Picchu.

Camping is not allowed here and it is usually a very crowded spot early in the morning as trekkers from around the world await the sunrise over the ruins. The unfortunate reality is that they are often disappointed; most of the year the sun rises from behind the surrounding mountains and doesn't appear until later in the morning, spoiling the effect. It is also often foggy. No matter, because nothing can take away from the sheer majesty of the city below. Words cannot do it justice, and so none will try. Enjoy the view. It is a walk of about 45mins down the fine Inca road from Inti Punku to arrive at the INC control and entrance to **Machu Picchu**, one of the Seven Wonders of the Modern World. Enjoy!

2 AROUND CUSCO

Biking down from the ruins of H'uchuy Cusco (Route 3)

INTRODUCTION

The massive and precise Incan stonework of Sacsayhuaman in Cusco

Cusco is one of the centres of Incan culture and its largest city, featuring numerous museums, shops, restaurants and a surprising number of Inca sites. Although it seems to have lost a bit of its lustre in recent years as more travellers seek out lower altitude and a more relaxed atmosphere in the Sacred Valley, it is still one of the most popular cities in South America. And while there are only a handful of trekking or biking routes that leave from Cusco, nearly all travellers finish their stay here. The city of Cusco is one of South America's gems and not only boasts various Inca historical sites but also is the departure point for trips into the Ausangate area, the Amazon jungle, and several of the routes to Choquequirao and Machu Picchu itself.

There are virtually unlimited choices for lodging and dining in the city of Cusco. All the tourist-orientated businesses are for the most part clustered around the city's central Plaza de Armas and are all a short walk to shopping and sites. The historic area of San Blas, an artsy type of neighbourhood just a few blocks uphill from the Plaza de Armas has a number of inexpensive hotels and traveller hostels. Accommodation ranges from shared bathroom backpacker hostels all the way up to four-star hotels, and pretty much everything in between. Restaurants vary from the upscale and trendy tourist haunts down to food vendors on the street corner. Choose a hotel near the Plaza de Armas to be centrally located. Note that businesses in Cusco change phone numbers and websites frequently and so some of the information reproduced below may be out of date.

ACCOMMODATION

One of the more expensive places to stay in town is the Hotel Monasterio, Calle Palacios 136, Plazoleta Nazarenas (www.monasteriohotel. com, tel: (51) 84 60 4000). Though ridiculously overpriced at over $300 (€218) per night, it does have a good central location and is located inside an old Inca stone palace, so the place oozes authenticity. Perhaps the best value in Cusco is the Hotel Torre Dorada, Calle Los Cipreses N-5 Residencial Huancaro (info@torredo-rada.com.pe, tel: 84 241698). It gets very high ratings and at around $110 (€80) for a double room offers a good combination of a quality hotel along with a reasonable price and very friendly staff.

Another upscale but less expensive stay can be found at Casa San Blas, Tocuyeros 566 (www. casasanblas.com, tel: (51) 84 237900). They have beautiful single and double rooms, both for the same price of $110 (€80). A beautiful boutique hotel with nicely decorated rooms and views of the city, it is a good high-end choice. A more reasonable option is the quaint Casona

Biking down the Huarocondo canyon, with the bridge to Soccma visible on the left (Route 6)

de Pleiades, Calle Tandapata 116 (www.casona-pleiades.com, tel: (51) 84 506430) at $65 (€50) for double and $80 (€62) for triple room. The rooms are very tastefully decorated with down duvets on the bed for those cold June nights, and there is a nice central meeting area. Also recommended is Tika Wasi, Calle Tandapata Route 491 Corner of San Blas and Siete Angelitos (www.tikawasi.net, tel: (51) 84 231609) with double rooms for $60 (€44) and triples for $75 (€54). This is a very nice little hotel with a large green courtyard and garden with views overlooking the city. It has wi-fi throughout the hotel and clean, modern rooms.

Those seeking the most inexpensive lodging should look for the hostels clustered around the Plaza San Blas. In particular check out El Artesano (tel: (51) 84 263968, email hospedajeartesano790@hotmail.com), which is located above the plaza (look for the bar called Km 0) and walk up one block to Suytucato 790. It is a quiet place but the walk up the steep street will tire you out! Those looking for a more youthful and boisterous stay should check out Loki, the hip backpacker hostel located on Cuesta Santa Ana 601 (www.lokihostel.com, tel: (51) 84 243705). Dorm rooms start at $8 (€6) per person, and there are a few private rooms for $27 (€20).

Cusco at sunset

DINING AND NIGHTLIFE

There are hundreds of restaurants in and around Cusco, and a wide range of prices and food types available. Most of the restaurants are centred between the Plaza San Francisco, uphill to the Plaza de Armas, and on up to the Plaza San Blas. Be sure to check out Ciccolina, Calle Triunfo 393, 2nd floor (www.CiccolinaCuzco. com, Tel: (51) 84 506430); entrees cost $7–$15 (€6–€11), and it specialises in freshly made pastas, steaks and other dishes with a Mediterranean flair. For exotic wood-fired pizzas – try the roasted vegetable – head for Baco, located near the Plaza at Ruinas No. 465 (email bacorestaurante@yahoo. com, tel: (51) 84 242808). Another popular gringo hangout, with very good reason, is Jack's Cafe, located on the corner of Choquechaca and Cuesta San Blas, between the Plaza de Armas and the Plaza San Blas (tel: (51) 84 254606). They serve classic 'food from home' – sandwiches on homemade bread, soups, salads, and some of the best and freshest espresso in town. Another good bet is Don Esteban Avenue del Sol 765 (tel: (51) 84 243629), a casual bakery/cafe with excellent espressos, whose owners also have a chic little cafe Don Esteban and Don Pancho, located at Portal Espinal 144 with great Peruvian cuisine.

For nightlife, there are a few discos located right on the Plaza de Armas that frequently change names (currently called Mama Africa and Mythology). They stay open all night and are the place to be for dancing and meeting young people from all over the world. Ukuku's is just a half block off the main square and has live music seven days a week. Also popular and right on the square is Norton's, a bar with a biker theme and a couple of pool tables and dartboards as well as famous hamburgers. Paddy's Irish Pub is right around the corner and has tap beers and an authentic pub atmosphere. Calle Tecsecocha, one block from the main plaza, is lined with discos and bars. There are always new bars and pubs opening in Cusco. Ask around when you arrive to find the latest favourite haunts.

ROUTE 3
To Calca via H'uchuy Cusco

Start	Tambo Machay, just above Cusco (3810m)
Finish	Calca (2960m)
Distance	25km
Total ascent	850m
Total descent	1700m
Difficulty	Moderate
Time	1–2 days hiking, 1 day biking
Trail type	Old Incan road, singletrack
High point	4320m (highest pass)
Bike or hike?	both
Agency/guide?	no

This is a great trek which leaves directly from Cusco, making it one of the more easily accessible treks for those with limited time. It is also an excellent mountain bike ride for advanced riders. H'uchuy Cusco means 'little Cusco' in Quechua and this was an important Incan site located on the descent down into the royal estates of Calca and Yucay. Nearly all of the route is above the tree line, providing excellent mountain views in all directions. However, this same lack of trees also means a lack of shelter from rain or intense sun, so bring appropriate gear. It is possible to camp in or near the ruins of H'uchuy Cusco, and if a night's camping is desired this is highly recommended. Many travellers trek the route to the site, camp there overnight and descend the next day. Otherwise, the route can be done in one long day.

There are a few possible start points for this trip including Tambo Machay, Sacsayhuaman, Chinchero, the Cusco–Pisac highway and others. The route described here leaves from Tambo Machay, one of a string of Incan sites laid out just above Cusco. Visiting all these sites is highly recommended and they are very close together in distance.

The trail begins at a ceremonial bath complex displaying the Incas' typical flair for the dramatic and difficult. The site of **Tambo Machay** is clearly marked at the main road from Cusco and is just across the highway from

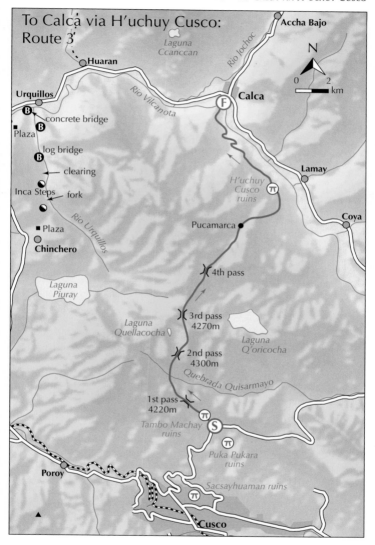

To Calca via H'uchuy Cusco:
Route 3

Accha Bajo
Laguna
Ccanccan
Huaran
Rio Jochoc
Urquillos
Rio Vilcanota
Calca
concrete bridge
F
Plaza
log bridge
clearing
Lamay
Inca Steps   fork
H'uchuy
Cusco
ruins
Coya
Rio Urquillos
Plaza
Pucamarca
Chinchero
Laguna
Piuray
4th pass
3rd pass
4270m
Laguna
Quellacocha
Laguna
Q'oricocha
2nd pass
4300m
Quebrada Quisarmayo
1st pass
4220m
Tambo Machay
ruins
S
Poroy
Puka Pukara
ruins
Sacsayhuaman ruins
Cusco

N
0   2
km

Puka Pukara (meaning 'red fort' in Quechua). Although there is no indication from the highway that it contains the trail to H'uchuy Cusco, rest assured that it does. To get on the trail, simply enter the site of Tambo Machay from the road and continue climbing above it. The trail quickly turns into a nice singletrack and climbs steadily northward and up. As is often the case in Peru, there may be several minor trails that branch off. Try to stay on the main trail, and as long as it continues upward in a northerly direction it is the correct one. Even if the main trail appears to split into several small ones, they all merge further uphill, something which is common when hiking in the Sacred Valley.

A little under 3hrs of easy walking brings you to the first pass, which lies at 4220m and has great views of Cusco and Tambo Machay, as well as views to the north. The trail has merged with the one from that climbs up from Sacsayhuaman, and is now following the original road used by Inca royalty to access their countryside retreats in the valley below. After a short 1hr climb comes the second pass, at an altitude of 4300m. ◄ Pass to the other side of the lake, taking the trail that goes around the end of the lake on the right-hand (northern) side. Follow the trail as it climbs up the gently angled ascent on the other side on up to the third pass, at 4270m. ◄ Take the trail over one more ridge, to the northeast to the last pass.

This is the valley that leads to H'uchuy Cusco and is marked with a small sign. Follow the trail down the valley, staying on the right-hand side until coming to **Pucamarca**, a typical Andean village whose rooftops and homes blend right in to the surrounding terrain, not surprising considering the village was built from the surrounding terrain. Continue descending from Pucamarca and soon large Inca terraces will appear along the right-hand side of the trail. Indeed, virtually the entire mountainside from here down to H'uchuy Cusco has been built up by the Incas. Soon the valley is choked off into a narrow ravine, and a very impressive and steep Inca stone staircase passes through the narrow canyon.

Below can be seen the small reservoir of Laguna Quellacocha (meaning 'lazy lake' in Quechua).

Here the much larger Laguna Q'oricocha (meaning 'lake of gold' in Quechua) is visible below on the right.

The path then briefly ascends, in classic Inca architectural style, to a dramatic viewpoint across crescent ravine covered entirely with Inca terracing. Upon circling along the top to the other side, the site of **H'uchuy Cusco** finally becomes visible. It has the usual impressive views in all directions, fulfilling both military and aesthetic purposes.

H'uchuy Cusco

There has been much speculation about the purpose of **H'uchuy Cusco** as well as about who built it. It seems likely that it was an early fort, perhaps built even before the arrival of the Incas, which they then improved upon, as was their habit. There is also an Incan road from here that goes over to Chinchero.

To return to Cusco or Ollantaytambo via the river valley below, there are two options. The first is the trail that goes northeast directly down to the river from the ruins to Lamay, via a bridge that was washed out at the time of writing but will no doubt soon be replaced. Or there is a trail and also a road that leaves from just 0.5km west of the ruins, both leading to **Calca**. The road is steep and made of very loose gravel and sand, and drops quickly down to the river below, then goes downriver 1km to the bridge at Calca that crosses the Vilcanota River to the main highway.

If you are mountain biking this route to Calca, there are various shortcuts that cut off the road switchbacks, and there is also a single-track that runs down the centre of the small canyon just to the left of the small road that descends to the river. Regardless of which route is chosen, whether trekking or biking, the views of the Cordillera Urubamba are excellent from the top and the descent a pleasant one.

ROUTE 4
The back way to Ollantaytambo

Start	Huarocondo (3330m)
Finish	Ollantaytambo (2850m)
Distance	28km
Total ascent	500m
Total descent	1000m
Difficulty	Moderate hike due to distance, easy mountain bike
Time	1 day hiking, half day biking
Trail type	Asphalt, dirt road, old Inca road
High point	Poroy (3530m)
Bike or hike?	both
Agency/guide?	no

This is the 'back way' locals use to travel between Cusco and Ollantaytambo. After Huarocondo the road drops down into a narrow and very scenic canyon, following it down into the Sacred Valley just east of Ollantaytambo. The train from Cusco to Machu Picchu also follows this route. There are several interesting Inca sites along the way that can be seen from the road, so even if you don't have a chance to hike it, consider hiring a taxi from Cusco to take this route to Ollantaytambo. It also makes an excellent route for mountain bikes or motorcycles.

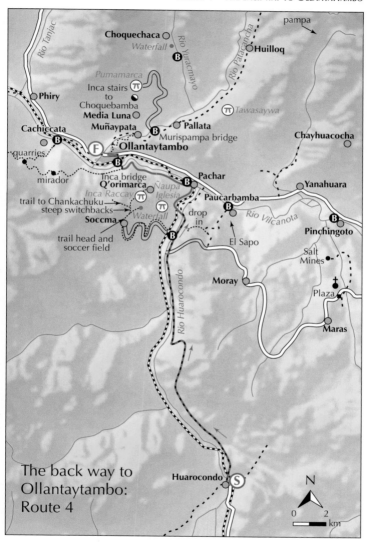

pampa

Choquechaca ○
Waterfall ⒷWIN
Río Yuracmayo
Huilloq ○

Pumamarca
Inca stairs ㊙
to
Choquebamba
Media Luna ○
Muñaypata ○
Phiry ○
Tawasaywa ㊙
Pallata ●
Murispampa bridge
Chayhuacocha ○

Cachiccata
Ⓑ
○
quarries
Ⓕ
Ollantaytambo
Ⓑ
Pachar
Ⓑ
Paucarbamba
Ⓑ
Yanahuara ●

mirador ●
Inca bridge
Q'orimarca ㊙
Ñaupa
Iglesia
Río Vilcanota
Ⓑ
Pinchingoto ●

trail to Chankachuku →
steep switchbacks →
Inca Raccay ㊙
Waterfall
drop
in
Soccma ●
El Sapo
Salt
Mines ●
trail head and
soccer field
Ⓑ
Moray ○
†
Plaza ●

Río Huarocondo
Maras

The back way to
Ollantaytambo:
Route 4

Huarocondo Ⓢ

N
0   2
km

The route is nearly all downhill from the high plains town of Huarocondo, so if walking the route, it is best to take transport to Huarocondo (or Anta, located right on the Cusco–Mollepata highway) and start there. If travelling this route on mountain bike, you could do the same and only bike the descent from Huarocondo to Ollantaytambo. Otherwise, it is a nice hike or bike ride all the way from Cusco with some moderate climbing along the way. The road down from Huarocondo meets the main Cusco–Ollantaytambo highway at Pachar, 7km from Ollantaytambo, and is an easy route to follow.

If starting from **Cusco**, take the main highway west out of town, and simply follow the signs for Izcuchaca. It is 26km from Cusco to Anta, and another 13km from Anta to Huarocondo. After arriving at Anta, turn right to pass through Izcuchaca and take the road onward to **Huarocondo**, which is paved and not heavily used.

> **Huarocondo** is a small town that is virtually unblemished by tourist activities or services and is famous for *chicharrones*, a snack of fried pork rind that is very popular with the locals. With its big central plaza, this is an excellent place to rest and have some lunch, some chicharrones washed down by a cold beer being highly recommended!

To leave Huarocondo, take the street that leaves the northwestern corner of the plaza. The local streets seem to close regularly for some type of construction and it can be a bit confusing, so ask a local to point out the right direction to Pachar. This route follows the train tracks that take passengers from Cusco to Machu Picchu. The road drops into the deep and narrow canyon shortly after leaving Huarocondo and continues down for 21km until meeting up with the Cusco–Urubamba–Ollantaytambo highway. ◄

Keep an eye out on the left for the terraces and Inca cave 'Ñaupa Iglesia', just before the road crosses to the left (western) side of the river.

From **Pachar**, an unremarkable village on the border of the Rio Vilcanota, the old Inca road goes off to the left directly onward to Ollantaytambo. Look for the small footbridge crossing the river, or ask a local. If travelling by

car or motorcycle, take the large orange bridge over the Urubamba and take a left, going west, and continue to Ollantaytambo which is 7km away. Otherwise, if biking or hiking this route, this is a great opportunity to arrive into Ollantaytambo as the Incas did. The trail follows the southern bank of the Vilcanota River, which was sacred to the Incas. As the trail continues west on a gentle downhill gradient, more and more Incan buildings appear on the surrounding hillsides and it becomes obvious that you are approaching an Incan city of major importance. The terrain on both sides of the river is impressively terraced, and it is easy to imagine the vast quantities of corn that were grown here in Incan times.

The trail ends at the bottom of town where the buttresses of the original Incan bridge that were the entrance to Ollantaytambo still remain. Cross the bridge and take the road, which diverges from the river here, the last 0.5km into town.

Biking down the narrow canyon from Huarocondo towards Pachar

ROUTE 5
To Urubamba via '44'

Start	Chinchero (3750m)
Finish	Urubamba (2880m)
Distance	21km; 10km from Km 44
Total ascent	100m; 0m from Km 44
Total descent	970m
Difficulty	Easy hike, moderate mountain bike
Time	2–3hrs hiking, 1–2hrs biking
Trail type	Incan road
High point	3750m at Chinchero or 3600m (at Km 44 on the Cusco–Ollantaytambo highway)
Bike or hike?	both
Agency/guide?	no

For those without a lot of experience, this is one of the better mountain bike rides in the valley – a smooth and moderate trail that passes through open meadows and is downhill all the way to Urubamba. Most of the route follows an old Inca road from Cusco to Urubamba, and there are stunning views of the Urubamba range the whole way down the trail. It's not the best hike in the valley due to its proximity to the traffic on the main highway to Urubamba, but on a nice day would still be better than taking the bus down. It is also one of the few mountain bike rides in the area that is suitable for beginners.

Start in **Chinchero** on the main Cusco–Urubamba highway if you want to exercise the legs a little, as there are about 10km of up-and-down road riding to warm up on before arriving at the trailhead. Or, if a pure downhill ride is preferred, simply watch the white marker posts along the highway and get out at the marker post of Km 44.

The trail proper begins on the west side of the highway, just past the **Km 44** marker post. Follow the trail as it goes down into the gully and water runoff channel. There are a few side trails and intersections along the way, but just continue straight and downward (north)

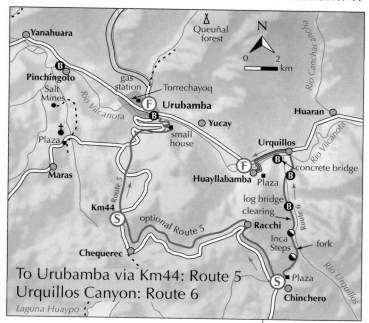

To Urubamba via Km44: Route 5
Urquillos Canyon: Route 6

directly towards the mountains, as the trail cuts through farm fields and family agriculture holdings, mostly of *maiz* (corn) and *trigo* (wheat). The trail will cross the asphalt highway twice during the first 5km. In each case, just look for the trail to continue on the other side of the highway.

After the second road crossing, the trail drops down further, parallel to the main road which is on the left. The path now follows a road several hundred years old that was used by the Incas travelling to Urubamba. After a long, fast stretch of downhill the trail crosses the paved road again just where it is making a sweeping right-hand curve. Cross the road and take the trail another 1km downwards until crossing the paved road for the final time.

A good view of the Cordillera Urubamba

Cross the road (which now makes a sweeping left-hand turn) and the trail arrives at a cluster of small houses located right on the corner. There is a new dirt road at this spot that goes straight up the mountain and is closed off with a small chain. Do not take this road. Instead, bikers of intermediate skill level or below should bypass the rest of this trail and get back on the paved highway here, to take the pleasant descent down to the river and the town of **Urubamba**.

More advanced bikers, or those hiking, should continue along the trail that runs straight downhill towards the river, away from the chained road entrance. ◄ The trail is a bit tricky to follow at this point as there are numerous footpaths heading off in every direction. The best line goes down at a slight right-hand angle, northeast towards the river. The trail splits several times but nearly all of them go down to the river, so choose the most obvious one or ask a local. The trail ends at the main bridge over the Vilcanota River, from where there is ample transport on to Ollantaytambo or back to Cusco.

Use caution on this section as there are numerous drop offs (and cacti) to contend with.

ROUTE 6
Urquillos Canyon

Start	Chinchero (3750m)
Finish	Huayllabamba (2910m)
Distance	11km
Total ascent	0m
Total descent	840m
Difficulty	Moderate hiking, difficult mountain biking
Time	3–4hrs hiking, 2–3hrs biking
Trail type	Incan road
High point	3750m
Bike or hike?	both
Agency/guide?	no
Route map	see Route 5

The canyon of Urquillos is a beautiful, technical and epic descent on a well-preserved Inca trail once used by Incan nobles to descend from Cusco down to their royal estates in the pleasant valley below. The best known of these estates is in Yucay, just downstream along the Rio Vilcanota from Huayllabamba, where the trail exits onto the main highway. This trail is an outstanding hike and is nearly all downhill, on Incan stairways most of the way. It is quite rocky as it descends Urquillos Canyon, and much of the trail is exposed to falls of 10m or more just off the trail. Thus it is only recommend for advanced mountain bikers riding a high-quality suspension mountain bike. For those with skills and a good bike, however, this route is one of the best in the valley and is a local mountain biking favourite.

Hikers of any ability will enjoy the walk immensely – aside from the exposure, it is not particularly strenuous or difficult. Urquillos Canyon is one of the very few canyons in the valley with virtually no inhabitants. There are small patches of native vegetation and trees, and overall it is a very pleasant place to be. There is little foot traffic on the trail, save for the occasional *burro* (donkey) making its way up from the valley bottom. There are excellent views from here of the Cordillera Urubamba and the many glaciated peaks it contains, including Chicón, Pumahuanca, Pitusiray, Sawasiray and others.

This trail is best done one way, downhill. Start in **Chinchero**, which is easily reached by public or private transport from Cusco, Urubamba or Ollantaytambo. The trail leaves from the northwestern corner of the central plaza of Chinchero.

This is where a popular **market** takes place on Tuesdays, Thursdays and Sundays. On these days it is quite full of vendors surrounded by their colourful wares, tourists walking by mumbling 'no gracias' in bad Spanish, and stray dogs and seemingly stray children wandering everywhere. Chinchero was an important Incan outpost along the route from Cusco to Ollantaytambo, and there is a sizeable amount of the settlement still intact. There is also an early Colonial church which is definitely worth a look if there is time. Entrance to the Chinchero site is included in the Boleto Turistico.

The descent down the Incan road from Chinchero to Urquillos

To begin the trail, take the cobblestone paved road from the west (bottom) end of the square. After a

Route 6 – Urquillos Canyon

short distance reach a T-junction, turn right and after just 3m take a left turn into a long, downhill dirt alley with low adobe walls on each side and a trail down the centre. ▶ Take this trail down; it will shortly curve to the right and break gloriously out into the open, an excellent dirt singletrack set among extensive farming terraces to the left and more terraces and Incan walls on the right. The trail starts fast, interrupted by only a few rocks and steps, before coming out to an outstanding section of Incan road, impeccably paved smooth with carved rocks and stones.

If this is all a bit tough to follow, ask a local to point out the way to Urquillos.

Then follows a series of impressive **Incan staircases**, one long set in particular which is a fun challenge for experienced mountain bikers. After a few stream crossings and another long staircase, the trail becomes smooth as it descends the right (east) side of this feeder canyon. Stay on the main trail until arriving at an intersection after 3km, where there is a **fork** in the trail. The path continues straight and starts climbing (an old Inca road that eventually reaches Huch'uy Cusco) but there is also a trail going down and to the left, into the canyon itself. This is the correct trail to take. Soon after, the trail breaks out into the open and begins descending the west side of this beautiful canyon. Continue descending through a never-ending series of Inca steps and drops until arriving at a small, grassy clearing. This makes a good place to rest and have some water and a snack.

After leaving the **small clearing** the trail winds pleasantly down the centre of the canyon in the shade, until coming to a small **log bridge**. Cross the bridge and continue. After another 1km it will arrive at a small pampa. It is important to look for this because it is here that you will find another log bridge, this one off to the left of the trail and very hard to see if not looking closely for it. ▶ The trail continues down, past small houses and farms before crossing a **concrete bridge** near the bottom, and arrives at the plaza of Huayllabamba, a small town along the Vilcanota River. Carry on to the main highway and you will find ample public transport going by in either direction to go to Pisac or Urubamba.

If you miss this bridge, the trail will still come out eventually on the main highway below.

3 AROUND URUBAMBA

Approaching the glacier of Chicón in the Sacred Valley (Route 11)

INTRODUCTION

The town of Urubamba lies in the heart of the Sacred Valley at the base of the Cordillera Urubamba, a large mountain range highlighted by the 5700m glacier Chicón and its tributaries. This range is part of the Continental Divide and separates the Sacred Valley from the descent down into the jungle and Amazon basin. A number of popular routes to Inca sites and day tours in the region leave from Urubamba, and there are also a couple treks that start here, climb up and over the Cordillera Urubamba and then plunge towards the Amazon basin.

Urubamba is not highly recommended as a place to stay, as it has an industrial feel and most of the accommodation is scattered along the highway. That said, it does have the attractive central Plaza de Armas and there is a growing number of places taking advantage of its lower altitude and more pleasant climate and the desire of many travellers to be based outside of Cusco. It is also centrally located between Cusco, Pisac and Ollantaytambo. Primarily known as a stopping place for large groups doing the standard Sacred Valley tour, it does have a large number of buffet-type restaurants for large groups. Other higher-end gourmet restaurants are opening up every year and some of them are worth a try.

ACCOMMODATION

There is a slew of new hotels open in the Urubamba area. Most of them cater to large groups and are a bit sterile. The best place to stay in Urubamba is Hotel Sol y Luna, Fundo Huincho Lot A-5 (www.hotelsolyluna.com, tel: (51) 84 201620). This is a boutique hotel with lovely landscaping and individual bungalows, and it is professionally run. Another good option is K'uchi Rumi (www.urubamba.com, tel: (51) 84 976 0356), which is also a bungalow-styled lodge, with seven rooms and a friendly staff.

DINING

An excellent high-end choice in Urubamba is Huacatay, Calle Jr. Arica 620 (www.elhuacatay.com, tel: (51) 84 201790). It serves Peruvian fusion cuisine and has a nice decor and an outside patio. A more casual choice is Café Plaza, located right on the Plaza de Armas in Urubamba, 440 Jirón Bolívar (tel: 84 201118), serving classic Peruvian food, soups, pastries and an assortment of local dishes.

ROUTE 7
Salt Mines of Maras and Moray

Start	Moray (3560m)
Finish	Pinchingoto (2890m)
Distance	14km
Total ascent	110m
Total descent	780m
Difficulty	Easy hiking, moderate mountain biking
Time	3–4hrs hiking, 2–3hrs biking (including time to visit both sites)
Trail type	Wide singletrack
High point	3560m (Moray)
Bike or hike?	both
Agency/guide?	no

This is a very popular route for both mountain biking and hiking, as it visits two interesting Inca sites: the Salt Mines of Maras and the site of Moray, both of which are unique and fantastic to visit. They do get a lot of visitors but most arrive and depart by bus or taxi and thus the trail linking the two attractions is little used and wonderful to walk or bike along. This route is almost entirely downhill, and so perfect for intermediate mountain bikers and almost any type of hiker. Either prearrange for a taxi to wait here, or else there is regular public transport to either Ollantaytambo or Urubamba and on to Cusco.

There are many different ways to do this trip but the best way is to first take a taxi directly to the site of Moray, as this is the high point, and there currently is no public transport of any kind to get there. The turnoff to Maras and Moray is located 12km above Urubamba on the main Cusco–Urubamba highway. It is not well marked but there is a small bus stop type of shelter as well as a forlorn old building across the street that apparently sells gasoline. There are private taxis waiting at this turnoff, so it is possible to arrive from Cusco or Urubamba by bus and go on to Moray from here in a taxi, which will cost about 20 soles. Pass through Maras and take the road all the way to **Moray**.

The visit to **Moray** is a very enjoyable one. A series of elaborate concentric circular terraces, it is claimed to have been a site for the Incas to experiment with growing crops at different altitudes, a sort of agricultural research centre. There are, apparently, significant differences in climatic conditions between the terraces, and seeds have been found from the time of the Incas. It seems more likely, however, that it was constructed as a ceremonial place to grow sacred crops, built long after the Quechuan people had perfected growing their crops at whichever altitude in their vast empire they wished. Certainly the construction is quite elaborate and extensive, containing hundreds of thousands of hand-placed stones. In any event, entrance costs 10 soles for adults or 3 soles for students; however the entrance fee is included in the Boleto Turistico.

The enigmatic circular terraces of Moray

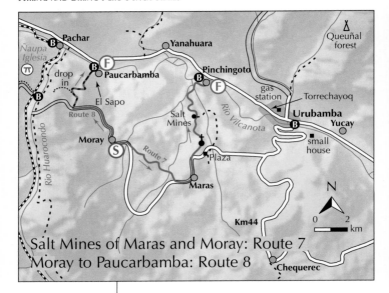

Salt Mines of Maras and Moray: Route 7
Moray to Paucarbamba: Route 8

After visiting the site, walk or ride back out 0.5km
along the same road you came in on. The road drops
into a small drainage, climbs back up, and after going
east 100m there is a sharp right-hand bend in the road.
At this spot there is a well-worn double-track trail going
straight ahead, and this is the trail that leads to Maras.
After a few hundred meters, there is a faint track leading
off to the right side. It goes a short distance to a pile of
rocks that was likely an Incan building of some short.
This is not the correct route, but if you are in no hurry
it is worth checking out. From here, there are no more
turns as the route traverses the altiplano via a maze of
different single-track trails, all which go in the same
direction towards **Maras**. There are a few small drainages to cross, and various foot trails going down and to
the left, but do not follow them. Stay on the high (right)
side of any trail junctions. There are excellent photo
opportunities at all points along this route, and the trail

is outstanding for walking and especially mountain biking.

After 7km of winding trail, and after the last small climb out of the final drainage, the trail returns to the main road just above Maras. Follow it down five blocks, then take a left towards the plaza, currently marked by a green house with an arrow on it pointing left. ▸

Upon entering the main plaza of Maras, continue straight and downhill, towards the northwest corner of the plaza and take the short, interestingly cobbled paved walkway to enter the grounds of the church. Cross the small lawn in front of the church heading south (downhill, towards the river). The lawn drops off steeply and here the trail begins – be sure not to take the wider dirt road that goes to the left, but the narrower footpath that descends directly downhill, in the direction of the massive Chicón glacier in the background.

From here, the trail heads down towards the river and Urubamba, into the canyon. The trail winds along the left (west) side of the canyon a few kilometres down to the **Salt Mines** of Maras.

Be sure to note the doorways of the houses along this street – most of them date from Colonial times and contain the original, massive stone doorway headers with elaborate carvings.

The **Salt Mines** is another interesting Inca site. It features a naturally salinated stream that has been diverted into hundreds of small, gravity-fed evaporation pools. The pools are individually owned and worked by families in the community and passed down to the next generation. These pools produce massive amounts of salt every month during the dry season from May to September, and have provided salt for the kitchen tables of Cusco, as well as an income for the local community of Maras, for hundreds of years. It is said that in Incan times, salt would be brought to the Peruvian coast and used to pack and preserve freshly caught fish from the ocean. This would then be run over the mountains by Inca chasquis (messengers/runners) using a relay system and taking advantage of the tambos (Inca relay stations and rest huts) in order to bring the Inca royalty fresh fish less than 48hrs after it was

The Salt Mines of Maras

removed from the Pacific Ocean. These days, how-ever, the community probably earns more from the entrance fees than from salt sales. This site is a must-see and there is only a 7 soles charge to enter.

To avoid the crowds, pay the fee but then continue through the gate instead of going down the main way. Go down the trail another 0.5km to the sharp 'S' curve in the trail. From there, you can access the pans just a few metres from the trail and get a close and upfront look at this ancient marvel. After visiting the salt pans, the trail continues down the canyon, crossing the Rio Vilcanota and exiting onto the main highway at **Pinchingoto**. Arrange to have a taxi waiting here, or else just simpy catch a passing combi to go to either Ollantaytambo or Cusco.

ROUTE 8
Moray to Paucarbamba

Start	Moray (3560m)
Finish	Paucarbamba (2875m)
Distance	11km
Total ascent	0m
Total descent	685m
Difficulty	Easy hike, advanced mountain bike
Time	2hrs hiking, 1hr biking
Trail type	Singletrack
High point	3560m (Moray)
Bike or hike?	both
Agency/guide?	no
Route map	see Route 7

A variation on the standard Maras–Moray circuit described in Route 7, this trip also starts from the site of Moray. However, instead of traversing over to Maras, this route follows a trail that drops down in to a scenic canyon characterized by a distinct red soil before finally exiting onto the Urubamba highway at the bridge of Paucarbamba. This makes for a very nice walk or bike ride. In fact, the descent is one of the best mountain bike downhill routes in the valley.

After visiting the site of Moray, begin descending the dirt road that continues past the site, heading down (north) towards the river. Note that this is the opposite direction the main traffic flow to Cusco. After only 0.5km, after the road makes a sharp turn to the left, there is another road going off to the right, directly towards the river. The road you are currently on continues straight, cresting a small hill before winding its way over to the road that comes down the canyon from Huarocondo. Be sure to not continue on the current road but rather turn right on the road heading down to the river.

Follow this trail downhill, after just a few minutes it will enter a small grassy area and turn into a singletrack shortly before arriving at, and crossing, a small double width dirt trail that continues on to the left. Here is the entrance to 'drop in' to the canyon. Simply continue down on the same trail you came in on, crossing the road and continuing down into the canyon. The narrow trail clings to the right side of the canyon as it drops down steeply.

The trail continues on towards El Sapo, which is the local name for the large red dirt hill a few kilometres down the canyon. The trail is a bit tough to find in a few places as it transitions, but the main idea is to be on the right side of the canyon, about halfway up – not down on the floor nor up on the crest. Using this advice as a guide, there should be no problem finding and following the trail, which continues winding its way down the canyon.

Descending from Moray with the Cordillera Urubamba in the background

This path has been used for hundreds of years to access the river from the altiplano, and vice versa. Countless cycles of rain and sun have turned the surface

Biking from Moray to Ollantaytambo

into a baked cement of mixed red and white clay. The trail is quite narrow and a bit tricky to descend on bike, but most parts are quite rideable and it is blazing fast. ▸

After 5km, the path will arrive at and cross another narrow dirt road. This one originates from Paucarbamba, where the trail is heading – but instead look for the singletrack to cross it twice and then continue down the right side of the canyon and **El Sapo**. For bikers, the trail really picks up speed here, as it runs along side a few *chakras* – small, family plots of land used for farming.

The trail eventually spills out on the same dirt road that was crossed a few times earlier, and from here the trail follows the road out the last 2km. The road comes out right at the bridge of **Paucarbamba**, crossing the Vilcanota River. You can arrange to have a taxi waiting here or else you can easily catch a passing combi, either to Ollantaytambo or the other direction towards Urubamba and Cusco.

Watch out for cacti, as they are everywhere around the trail.

ROUTE 9
Abra Azulcocha to Calca

Start	Abra Azulcocha (4450m)
Finish	Calca (2960m)
Distance	26km
Total ascent	0km
Total descent	1490m
Difficulty	Easy hiking, moderate to difficult mountain biking
Time	4–6hrs hiking, 2–3hrs biking
Trail type	Incan road, rugged dirt road
High point	4450m (Abra Azulcocha)
Bike or hike?	both
Agency/guide?	no

This is an excellent hike, as well as one of the best mountain bike rides in the entire Sacred Valley. There is a spectacular Inca trail that descends from the high-altitude pass of Abra Azulcocha, at 4450m, and drops through a narrow *quebrada* (canyon) down to the former Inca town of Calca. Along the way it drops nearly 1500m over a distance of 26km, from the stark alpine landscape of the altiplano through an ever-thickening forest, and passes over some magnificent stretches of Inca road before dropping into an isolated canyon complete with pre-Inca high cliff burial sites located high up the walls of this isolated canyon.

If hiking, it is best to take transport up to the pass to avoid a long and high climb. Most mountain bikers also choose to shuttle up to the top by motor vehicle; otherwise this is an excellent climb up on the bike – the road up to the pass is gorgeous and has little traffic. This route used to see only a few vehicles a day but in the last couple of years traffic has steadily increased. Budget and/or independent travellers should have relatively little difficulty finding public transport leaving from the bus terminal in Calca, destined for Lares, then simply getting out at the top of the pass. On the way up from Calca you will pass the recently uncovered site of Ancasmarka at 3850m.

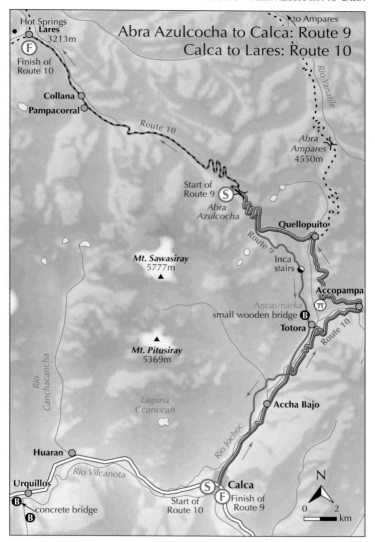

Abra Azulcocha to Calca: Route 9
Calca to Lares: Route 10

to Ampares

Hot Springs
Lares
3213m
Finish of
Route 10

Río Yanatile

Collana
Pampacorral

Route 10

Abra Ampares
4550m

Start of
Route 9
Abra Azulcocha

Route 9

Quellopuito

Mt. Sawasiray
5777m

Inca stairs

Accopampa

Ancasmarka
small wooden bridge

Totora

Route 10

Mt. Pitusiray
5369m

Río Canchacancha

Laguna Ccanccan

Accha Bajo

Río Jochoc

Huaran

Río Vilcanota

Urquillos
concrete bridge

Start of
Route 10

Calca
Finish of
Route 9

N

0   2
km

Hiking and biking trails on the high Andean scree slopes

From here, there is also an unimpeded view of the Incan road that you are about to descend, as well the beautiful farming valley it passes through. Try to notice where it meets the main road, as this is an important part of the route finding.

From the pass of **Abra Azulcocha**, a bit of reconnaissance is required, and finding the right trail down is a bit tricky. If the weather is clear, looking down towards the southeast you should be able to see the Inca road down in the valley below, descending down the right-hand side. Try to see the spot again where the Incan road crosses the dirt road for the last time, before they head in separate directions. That is the most important part of the route finding, as the Incan road continues from there down into the canyon. You can either take the road down or look for the many shortcut footpaths that go in a fairly straight line down towards the head of the canyon and intersection of the road and Incan trail. The road is best if visibility is poor or if there is uncertainty about the group's ability to navigate there.

Otherwise the route is fairly easy to find, as the series of shortcuts all drop steeply off the main dirt road in a southeasterly direction and cross the main road three times. These paths are also the way to descend on mountain bike, and they soon link up to the upper section of the Incan road itself. Continue down to the intersection, then take the Incan road down the west, or right-hand, side of the canyon. At this point there are two trails, one about 20m higher than the other. Take either one, as they merge about 2km down the trail anyway. ▸ The trail winds down and around the mountainside a bit before plunging down into the canyon. Further down, there are some very good stretches of original Incan road, complete with stone steps and paving.

This is one of the best preserved Incan roads in the Sacred Valley, and also one of its finest bike descents.

After about 6km of descent, there will appear a curved Inca staircase, a narrow winding set of steps down to the first bridge. ▸ Cross the bridge and continue down the left (western) side of the canyon. Just after the bridge, there is a small trail going off to the left up into the cliffs. Until recently there were two well-preserved pre-Inca mummies just sitting up against the cliff; however, they are no longer there (hopefully they were removed by the proper authorities and not by scavengers). Looking up you can still see the burial tombs in the cliffs above.

Be careful on this stretch, as a fall off the left side could be fatal.

Continue down more Inca steps and steep, paved road sections and after a few kilometres more the trail will cross the river again, via a small wooden bridge, to the right-hand side of the canyon. The canyon is quite narrow and scenic here. Another 5km of rocky descending and the trail will reach the final bridge. Cross here to the left side of the canyon and continue downhill.

Soon, some houses will appear that signal the outskirts of the approaching small village of **Tortora**. The trail ends here and merges with the main road. From here, the road continues back down and returns to **Calca** via a series of long and sometimes steep switchbacks. There is a trail that shortcuts many of the switchbacks – just keep an eye out for the trail dropping off the right side of the road, usually located just before or after a sharp turn. These shortcuts are a much better option when hiking than taking the road; they are also quite enjoyable for bikers but be advised some of them are rated difficult.

ROUTE 10
Calca to Lares

Start	Calca (2960m)
Finish	Lares (3200m)
Distance	49km
Total ascent	1520m
Total descent	1280m
Difficulty	Easy to moderate
Time	From Calca: 2 days hiking, 4–7hrs biking; from Abra Azulcocha: 3–4hrs hiking, 1–2hrs biking
Trail type	Incan road, rugged dirt road
High point	4450m (Abra Azulcocha)
Bike or hike?	both
Agency/guide?	no
Route map	see Route 9

Instead of reaching the pass and returning back down to Calca like Route 9, this route drops down the eastern side of the pass and down into the high jungle town of Lares and its famous hot springs. It is more popular as a bike ride descent than a hike, but a fair number of trekkers choose to hike down to Lares from the pass of Abra Azulcocha via an old Incan road in good condition.

Most people do this route by taking motorized transport above Calca to the pass of Abra Azulcocha, and then descending on foot or mountain bike to Lares.

The road down to Lares makes an excellent bike ride for beginner and intermediate riders, while experts can find a variety of singletrack near and alongside the road to keep them more than challenged. It is perhaps not ideal for hiking, as the trail closely follows the road; however, there is not much traffic and the scenery is excellent. Lares is located just under 20km below the pass, with the hot springs themselves another 1–2km outside of town.

On leaving the plaza in **Calca**, the road will climb up the canyon, passing the small community of **Accha Bajo** and then past the recently uncovered site of **Ancasmarka** at 3850m, where there are extensive terraces and lookout

Riding the trail down to the Lares hot springs

posts that were that were an important part of the valley's defence in Incan times. The site probably predates the Incas and features pre-Incan construction techniques such as those found near Pumamarca, Abra Malaga and other sites around Ollantaytambo. It is worth a look around, especially because of the excellent sight lines it commands. There are several large herds of llamas here also. The road then continues climbing another 10km, passing the turnoff for Ampares (stay left at this intersection) before finally reaching the pass of **Abra Azulcocha** ('blue lagoon' in Quechua) in the heart of the Cordillera Urubamba mountain range. The altitude here is 4450m above sea level.

From here, take the road down the first few kilometres, there are various shortcuts through the switchbacks ideal for mountain biking or hiking. Soon, the original Incan road that comes down from the pass is visible off to the left. This offers a more pleasant hike than walking on the road and so should be taken if hiking. If mountain biking, it is an option only for more advanced riders, otherwise follow the modern dirt road as it descends the valley.

The trail continues to descend through the Pampacorral valley, until at 11km below the pass lies the

115

It is a pastoral area, so large herds of sheep and llamas are likely to be spotted.

tiny mountain hamlet of **Collana**. There are no services here. ◄ Here, the old Incan road merges with the modern dirt road that comes from the pass. All hikers and bikers should continue down the road to Lares, 8km further on. The valley and scenery here is quite spectacular, and you can feel the air becoming warmer and thicker as you descend towards the Amazon. The river is a steep drop below on the right so use caution, particularly if mountain biking, as there are some dangerous corners.

There is very little development in this area, save for a few small isolated Andean communities. There are no services between the pass and the town of Lares, so be sure to be well hydrated and carry plenty of food and water supplies. The town of **Lares** is very small, just a few stores and basic hostels on one main drag, before the road continues its downward journey eastward towards the jungle. There is a good selection of snacks, sodas and beer available in Lares, although refrigeration apparently hasn't yet made it this far, so hopefully you like your beverages lukewarm!

The **hot springs** of Lares are 2km outside of town; ask someone in town to point out the correct street, as they are not marked and it is fairly difficult to find it without someone pointing the way. At the hot springs you will find basic snacks and the occasional señora cooking up some hot food, but it really is best to bring along everything you need to eat, along with a small stove and supplies. There are four tent sites at the hot springs that can be rented out for 5 soles a night. There are also a few bungalows built right on the hot springs that in theory can be rented to guests, but more often than not they are 'closed for repairs'. Administered by the municipality, they do not appear to be very well run, but it is worth a try if you are not interested in camping. Otherwise, there are three or four very basic hostels right in the town of Lares, charging 10 soles per person. Entrance to the hot springs themselves costs 10 soles a person for foreigners. Bring your own towel as they are not provided nor available.

ROUTE 11
Chicón summit

Start/Finish	Urubamba (2880m)
Distance	32km round trip
Total ascent/descent	2640m
Difficulty	Very strenuous, due to steepness and altitude
Time	2 days hiking to reach the summit and return
Trail type	Mountain trail
High point	5520m (Chicón summit)
Bike or hike?	hike
Agency/guide?	yes (to reach the summit)

This is a climb to the summit of the mountain called Chicón, which looms over the Urubamba valley. It is sometimes called Media Luna ('Half Moon') by the locals. Culminating with a close-up view of the beautiful but rapidly disappearing glacier of Chicón, it is a relatively straightforward hike up the valley and up onto the glacial saddle itself, from where you can enjoy the phenomenal view and then return back down, or strap on some crampons and continue up to the summit. This mountain sees very little tourist traffic and is a great opportunity to climb a glaciated mountain without the several days that is usually required.

The route from the glacial saddle to the summit requires ropes, crampons and glacial rescue equipment as well as the knowledge how to use it. You will also need a guide – contact a qualified agency in Cusco or Ollantaytambo. No special equipment is needed if you are climbing just up to the base of the glacier. Urubamba is the point of departure for this trip and anything you need to purchase for the trip, including all types of food and camping equipment, can be found there.

From the gas station in the centre of **Urubamba**, go uphill (north) directly towards the Chicón massif. The paved road shortly turns to dirt as it continues up the mountain valley, then after about 4km becomes more obscure as it slowly turns into more of a double path, rather than any kind of a road. Nearly every road in the Sacred Valley is being pushed further upward into the valleys, so it is

Mt. Pumahuanka
5330m

Abra
Poqucasa
4800m

Chicón: Route 11

N

0   2
km

Cuyoq

upper
camp

saddle

Pampas 1,2 and 3

H'uchuy
Cocha

Mt. Chicón
5520m

dead end
4wd

Paccha

lower camp

Inca
Raccay

fork separate
from canyon
3940m

Chayhuacocha

Queuñal
forest

Yanahuara

Pinchingoto

gas
station

Torrechayoq

Salt
Mines

Urubamba

Rio Vilcanota

Yucay

Huaran

Plaza

small
house

Urquillos

Rio Vilcanota

Maras

Huayllabamba

Plaza

concrete bridge

Rio Canchacancha

pampa

difficult to say how high the road might reach by the time
you read this book.

In any event, after the road peters out continue
upward along the trail. It is a bit tricky maintaining the
way here, as there are various footpaths heading off in
all directions and there are no trail signs of any kind. The
best way is to stay in the centre or slightly left (west) of the
giant valley that the trail ascends. For most of the route,
at any intersection the correct trail is on the left side,
slightly up on the ridge but not too much. Take care not
to take any of the trails that lead too steeply off to the left
(up the ridge) but rather keep going at a gentle gradient

upwards, easing left at any intersection. From where the road ends (4km from the town of Urubamba) there are approximately 3km as the valley climbs – take care to stay on the valley floor and not climb too high up the left, or west, side.

The trail climbs through some deciduous forests, including a small forest of the native tree **Queuñal** which is rarely seen any more. There is a campsite here. Further up, the vegetation begins to thin out, leaving only knee-high shrubbery and thus the views of the peak you are climbing begin to appear. At 7.5km from town, the trail will begin climbing steeply up the left-hand ridge of the valley. The main trail continues upward but it is heading into a dead-end box canyon with sheer walls that should be visible by this point. At a **fork** in the trail (3940m altitude) take the left branch. The area is excellent for grazing and there are usually many cows. However, the looming sheer granite walls do not allow passage to any but the hardiest of climbers and so this area should be avoided by being sure to climb above it on the left-hand side.

The trail gains the high ridge line that separates this valley from the one just to the east of the glacier Pumahuanka, which is an excellent climb in its own right. ▶ After gaining the ridge, the trail stays slightly below it and goes straight up and northwards towards the glacier. Some 11km from Urubamba, at an altitude of 4680m, lies the lake of **H'uchuy Cocha** ('little lake'). This is a suitable place to camp, and if it is late in the day, it is a good choice. To reach this lake from town takes 4–6hrs of walking, so be sure to leave early in the morning.

To get to the glacier, continue up the rock scree where there is a faint trail. There are several false approaches, but finally the glacier itself appears, magnificent and much larger than it seemed from below. Only while standing at its base – marked by a large, beautifully coloured glacial lake – does its true size become apparent. The lake's head wall is at least 15m of sheer, blue glacial ice. This is the **Upper Camp**, the last suitable spot to camp, and also a good spot to turn around if you are not planning to attempt the summit.

If it is late in the day there are suitable camping spots here, but it is better to continue up to the lake.

From here, the route continues upward, skirting the lake on the right (eastern) side and takes advantage of an iceless rock ridge line that gains quite a bit of altitude on Chicón's southern face before finally hitting the mountain's highest and final exposed rock, which lies at approximately 5000m and 2–3hrs of climbing from the lake below. There is then another 300m of ice climbing to reach the glacial **saddle**.

There is not a good place to camp, except for true alpinists.

◄ While the final summit route ahead is not technically difficult, it is nonetheless a labyrinth of shifting crevasses and thus a very serious climb and one that could easily take a life. In this case, a set of crampons and an ambitious, can-do attitude will not be sufficient – true crevasse rescue gear and, more importantly, the well-practised knowledge of how to use it, is essential to complete the route. As technical climbing and route-finding is outside the scope of this book, it is recommended that you hire a professional agency out of Cusco or Ollantaytambo. Insist that the guide be mountain

Campsite at the glacial lake at the base of Chicón

certified and also make sure they speak your maternal language fluently – a crevasse rescue attempt at 5000m in a storm at night is no time or place to be trying to overcome language barriers. Enjoy the views from **Chicón summit**, at 5520m. Descend by the same route.

ROUTE 12
To Lares via the Pumahuanka valley

Start	Urubamba (2880m)
Finish	Lares (3200m)
Distance	24km from trailhead
Total ascent	1540m
Total descent	1220m
Difficulty	Strenuous
Time	9–12hrs hiking
Trail type	Singletrack trail, dirt road
High point	4420m (Abra Poqucasa)
Bike or hike?	hike
Agency/guide?	no

This is a very nice hike up and over the Cordillera Urubamba and down to the hot springs of Lares. It features Inca as well as pre-Inca ruin sites, views of several nearby glaciers, alpine lakes, and one of the nicest campsites you will ever find. It is not a secret route by any means, but it is one of the less-travelled valleys that connect the Sacred Valley to Lares, and it is not common to see other groups on this trip. This route can be done as a very long day hike, but it is better to spend a night camping in the mountains instead, and reach Lares the following day.

It is possible to do this route on a mountain bike, but only if you don't mind carrying the bike for several kilometres on each side of the rocky pass.

There are a few different roads that head up the Pumahuanka valley, and it can be tricky to find the correct one. Start from the centre of **Urubamba**, at the **gas station** (el grifo) at the main intersection in town. Go

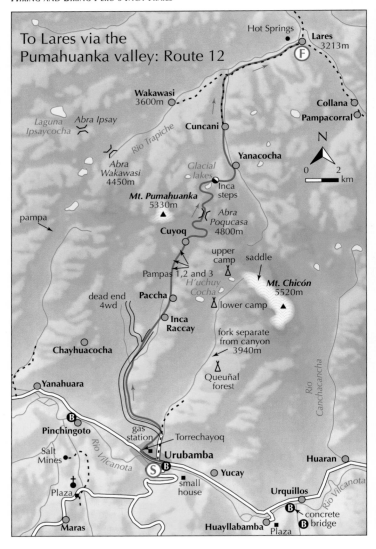

Crossing a section of Inca trail

west on the main highway, towards Ollantaytambo. Just past the bus terminal, a road climbs up and to the right. Take this for several blocks to the street of Torrechayoq. Turn here and follow it as it climbs steeply through the gritty urban centre of Urubamba. Continue on the road as it turns left, heading westward and climbing up the Pumahuanka valley. Follow the road 6km upward, where it reaches a split in the valley and a small concrete bridge over a river. There should be a well-worn trail continuing up the valley, on the right-hand side just before the bridge. This is the trail to Lares.

The trail winds up through a quiet forest of Unca trees, and 4km after leaving the road comes upon the restored, pre-Inca site of **Inca Raccay**.

The architecture of **Inca Raccay** ('place of the Inca' in Quechua) suggests it served as an outlook post to monitor the comings and goings of valley traffic back before the Incas arrived. This is a nice place to take a rest and have something to eat and drink.

Upon leaving the site, take the trail up and continue ascending the right (eastern) side of the canyon. A few kilometres ahead lies the tiny community of **Paccha**.

Paccha means 'waterfall' in Quechua and is sometimes called Pacchapata ('place of the waterfall'). It is a lovely example of a typical Andean high-mountain community, living in utter harmony with the land. There is a small trout farm that serves the community, as well as the usual holdings of potatoes, maize and other crops.

The trail goes down into the community, but this is not the correct way to Lares. The proper trail continues on the same side up the canyon, above Paccha and its namesake waterfall, for another 2km and reaches the first of four pampas suitable for camping before the pass. ◀

Unless it is late in the day, it is better to continue climbing.

The trail crosses over to the left (western) side of the valley just above the waterfall via a small wooden bridge. The trail climbs steeply up traditional Inca paving stones for a little less than 1hr before arriving at the next campsite, a truly stunning grotto in the forest complete with a curving stream running through it. It is a very peaceful place and looks a bit like the signature hole at an exclusive country golf club. Make camp here if possible. If not, there are still two more pampas up ahead where it is possible to camp.

After the **last pampa**, the trail passes through an area the locals call Cuyoq as it begins the long, final climb to the pass of **Abra Poqucasa**. The path is obvious, and when the terrain turns to solid rock and develops a lunar feel, take comfort that the pass is near.

The **Abra Poqucasa pass** is marked with a cross and a few religious poems painted on a large rock. There are also numerous rock cairns built to mark the pass, as well as a gift to the *apus* (mountain gods) who are believed to guard over these mountains. There are magnificent views in all directions, you can see as far away as the Moray plateau,

On the trail to Pumahuanka

Ausangate to the southeast, Salkantay on a clear day can be seen to the southwest, to the northwest is Pumahuanka, and to the northeast there are good views of the Sawasiray glacier above the Calca valley.

Take the trail down over the rugged rocky trail, some of it still showing traces of the Inca road that preceded it. The path passes by several small glacial lakes before passing on the left (western) side of the last and largest one, **Yanacocha** ('black lake' in Quechua), and into a steep descent of the valley. Several parts of the trail are original Inca staircases. Finally the trail emerges into the short grass of the high puno, a high-altitude treeless landscape characteristic of the Andes. On this part of the descent the weather is usually more pleasant and starting to warm a little after the brutal cold near the pass.

The trail continues down until it reaches **Cuncani**, which used to be just a small stop along the trail but

Glacial icefalls have become common in recent years

a road has now been built up from Lares and so it has grown a bit. The walk down to Lares from here is on the road itself but is still pleasant as it winds its way down the valley past several small villages and houses. Be sure not to walk all the way into the town of **Lares** itself, which is 9km below Cuncani. Instead, keep an eye off the left side of the road as it nears town: the hot springs are located 2km outside of town and are visible from the road. After paying the entrance fee and taking a shower before entering, soak your weary muscles in the hot and medicinal waters of Lares.

Return to Cusco or Ollantaytambo either by private transport that you have prearranged to meet you, otherwise there is now a fairly reliable stream of public and semi private vehicles for hire – inquire in town.

4 AROUND OLLANTAYTAMBO

Trekking towards the Huayanay glacier (Routes 27 to 29)

INTRODUCTION

The majestic Incan fortress of Ollantaytambo

Perhaps the crown jewel of all the Sacred Valley, due to its central location, lower altitude, moderate climate, and its countless Inca sites within a half-day walk, Ollantaytambo lies in a spectacular valley at the confluence of two important rivers: the Urubamba/Vilcanota and the Yanamayu. It is gaining a reputation as the Adventure Capital of Peru, and is the best place from which to base your adventures. From here you can trek or mountain bike to Machu Picchu, Quillabamba, Choquequirao, and nearly every other major site in the Sacred Valley. The town itself retains its original layout, Inca architecture and culture, and small village charm. It is also known for the massive and spectacular Inca fortress that looms over the entire town.

Ollantaytambo has surged in popularity as word has spread among travellers that this is the place to be for its relaxed atmosphere, authentic preserved Inca architecture and culture, so many archaeological sites and a central location close to Machu Picchu. It is a great place to relax has some of the best opportunities for people-watching in the entire valley.

ACCOMMODATION

Pakaritampu in Av Ferrocarril s/n (by the train station), is a beautiful, three- to four-star hotel with large grounds to walk around in and a few llamas lounging around its Inca terraces (tel: (51) 84 204020, email: piramide@ pakaritampu.com, www.pakaritampu. com). The rooms are well decorated and light and airy. It is a very peace- ful place and recommended for those looking for a little luxury, but it won't come cheap at $120 (€87) for a matri- monial or double.

Next best choice and a little easier on the budget (although not by much) is El Albergue (tel: (51) 84 204014, email: reservations@elalbergue.com, www.elalbergue.com). Located by the train station, it can be a bit noisy but only for the brief moments of train arrivals. The hotel has a long history: it was opened by Wendy Weeks and her partner Robert Randall in the 1960s and was the first lodging in this town. It features a simple yet classic decor, and perhaps best of all a wood-fired sauna for those cold Andean winter nights. Matrimonial/double rooms are priced at $90 (€65).

Longtime trekker and biker favourite is KB Tambo Hotel, Calle Ventiderio s/n (www.kbperu.com, tel: (51) 84 204091). Located just below the main plaza on the main road, this boutique budget hotel has a charming garden, rooftop deck and jacuzzi with views of the entire town. The rooms are modern with giant windows, most overlooking the ruins. Matrimonial/ double rooms cost $40 (€29), a suite $60 (€44).

Next door to KB Tambo Hotel is Hotel Sol (www.HotelSolPeru.com, tel: (51) 84 204130). Newly built alongside the river, it has rooms with private balconies and in-your-face views of the fortress. Large, bright and airy with lots of open space, it has the feel of a modern, upmarket hotel while still retaining a great deal of local, small town charm.

Another option is Hostal Iskay (www.HostalIskay.com, tel: (51) 84 204004), which has singles for $30 (€22), doubles for $45 (€33), and peaceful views of the ruins.

Finally, for those on a tight budget, try Hostel Chaska Wasi, Calle Chaupicalle (katycusco@yahoo.es, tel: (51) 84 204045), run by a lovely local woman named Katy who takes good care of her guests, and the rooms are very inexpensive at around 25 soles per person.

There are new, cheaper hostels opening up constantly. Those on a really tight budget can look around the Plaza upon arrival, or ask for the neighbourhood of San Isidro, which has a number of inexpensive back- packer hostels.

DINING AND NIGHTLIFE

The most popular place in town to eat is Hearts Cafe, a non-profit cafe centrally located across the street from KB Tambo. Proceeds go towards projects benefiting women

The historic Inca village of Ollantaytambo

and children in the Sacred Valley, but that is not the only reason to eat there. Their massive portions and tasty breakfasts set the tone for this Peruvian–British food palace. Up on the plaza, the restaurant La Ñusta is an institution and was one of the first restaurants to open in town. Try the quinoa pancakes for breakfast. Finally, no visit to Ollantaytambo would be complete without a glass of wine or water at the cosy bar next to the fireplace at Mayupata, the classiest joint in town – also the most expensive. They have great pizzas as well as more elegant dishes, and a large dining room that is good for groups. The nightlife in Ollantaytambo can be surprisingly rambunctious; try the El Gonzo's bar just off the main square.

ROUTE 13
Pumamarca

Start/Finish	Ollantaytambo (2850m)
Distance	14km round trip
Total ascent/descent	500m
Difficulty	Easy to moderate
Time	3–4hrs hiking, 2–3hrs biking. Allow extra time (30–60mins) to visit Pumamarca
Trail type	Rugged dirt road and singletrack trail
High point	3350m (Pumamarca)
Bike or hike?	both
Agency/guide?	yes

Pumamarca is a popular site with the locals for hiking and mountain biking, and is highly recommended for anyone with a half-day to spare in Ollantaytambo. A fun and easy half-day bike ride, or walk, from Ollantaytambo this trail goes up to the pre-Inca site of Pumamarca. This site was probably a military outpost for the tribe that inhabited this area before the conciliation of power brought on by the Inca Pachacutec around the year 1420. The Incas, as was their custom, enlarged and improved the place, and there are impressive sight lines to all the nearby mountain passes. The views from the site are excellent and overall it is a very pleasant way to spend a few hours – bring a picnic lunch.

The bike ride from the site back down into Ollantaytambo is a locals' favourite, as the fast and technical descent has a bit of everything. Otherwise, it is also a very pleasant and quiet walk back down into Ollantaytambo.

There are several ways to do this route. The best way is to walk there and back from Ollantaytambo, which takes about 2hrs each way, and is a total distance of 14km. Or take a taxi up to the ruins, and then walk back down. This trip also makes a great bike ride, either riding up and down from Ollantaytambo or taking a taxi up and biking back down. Finally, it is possible to just take a taxi up, have the driver wait while you visit the ruins and then drive back down.

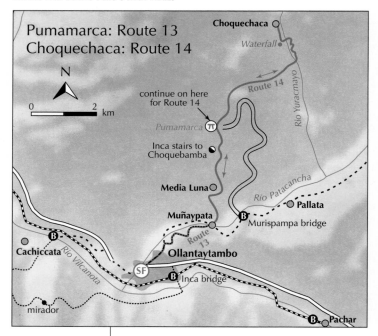

Pumamarca: Route 13
Choquechaca: Route 14

In all cases, start from KB Tambo Hotel, which is just below the main plaza in **Ollantaytambo**. Take the dirt road heading upwards, north and away from the hotel. After 1km there is a bridge crossing the **Patacancha River**. Fifty metres after crossing the bridge, a trail branches off to the right alongside the river. If you are walking, or want a more challenging section on the bike, take this trail. Otherwise, continue upwards on the road.

After a few kilometres the trail rejoins the main road at a few houses known collectively as **Muñaypata** for about 50m, then the trail leaves the road, off the left side. Look for a two-storey red house – the trail disappears behind it just to the left. Walkers should take this trail; bikers of all levels should continue on the road to the second bridge at Murispampa. A short climb later the path arrives at the impressive and just cleared Inca site of **Media Luna** ('Half Moon'). Be sure to turn sharply up and away from them here at the junction, to the right. ▶

The trail keeps ascending before going past the awesome Inca terraces of Muscapuqio ('place with water' in Quechua) which are below the trail, towards the road. From here, the trail goes directly to Pumamarca over the next 3km. Halfway up, there will appear an Inca staircase ascending the mountain off to the trail's left. This is the Inca route up to Choquebamba, a different site that is not part of the Pumamarca route. ▶ Do not take this staircase but continue straight on until, after passing a quaint mountain house on the shoulder of the ridge, you see a set of round pre-Inca storage buildings (*chullpas*) off to the right across a small pampa. The road and the trail meet up again here, and it is just a short 10min walk up and into the site of **Pumamarca**.

Return via the same trail or take the rough dirt road that climbs from the main road from the bridge at Murispampa.

Do not enter Media Luna but instead take the switchback up and to the right.

Here you begin to realize the sheer volume of Incan works constructed, just in this one valley alone.

The pre-Incan site of Pumamarca

ROUTE 14
Choquechaca

Start/Finish	Ollantaytambo (2850m)
Distance	14km one way, 26km round trip
Total ascent/descent	1310m
Difficulty	Easy to moderate
Time	Full day hike, or overnight if desired
Trail type	Mountain trail
High point	4160m (Choquechaca)
Bike or hike?	hike
Agency/guide?	no
Route map	see Route 13

This is a very pleasant trail that climbs past Pumamarca, up the Halancoma river valley through native forest before arriving at the small mountain community of Choquechaca. There are only about a half-dozen or so families living in this small pampa near the base of the Halancoma glacier. An excellent day hike from Ollantaytambo, the route starts in Ollantaytambo and goes through the little visited pre-Inca site of Pumamarca before climbing up a nicely forested valley to Choquechaca. From there, you can continue up to the base of the Halancoma glacier, and there are some worked Incan stones along the way. You could also camp and return to Ollantaytambo the next day. This route is not suitable for biking.

From **Ollantaytambo** follow the directions to **Pumamarca**, as in Route 13. If you are planning to camp overnight, consider hiring mules in Ollantaytambo to carry the gear. After visiting the ruins, go to the upper portion of the site, which is straight north or simply uphill. You will be looking up the Halancoma valley, and a few trails will appear.

The trail you want lies up the valley but on the other side of the river. There are ample game trails here, so don't worry too much about which is the exact trail, but rather progress up-valley while at the same time gradually working towards the river below.

Upon approaching the river, be sure to only take larger trails and not the very small game trails. Cross the **river** on a small bridge and then begin climbing up the other side of the valley. This part of the trail is quite beautiful and features one of the few remaining sections of old growth forests left of the native tree Queuñal. A few kilometres up, the trail passes near a small but lovely **waterfall** and there is a nice clearing to take lunch, or even camp if it is really late in the day – otherwise it is much better to press onwards and upwards.

Just above the Andean village of Choquechaca

From here it is 1–2hrs further up the trail to Choquechaca. There are no landmarks along the way but it is nearly impossible to get lost, as the trail follows the river and then winds its way up past small family farms to **Choquechaca**, a good place to camp for the night. Otherwise, enjoy a nice picnic, and then return via the same trail to Ollantaytambo.

ROUTE 15
To Lares via Abra Wakawasi

Start	Yanahuara (2870m)
Finish	Lares (3200m)
Distance	28km
Total ascent	1580m
Total descent	1250m
Difficulty	Moderate hiking, difficult biking
Time	2 days hiking or biking, possible in 1
Trail type	Mountain trail, rugged dirt road
High point	4450m (Abra Wakawasi)
Bike or hike?	both
Agency/guide?	no (but porter/mule for a bike)

A very popular route to the hot springs of Lares, and for good reason – the trail is quite manageable and passes up and over a high alpine pass with three beautiful glacial lakes just below it, perfect for camping. This route also makes an excellent mountain bike ride, as almost all of the descent from the pass down into Lares is rideable. However, the climb up and out of Yanahuara is a bit fierce and will require pushing or carrying the bike. It may be possible, as well as desirable, to hire a porter or mule to bring the bike up most of the way up, depending on your physical fitness.

This trip begins in **Yanahuara**, a small community located about 15km downriver from Ollantaytambo, about 7km to the west of Urubamba. Ask any local, or look for a large 'Casa Andina' sign on the main highway and turn north, uphill and away from the Vilcanota River. Take the road up, about 1km from the bottom, to a fork in the road and take the right fork. Take a moment to look up and it can be seen that the valley is split into two here by an obvious mountain spur coming down nearly to town. The route to the pass is the one slightly off to the right, up the valley.

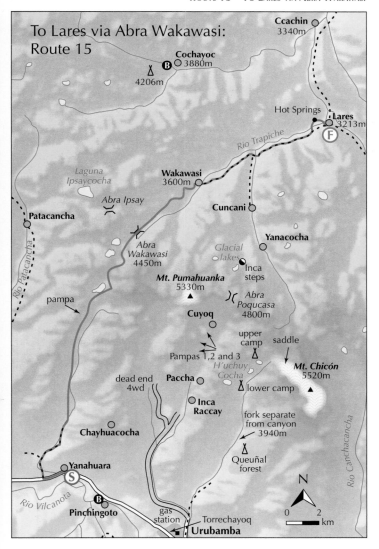

To Lares via Abra Wakawasi:
Route 15

Ccachin
3340m

Cochayoc
3880m

4206m

Hot Springs

Lares
3213m

Rio Trapiche

Laguna
Ipsaycocha

Abra Ipsay

Patacancha

Wakawasi
3600m

Cuncani

Abra
Wakawasi
4450m

Yanacocha

Glacial
lakes

Inca
steps

Mt. Pumahuanka
5330m

pampa

Abra
Poqucasa
4800m

Cuyoq

upper
camp

saddle

Pampas 1,2 and 3

H'uchuy
Cocha

Mt. Chicón
5520m

dead end
4wd

Paccha

lower camp

Inca
Raccay

fork separate
from canyon
3940m

Chayhuacocha

Queuñal
forest

Rio Canchacancha

Yanahuara

N

Rio Vilcanota

Pinchingoto

gas
station

Torrechayoq

Urubamba

0   2
km

After the main fork, follow the road uphill as it turns quickly from pavement to dirt, winding its way past the various new boutique hotels that are sprouting up like weeds. The road currently climbs another 4km before ending, but it is likely that in the future it will continue to be extended up the mountain, For now, though, it remains a trail that goes through a very pleasant mountain valley without any motor traffic.

Continue upward as the trail turns to just a small footpath and then arrives at a fork, with two trails of about equal size, both going uphill. The right path stays low and follows closely the small river at the centre of the valley. This is not the route to Lares, although it is a lovely walk; if perhaps a few of your group weren't planning to do the overnight hike, this would make an ideal half-day route. The trail along the river continues upward for quite some distance and there are many small Inca works in this valley – as yet they are not well known but a few hours walk and a sharp eye will almost certainly be rewarded.

Crossing a river on the trail to Lares

The correct route, however, climbs up and away from the river to the left. The trail will begin to climb

sharply. Now begins one of the more strenuous parts of the hike, so this is a good time to stop and make sure the whole group is together at this point and that everyone has water, etc. Keep climbing upward and stay on the main trail. Eventually, after 7–8km of ascending from Yanahuara, the trail levels out a bit and begins traversing the high pampas common at this altitude. ▶ Here begins a long ridge-top traverse, above on the right side of the valley, until it arrives at a strange-looking field of rocks and water which is 9km from where the trail began, down below.

The altitude here is about 3600m.

Here you must cross to the other side of this enormous pampa, but the route finding is relatively straightforward and the trail that crosses to the other side is obvious. It will probably begin to get a bit chilly at this point, and here at the pampa is another good spot to regroup and make sure all are accounted for. If it is quite late in the day, this is a suitable enough place to camp but otherwise the preferred spot is 1hr further up the trail. Continue along the narrow, rocky trail as it climbs up a spine of the Pumahuanka massif until you reach a lovely high alpine meadow with three glacial lakes and a flat place to camp. The next day's climb can be seen framed against the steep wall to the north; but for now pitch the tents and enjoy your favourite beverage while staring at the eerily coloured blue glacial waters of the lakes.

The next morning starts with a very steep and stiff 1hr climb to the pass of **Abra Wakawasi** at 4450m. ▶ From the pass, the trail begins descending to Lares and there really is only one route. However, the foot traffic through the years has worn literally hundreds of different footpaths on the way down. It can make it seem confusing, but a long as you stay on the bigger paths and goes downward, there is virtually no chance of getting lost. Nearly all of the trails converge further down the trail. A general rule is to stay 'high' up on the ridge unless all trails lead downward. Many footpaths will lead down to the river you are following, but the Incas usually built their main roads 100m or so above the rivers themselves and this route is no exception.

The pass is marked by several cairns and can be very windy and cold, although the views are always magnificent.

A Quechuan local, pondering his crops

The trail continues downward through beautiful, classic high Andean scenery: bright white mountain glaciers, green valleys with several rivers running through them, and a few small children in their woollen *chullos* (woven stocking caps) tending their flock of sheep or llamas. After 8km, the weaving village of **Wakawasi** appears, at an altitude of 3600m.

> Here at **Wakawasi** the locals continue to lead virtually the same lifestyle that their ancestors have before them for hundreds of years. At the time of writing there is a road being constructed from Lares, far below, up to this village. It is not certain to up to what it altitude it will be built. No matter – this is a gorgeous trekking route that still passes through some wonderfully authentic culture.

From Wakawasi the road continues downward another 8km to the town, and hot springs, of **Lares**. The hot springs are located just outside of town, on the road you will be descending on. Keep an eye out on the left after descending 8km, or about 2hrs of walking. Eventually, the hot springs complex of Lares will be visible below, off the left side, otherwise just keep asking the locals as you get close for the location of the *baños termales*.

This route is superb for mountain biking, and the descent from the pass down to the hot springs is one of the better adrenaline fixes that the Sacred Valley has to offer. If doing this descent by mountain bike, use extra caution and show extra respect at all encounters with others. This is a popular route and it you should expect to meet other groups. Nonetheless, it remains one of the area's real jewels.

ROUTE 16
To Lares via Patacancha

Start	Ollantaytambo (2850m); Patacancha (3650m)
Finish	Lares (3200m)
Distance	38km from Ollantaytambo, 19km from Patacancha
Total ascent	1610m (810m if starting from Patacancha)
Total descent	1260m
Difficulty	Moderate hiking, difficult biking
Time	2 days hiking or biking, possible in 1 long day
Trail type	Mountain trail, dirt road
High point	4460m (Abra Ipsay)
Bike or hike?	both
Agency/guide?	no

This trek to Lares passes through the weaving and cultural mecca of Patacancha before *bolteando la abra* (crossing the pass) of Abra Ipsay in the Cordillera Urubamba and dropping down into Lares. As it is one of the most popular trekking routes in the Sacred Valley, it is not the best choice for those seeking isolation away from other tour groups. Nonetheless, it is a spectacular trek or bike ride that passes through several tracts of native trees as well as several beautiful alpine lakes near the high pass. As if that wasn't enough, after the pass comes an hours-long descent that ends up at the thermal hot springs of Lares, where you can soak sore muscles after the long journey, just like the Incas themselves no doubt did!

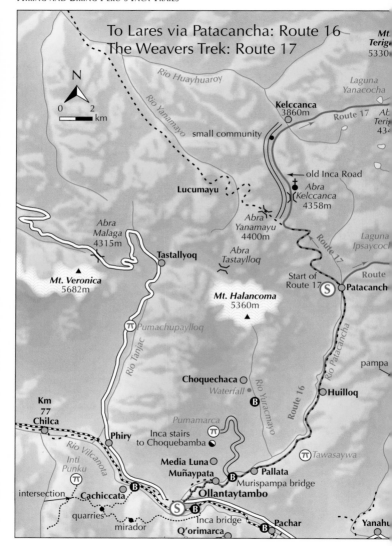

To Lares via Patacancha: Route 16
The Weavers Trek: Route 17

The natural thermal hot springs of Lares

This route can begin either in Ollantaytambo or else further up the valley at Patacancha, which can be reached via taxi as the road is in good condition and has recently been improved. If looking for mules to carry the gear and/or a guide, the best bet is to hire an agency in Ollantaytambo.

From **Patacancha**, start at the village school and take the trail that begins behind it and heads due east, up the mountainside. Follow this trail as it ascends the ridge line until, after about 3km the high alpine lake of Ipsaycocha will come into view. ◀ After another 2km of climbing the trail arrives the pass, called **Abra Ipsay**. From here the views of the surrounding Cordillera are spectacular and extend for kilometres in all directions. After enjoying the vista, begin the descent down towards **Wakawasi**, which is located 5km below the pass.

Hard to believe, but there are small mountain trout living in these frigid, remote waters!

> **Wakawasi** is a well-preserved indigenous community known for its traditional weaving practices and accompanying llama herds. Here, the people continue to live a lifestyle that has changed very little over the centuries, and this is a good place to

stop and have lunch and chat with the locals, and perhaps even throw down a few glasses of chicha!

From Wakawasi, the trail becomes a road and continues descending down to **Lares**. It is 9km from Wakawasi to the hot springs, which are located 2km before arriving into the town itself. Look for the shortcuts along the road's switchbacks to make the walk (or bike ride) go even quicker, so as to be soaking in those hot waters as soon as possible.

ROUTE 17
The Weaver's Trek

Start	Abra Yanamayu (4440m) or Patacancha (3650m)
Finish	Lares (3200m)
Distance	45km from Abra Yanamayu, 54km from Patacancha
Total ascent	1250m (2050m from Patacancha)
Total descent	2500m
Difficulty	Moderate hiking; difficult biking
Time	2–3 days hiking or biking
Trail type	Incan road, singletrack trail and dirt road
High point	4440m (Abra Yanamayu)
Bike or hike?	both
Agency/guide?	no
Route map	see Route 16

This route to the hot springs of Lares passes through not only the gorgeous scenery typical of these parts of the Andes, but also through two communities – Kelccanca and Ccachin – known for their traditional weaving culture, which is still going strong and being passed down from generation to generation. While in most of the country the old ways are being displaced in favour of modern sewing machines and synthetic fabrics, these remote mountain communities have preserved their cultural authenticity while producing beautiful textiles such as *mantas*, the mid-sized Quechuan blanket worn on their back that serves as a baby carrier, food and clothing storage, and all around backpack for the local people.

The smooth, high altiplano above Patacancha on the way to Lares

This is a one-way trek. It is recommended to take motorized transport from Ollantaytambo up to the start at the pass of Yanamayu ('black river' in Quechua) above Patacancha. It is also possible to start the trek from Patacancha instead, if a few extra hours of hiking are desired. If you are planning to travel with mules or horses they should be procured from one of the many agencies in Ollantaytambo, with at least one day's advance notice. Whether leaving from Ollantaytambo or Patacancha, simply travel up the dirt road to the pass, **Abra Yanamayu**.

There is a small building at Abra Yanamayu, a small church typical of the high Andean road passes. These are built to give thanks for the safe journey so far, and to pray for continued blessing down the other side. Otherwise, there is nothing here and it is a windy and desolate place.

The road forks here and the correct one must be chosen. The main road goes left over the pass and descends in a northwesterly direction down towards Occobamba and the high jungle. The small church is located directly on this road, but this is not the road to take. Instead, there is another smaller and recently built road that heads right, to the northeast. This is the correct way, so begin here as the road stays high on the ridge line and traverses the head of the main valley that goes down to Ollantaytambo. After just 1km on the road there is a choice whether to take the new road (currently being constructed) or the original Inca route through the pass. The old Inca road option drops down a bit to the right-hand side, into the high pampa. From here it is just a short walk to **Abra Kelccanca**, the pass above Kelccanca, which is really just the high point of the pampa and is marked by a tiny shrine dedicated to the apus, or gods.

After a few kilometres, the new road and Incan road both enter a drainage, though on different sides. There really is no other exit from this drainage and so the exact trail does not need to be followed at first, but soon a side must be chosen as the ravine becomes deeper and not suitable for travelling. Cross early and continue downward on the Inca road on the east side of the valley. This part is technical; if you are biking and do not possess advanced skills, the better option is to take the newer road down to Kelccanca. Both the new and old road descend the valley for about 4km until arriving at a very small community consisting of no more than 10 houses. From here, it is about 2km more down valley along the Incan road to arrive at Kelccanca.

> **Kelccanca** is in a beautiful Andean setting and is a small community that subsists on agricultural and textile weaving. There are a couple of round, tent-like buildings with brightly coloured canvas roofs that appear almost like a circus as you approach the hamlet. Kelccanca lies at the intersection of two high alpine valleys, the one you just came down and the one that is about to be ascended. This second valley, which descends from Abra Teriguay, leads to a pass on the shoulder of the mountain

from which it gets it's name. To the left, or east, the two valleys merge and continue descending, eventually reaching the Amazon jungle.

Anyone who got a late start, encountered delays, or had decided to bike or hike up to the pass from Ollantaytambo would best camp near Kelccanca. This route, however, must go on to Ccachin and to do so requires climbing up to the pass. It is a stiff climb and as always, it is wise to regroup the whole party before starting. To begin climbing the pass late in the day, without the whole group, or in bad weather should be avoided if possible.

It is 3–4hrs of steady climbing from Kelccanca to the pass. Along the way there are a few large, flat spots suitable for either lunch or camping sites, including a very nice campsite at **Laguna Yanacocha**, which lies 1.5km below the pass. Arriving at **Abra Teriguay** (4345m), named for the glacier just behind it on the north side, the pass itself has no distinguishing features save for a few rock cairns placed at the top. After crossing the pass, continue down the other side, staying to the right-hand side of the river. The path meanders down at a gentle incline.

About 1.5hrs further is a good place to camp, where there are a few small houses and space to put up tents. Looking across the valley to the left you can see a large, red-coloured mountain. This is known locally as Puka Orqo ('red mountain' in Quechua). From here it is another 4km to where a small bridge crosses the river to the left. This is the bridge of Cochayoc, and at the time of writing a new road was being constructed to connect Costaylloq with Ccachin from below. Take this bridge, then it is 6km from here down to **Ccachin** – again this can be reduced by taking the many footpaths along the descent that shortcut some of the road's switchbacks.

From Ccachin it is 8km up to the hot springs of **Lares**. This walk is quite lovely and follows the old Incan road that connects Lares to the jungle. An alternative option is to walk out from Ccachin down to the main road at Choquecancha. In recent years road traffic

here has increased considerably, so if it is late in the day or the group is tired, it is possible to wait on the main road to catch a ride up to Lares, which is 12km further uphill. From Lares, there is occasional public transport on to Calca but a better bet is to have private transport arranged. There are a few basic hostels and restaurants in the town of Lares but the key words are 'basic' and 'few'.

Locals in Ccachin showing off their textiles

ROUTE 18
Inca Raccay and Q'orimarca

Start/Finish	Ollantaytambo (2850m)
Distance	46km round trip, 32km starting from Pachar
Total ascent/descent	1260m
Difficulty	moderate hiking, moderate to difficult biking
Time	6–8hrs starting from Pachar
Trail type	Dirt trail singletrack
High point	4110m (Q'orimarca)
Bike or hike?	both
Agency/guide?	no

This is a great day tour from Ollantaytambo that features a mild climb up a gorgeous Andean valley. The trail first arrives at the base of a beautiful waterfall, and then continues on to Inca Raccay, a little-visited Inca ruin perched at the top of the waterfall, with an option to hike further up the canyon to Q'orimarca, another Incan site. This is not a highly travelled route and sees few tourists, but is well worth the effort and highly recommended. The whole trip is possible in one day but it is best to begin hiking at Pachar or even Soccma as the terrain is very steep.

Take the highway leading out of **Ollantaytambo** towards Cusco for 7km and turn off at the small community of **Pachar**, located just off the road on the right. Finding the road up the canyon is a bit difficult as it leaves the village of Pachar, ask any local to point you in the direction of Huarocondo or keep heading up towards the canyon opening. To get to the Soccma turnoff, it is a easy and pleasant ascent of 6km on a dirt road with very little traffic – it should take about 1hr 30mins on foot or by bike.

There are several sets of **Inca ruins** along the way, including the site of Ñaupa Iglesia, a small cave with an excellent carved rock shrine, accessed by some impressive Inca terraces and steps. Also, look for some pre-Incan pictographs (rock paintings) that

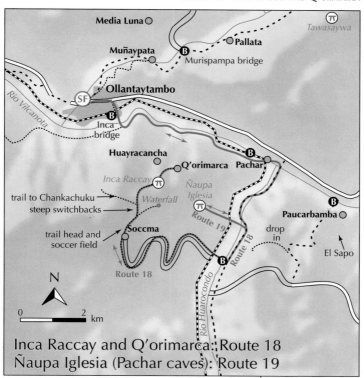

Inca Raccay and Q'orimarca: Route 18
Ñaupa Iglesia (Pachar caves): Route 19

can be seen right from the road, they are on the right hand side approximately 2km after passing Ñaupa Iglesia.

Some 4km further up the canyon, there is a small bridge on the right that accesses the road to **Soccma** and is marked with a small sign. Soccma is a further 5km up this bumpy, dirt road. If you prefer, you can take a taxi from Ollantaytambo to Pachar, which should cost about 30–40 soles, or even all the way up to Soccma and start the route from there.

Once in Soccma, which is 11km from Pachar, look northwest (up valley) to get your bearings. From there, you can see clearly the canyon that the trail is heading into, which gets quite narrow before pinching off at the top. There is a prominent trail on the left side of the canyon, and this is the one to take. To get there, look for the **soccer field**, which is next to the first group of small houses in the village. The trail leaves from here, just off to the left. There will be many different foot trails but most eventually spill out on this trail. This is actually the trickiest part of the route – the rest of the way is obvious and easily followed. Once on the main trail, continue climbing up the valley. ◄

In the valley below to the right are a succession of chakras (small farms).

After a couple of kilometers, you will arrive at the intersection of two trails. The first is a trail going off to the right; this trail does not go to the top but rather goes to the base of the waterfall and makes a good short detour. The left hand trail ascends a series of steep switchbacks, and this is the trail that must be taken up to the sites of Inca Raccay and Q'orimarca. Begin climbing up the switchbacks. Midway through the switchbacks there is a small junction: the main trail heads right (west) and up the canyon, the other goes to left (east) into a smaller canyon, leading to the village of Chankachuku – do not go this way.

Continue up and to the right (north) for another 1km, where after rounding a corner there is a magnificent waterfall visible on the other side of the narrow gorge. You will easily spot the ruins of **Inca Raccay**, straddled dramatically atop a narrow ridge directly above the waterfalls. Continue climbing for a few more kilometers until the trail veers down and arrives at the river crossing.

On the other side of the river, to the right, is a short side trail down to the ruins of **Inca Raccay**, also known as Perniylloq, 3622m above sea level. It is less than 1km to the ruins and definitely worth the time to visit. This site was likely built before the Incas and it has a similar style to Pumamarca above Ollantaytambo. Both have a dramatic and also strategic location overlooking their respective valleys.

The main trail continues climbing after crossing the river. Looking up you will see the main trail veering to the right (north), while a smaller trail climbs a few hundred metres to the tiny 'village' of **Huayracancha**, enthusiastically manned by the vibrant señor Vidal Ccasa who will be quite happy to offer any hospitality he can. This has been known to include large quantities of *chicha*, the local homemade corn beer. If you ever wanted to throw down chicha with the 'real' locals, this is as good as place as any! Try to bring some tea or sugar from town for him and his family as a fair trade.

Returning to the main trail, it is a short climb of less than 2km across the pampa to the intersection for the pre-Inca site of **Q'orimarca**. Go right and traverse across before ascending a few switchbacks and arriving at Q'orimarca, an assortment of terraces and walls built sometime in the 13th century and located at an altitude of just under 4000m. ▶

The pre-Incan site of Inca Raccay

The view is quite lovely from here and there is a good look at the trail that you just came up.

153

Hiking up towards Q'orimarca

Those who pushed a mountain bike up here will now get to begin one of the finer singletrack descents in the Sacred Valley, a blistering drop all the way down to Ollantaytambo. Otherwise those on foot can now begin walking back down to Soccma – take care as a lot of the trail is loose gravel next to a precipitous fall. From Soccma continue down to the bridge and the dirt road back to Pachar.

To return to Ollantaytambo either arrange to have a taxi waiting at the end of the day, or else walk down the mountain from Soccma to the Huarocondo–Pachar road, where it is generally possible to catch a ride from a passing truck but by no means guaranteed. The other option is to have the same taxi that dropped you off return to pick you up, If biking this route, it is no problem to ride back to Ollantaytambo as it is nearly all downhill from the waterfall.

ROUTE 19
Ñaupa Iglesia (Pachar Caves)

Start/Finish	Ollantaytambo (2850m)
Distance	24km round trip or 10km from Pachar
Total ascent/descent	200m
Difficulty	Easy hiking, easy to moderate biking
Time	5–7hrs hiking, 3–5hrs biking
Trail type	Dirt trail
High point	3050m (Ñaupa Iglesia)
Bike or hike?	both
Agency/guide?	no
Route map	see Route 18

A very interesting short day trip from Ollantaytambo, this site has just recently been uncovered and restored and features some fantastic Inca terraces, as well as a cave decorated with some of the finest carved stones in the Sacred Valley. The site has not been professionally excavated and it is not yet certain when it was built or what its purpose was. It certainly was a very important site, however, as indicated by the extensive terracing and quality stonework. Very few Incan sites in the Sacred Valley were religious sites, but this cave appears to be one of them.

There are different ways to do this trip, either walking from Ollantaytambo or taking a taxi directly to the base of the terraces, from where it is a 15min walk to the ruins. A third option would be to get dropped off at the base of the ruins and walk back to Ollantaytambo afterwards. Renting a bicycle in Ollantaytambo is another good option as the trail is flat along the river to Pachar, and from there the climb up the road to the base of the cave is short and not very steep.

From **Ollantaytambo**, either bicycle, walk, or take a taxi 7km outside of town, east on the road towards Cusco. The turnoff is referred to as **Pachar**, which is the name of the community just a short way uphill. There is a bright orange bridge crossing the Vilcanota river – cross this bridge and at the end of it take a right and follow the road upwards. If coming instead via the Incan road from

Ollantaytambo which leaves from the bridge at the bottom of the road out of town, you will come out onto a dirt road – take a right and go uphill. From where the Incan road meets the dirt road, it is 3km up the road to the trailhead for the cave.

The trail starts right where the road dips down a little and crosses a bridge over a small river and the train tracks. (If you go too far, it will soon become obvious as the road will go past the extensive terracing marking the site on the right-hand side.) Simply follow the well-worn footpath from the bridge along the railway tracks, heading uphill. Follow the train tracks for about 100m before the trail climbs up and to the right. From here it is a short 15min walk through the impressive terracing up to the site of **Ñaupa Iglesia**.

The carved temple rocks in the caves of Ñaupa Iglesia

Ñaupa Iglesia was a very important site and features fine Inca rock carving. Given the quality of the stonework here, Ñaupa Iglesia was likely a religious

Hiking up the terraces lining the mountain below Ñaupa Iglesia

shrine and/or a royal burial place. An entire wall inside the cave has been shaped and smoothed, and there is a throne at the mouth of the cave that has been perfectly carved out of solid rock. There are a few small but distinct Incan buildings surrounding it, a commanding view of the entire valley, and it appears to be connected to the site of Inca Raccay and Q'orimarca (Route 18) via an Incan trail but the trail has not been restored and is obscured and in poor condition. However, this site was not described in any of the Conquest literature and thus very little is known about it.

After visiting this small but impressive site, return via the same route back to Ollantaytambo or for a longer trek continue on to Soccma as described in Route 18.

ROUTE 20
Las Canterras quarries and Inti Punku

Start/Finish	Ollantaytambo (2850m)
Distance	20km round trip
Total ascent/descent	1040m
Difficulty	Strenuous, due to steepness and sun exposure
Time	6–8hrs
Trail type	Singletrack trail
High point	3890m (Inti Punku)
Hike or bike?	hike
Agency/guide?	no

An epic day trip from Ollantaytambo that first arrives at the Inca quarries of Las Canterras, with the option of continuing up to the mountaintop Incan lookout of Inti Punku. At Las Canterras there are the remains of the Inca workshop that produced the giant carved stones used to build the fortress of Ollantaytambo. Inti Punku ('sun gate' in Quechua) is a small Inca site but one of the most majestic in the whole area, perched atop a mountaintop ridge line with outstanding views in all directions, including the 5700m glacier Veronica. This trip is highly recommended and sees relatively little traffic despite its location right above Ollantaytambo.

There are two good options for doing this route, either hiking or on horseback. The climb is quite fierce, so if you have interest in going horseback riding this would be a good route on which to do so. Horses can easily be hired in Ollantaytambo but should be arranged the day before so as to get an early start, which for time and weather reasons is very important. It is not possible to ride up as the trail is too steep.

The trail leaves from the 'Inca Bridge' at the bottom of **Ollantaytambo**. Cross the bridge over the Rio Vilcanota and take the trail downriver, to the right (west). The trail has several spurs, most of them heading down to the right, towards the river. Ignore these and continue climbing. The trail ascends gently and offers up great views of

The palace of Manco Inca in Ollantaytambo, 'Quello Raccay'

Ollantaytambo and the surrounding area. ▶ After another 2km of climbing the trail arrives at a large open area that is used as a **mirador** (viewing area) for the Inca pyramid below of Pakaritampu and its 'special effects' that occur during the equinoxes and summer and winter solstice. This makes a good place for a quick rest before resuming the ascent.

There are two small trails that intersect the main trail; just stay left at any intersection and keep ascending. Continue climbing up for another 2km and the trail arrives. The first destination is **Las Canterras**.

Be sure to look off to the right, across the river, after 1km or so of walking for a good look at the Incan palace, called Quello Raccay ('yellow place'), once occupied by Manco Inca.

The quarries of **Las Canterras** is where the Incas mined and shaped the massive stones that they used to build the fortress of Ollantaytambo. From here on the hillside, you can look across the valley on the other side of the river and clearly see the back of the fortress, as well as the long ramp that was built by the Incas to bring the stones up to the

159

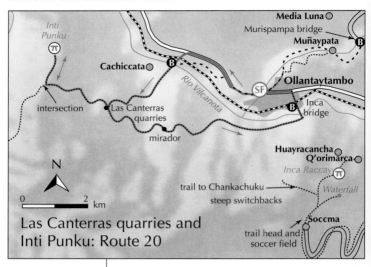

Las Canterras quarries and
Inti Punku: Route 20

*Excellent example,
in the quarries of
Ollantaytambo, of
the wheel the Incas
didn't have*

complex. The great explorer Vince Lee duplicated this feat, proving how it could have been done. At the quarries, there is ample evidence of the work that was being done when the Spanish Conquest came. There are lots of stones that were being worked on and shaped, as well as the remains of some basic worker housing. There are also good views of the Ollantaytambo town and valley, as well as the glacier of Mt. Veronica.

The quarries are about two thirds of the way up to the top and the site of Inti Punku. After leaving Las Canterras, continue climbing northwest, in the direction of Mt. Veronica and the trail becomes more obvious. As always, there are side trails that go off in all directions. Many of them rejoin the main trail anyway further uphill and are fine to take. The best advice is to stay on the largest trail and to continue going up and to the northwest, towards the glacier. The climb steepens before finally arriving at the last rest spot, a small flat place with a small house that serves as a rest area for the locals who graze their livestock here. The trail up to Inti Punku can be clearly seen – all that is required is to muster up a little more energy for the final climb.

The final approach to **Inti Punku** is classic Inca architecture. That means it consists of increasingly suspenseful hiking as the trail climbs to its climax, followed by a false summit, then one more amazing section of Incan road leading to the site itself. When the weather is clear between April and October, this last section is truly breathtaking as it climbs up the ancient stone steps to the perfectly placed doorway of Inti Punku, with the huge white glacier of Veronica just behind it.

Inti Punku was most likely an astronomical as well as military lookout site. It has protective views in all directions, particularly the four valleys that allow access to Ollantaytambo – one from Machu Picchu, one from Cusco, one from Salkantay, and one from Abra Malaga and the jungle beyond. However, it also has astronomical connections as well; for example on the summer solstice when the sun first hits the eastern window, it goes out the back side of the building and the western window and shines directly toward Machu Picchu. All in all, an amazing site.

Inti Punku, 'the sun gate', above Ollantaytambo

To return, follow the trail back down the way you came up. There is another way down that is very easy to find, as it follows a natural walking line down to the small community of **Cachiccata**. The trail splits 2km below the site of Inti Punku, and the trail going off to the left, north towards the Veronica glacier, leads down into Cachiccata. From there, it is a 15min walk out to the main paved road, where you can flag down a passing truck or bus, or simply walk the 20mins back into Ollantaytambo along the road.

ROUTE 21
The Veronica glacier

Start/Finish	Pisca Cucho (2700m)
Distance	24km round trip
Total ascent/descent	2050m
Difficulty	Strenuous due to altitude and steepness
Time	3 days hiking (plus any time spent on the glacier)
Trail type	Mountain trail
High point	4750m
Hike or bike?	hike
Agency/guide?	yes (to reach the summit)

This trek leaves Pisca Cucho ('five corners' in Quechua), which is near the beginning of the Inca Trail, and so it is a good choice for spending some time hiking and acclimatizing before starting the trail. It also makes a good side trip from Ollantaytambo. The route skirts the southwest flank of Veronica and climbs up to a saddle with gorgeous views and even access to the glacier itself for the more adventurous. Besides climbing the Chicón mountain in Urubamba, this is the closest access to the many beautiful glaciers you will see while travelling around the Sacred Valley.

This is a heavily crevassed glacier and if you wish to climb beyond the saddle climbing equipment and the knowledge how to use it is essential. In favourable conditions, it is possible to reach the summit in two days from here but there are frequent avalanches and ice falls.

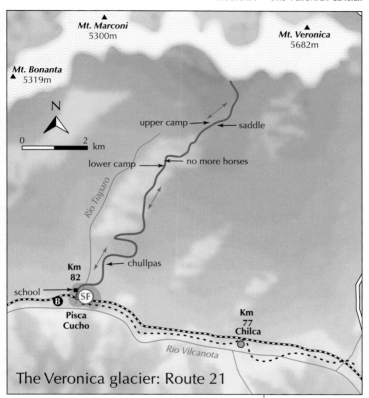

The Veronica glacier: Route 21

Plan to arrive in Pisca Cucho well prepared, as there is very little in the way of supplies, so be sure to stock up in Ollantaytambo. Horses can be arranged a day in advance here or in Ollantaytambo; the route is fairly steep uphill hiking for most of the way. The best place to start from is Pisca Cucho, which lies just off the road shortly before it reaches a dead end at the start of the Inca Trail itself (Km 82). To get there, go west from Ollantaytambo on the paved road towards Abra Malaga; 7km from Ollantaytambo, there are a few houses and a spur road

The glaciated western peak of Mt. Veronica

off to the left. This small group of houses is known as Phiry. Turn left here and take the dirt road 8km along the river, past Chilca (Km 77) and arrive at **Pisca Cucho** (Km 82). Perhaps the best place to sort gear and/or meet the arriero is at the school – just ask anyone in town to point out the 'escuela'.

The trail lies off the north side of the road. From the school, go out to the road and go right, east towards Ollantaytambo, for 0.5km. There on the left is the road which accesses the canyon the trail climbs up into. Take the road directly towards the mountain of Veronica, which lies straight ahead. ◄ The road turns into a trail as it begins climbing the southwest flank. It makes various twists and turns as it climbs up, and there are a few trails heading off towards various family farms, but just stay on the main trail and always in the general direction of the peak itself. After a few kilometres there are a few pre-Inca chullpas, round structures that were probably used to store food supplies such as corn.

There are always new road spurs being built here, so the best advice is to keep heading toward the mountain.

164

Continue ascending, past the open field and up a series of switchbacks. After 4km, the trail turns to the east and enters one of the tributaries of the Veronica glacier. This is the **lower camp** and beyond here the trail is not passable for horses or mules and so all gear must be carried from here on up. There aren't any other campsites until the high saddle, which is still 3hrs walking up ahead; best to stay here if it is late in the day.

The route is difficult to follow in this part of the canyon ascent. There is a trail high along the ridge line on the right-hand (south) side that is probably best to follow, as the vegetation down on the floor of the valley is very thick and hard to navigate. The best advice is to keep ascending the canyon while staying as high up on the right-hand ridge line as is possible. From here, you can see your destination, the high saddle up ahead, so use that as a guide as well.

After gaining the small **saddle** in the notch, the glacier is visible for the first time and is another 0.5km up

Ascending towards the glacier of Mt. Veronica

165

The scour marks from countless years of the ice scraping down the rock has left a very interesting surface to walk on.

ahead. This is the last suitable place to camp, and is known as the **upper camp**. The trail continues on up to the **glacier**, which unfortunately is rapidly receding. ◄

From here you can simply climb around and then return back to Pisca Cucho and Ollantaytambo the way you came, or climb the glacier to the summit, if suitably experienced and equipped.

ROUTE 22
Patacancha valley

Start	Trailhead at Tastallyoq (3860m)
Finish	Ollantaytambo (2850m)
Distance	29km
Total ascent	580m
Total descent	1590m
Difficulty	Moderate
Time	6–7hrs hiking, 5–6hrs biking
Trail type	Dirt trail
High point	4480m
Hike or bike?	both
Agency/guide?	no

This is a very pleasant day hike or ride that takes you up and over a high mountain pass and down into the valley of Patacancha. Nice views, isolation and a few remote alpine communities are the highlights of this trip.

The trail leaves right from the main highway going up to Abra Malaga from Ollantaytambo. If hiking this route it is best to take a taxi up to this corner, known to the locals as **Tastallyoq**. If you tell the driver you are going over to Patacancha, he will know where the trailhead is. If biking, either bring the bikes up in a taxi, otherwise it is a pleasant 3hr climb up from Ollantaytambo on the paved road.

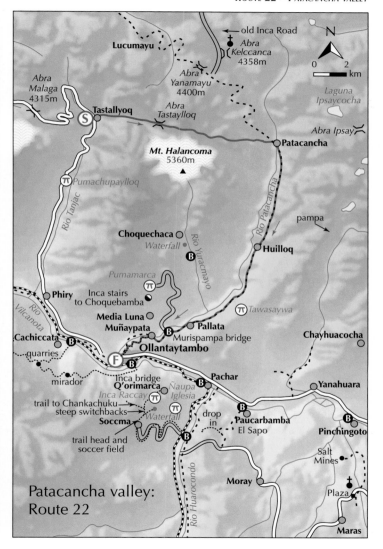

← old Inca Road

N

0   2
km

Lucumayu

Abra Kelccanca 4358m

Abra Yanamayu 4400m

Laguna Ipsaycocha

Abra Malaga 4315m

Tastallyoq (S)

Abra Tastaylloq

Abra Ipsay

Patacancha

π *Pumachupaylloq*

Mt. Halancoma 5360m ▲

Rio Tanjac

Choquechaca ○ *Waterfall*

Rio Yuracmayo

(B)

Rio Patacancha

pampa

Huilloq

Pumamarca

π

Phiry ● Inca stairs to Choquebamba

Rio Vilcanota

Media Luna ○

Muñaypata

Cachiccata

Pallata

π *Tawasaywa*

(B) Murispampa bridge

Chayhuacocha ○

(B) **Ollantaytambo**

quarries ●

(F)

(B)

mirador ●

Pachar (B)

Yanahuara ○

Inca bridge **Q'orimarca**

π *Ñaupa Iglesia*

Inca Raccay π

trail to Chankachuku steep switchbacks →

Waterfall

drop in

(B)

Soccma

Paucarbamba El Sapo

(B)

Pinchingoto

trail head and soccer field

(B)

Salt Mines ●

Patacancha valley: Route 22

Moray ○

Rio Huarocondo

Plaza

Maras

*On the trail from
Tastallyoq to
Patacancha*

The trailhead is nothing more than a small foot trail heading off the right-hand side of the road. There is a small river valley here and foot trails going up each side of it. The best side to climb up is the right (south) side. The trail ascends upwards at a modest gradient for a little way through the remote countryside; there a few scattered houses but otherwise nothing else of significance. After 5km of climbing from the trailhead there is a final rocky ascent and you arrive at the pass, **Abra Tastallyoq**.

After the pass, the trail drops down to **Patacancha** via 6km of very enjoyable hiking through beautiful terrain and there will be few if any other tourists – and not very many locals either. The trail spills right out on to the road in front of Patacancha. From here it is 17km back down to Ollantaytambo, or you can look for a truck or taxi that is heading down the mountain past **Huilloq** and into town.

ROUTE 23
To Quillabamba via Abra Yanamayu

Start	Ollantaytambo (2850m)
Finish	Quillabamba (1060m)
Distance	380km
Total ascent	1950m
Total descent	3740m
Difficulty	Moderate
Time	3–6 days by bike or motorcycle
Trail type	Rugged dirt road
High point	4400m (Abra Yanamayu)
Hike or bike?	bike
Agency/guide?	recommended

This route is truly an epic adventure, crossing the 4400m pass of Abra Yanamayu and from there dropping thousands of metres down to the edge of the Amazon basin. This trip is best done as a mountain bike or motorcycle trip. It could be done trekking, but there is no foot trail, just a rugged dirt road, and it is a long journey. The scenery along the way is wild and stunningly beautiful. After crossing the pass of Abra Yanamayu there are no Incan sites to see, though they are undoubtedly there, buried under a few centuries of jungle growth.

This road was opened to traffic for the first time in 2006, when the final stretch above Occobamba was completed. At the time of writing, the road is still quite sketchy and in a few places not drivable. Part of the route, specifically most of the lower river crossings, is passable by 4WD vehicles only. The road can be quite dangerous during the rainy season due to landslides, and thus is not recommended at all from October to April. There are few or no services available until Quelluono, thus all food, water and fuel must be brought along from Ollantaytambo.

Begin at the road heading up the mountain from just below the plaza in Ollantaytambo, behind KB Tambo Hotel. The pass is 31km up the road, passing many Inca sites and terracing as well as the weaving communities of **Huilloq** and **Patacancha**. Six kilometres after Patacancha,

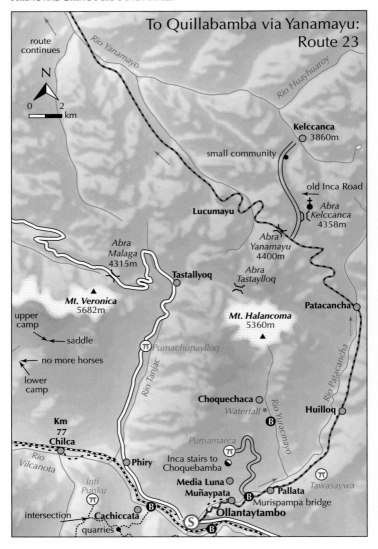

To Quillabamba via Yanamayu:
Route 23

route continues

N

0   2
km

Río Yanamayo

Río Huayhuaroy

Kelccanca
3860m

small community

old Inca Road

Lucumayu

Abra Kelccanca
4358m

Abra Malaga
4315m

Tastallyoq

Abra Yanamayu
4400m

Abra Tastaylloq

Mt. Veronica
5682m

Patacancha

upper camp

saddle

no more horses

lower camp

Mt. Halancoma
5360m

Pumachupaylloq

Río Tanjac

Río Patacancha

Choquechaca

Waterfall

Río Yuracmayo

Huilloq

Km 77
Chilca

Pumamarca

Río Vilcanota

Phiry

Inca stairs to Choquebamba

Inti Punku

Media Luna
Muñaypata

Pallata

Tawasaywa

intersection

Cachiccata

quarries

Murispampa bridge

Ollantaytambo

S

there is a road on the eastern side of the valley, disappearing up and over a ridge. This goes over the pass and down to Kelccanca and eventually Lares, as described in Route 15. Ignore this road to the right and continue up, cresting the pass which consists of nothing more than a windswept landscape and a small church.

Motorcycling in the Sacred Valley is always an adventure

> The **Abra Yanamayu** pass is situated at 4400m above sea level and forms part of the Continental Divide. From here looking eastward, the next point at which the earth rises this high would be Mt. Kilimanjaro in Tanzania. East from this pass, all water flows out through the Amazon jungle basin to the Atlantic Ocean. The majority of this massive descent and drop in altitude (over 3500m) occurs on the road about to be taken.

From the pass the road begins descending, passing a few simple huts along the way before crossing to the eastern side of the river just after the village of

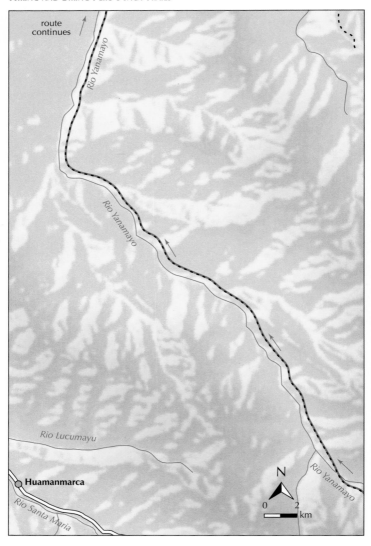

route
continues

Rio Yanamayo

Rio Yanamayo

Rio Yanamayo

Rio Lucumayu

Huamanmarca

Rio Santa Maria

N

0   2
km

Lucumayu, located 13km below the pass, with its beautiful newly built school, faced with stone and overlooking the valley.

A few kilometres below, the river crosses again to the western side of the river, having descended over 700m from the pass. Here begins one of the more dramatic stretches of the route. The road clings precariously to a slope base of gravel and scree, angled at over 45 degrees. Take care as any slip would be fatal. The road continues down the canyon, finally levelling out a bit and the vegetation begins to thicken.

The altitude here is about 2700m and the air continues to get warmer. ▶ The small town of **Occobamba** lies a bit further downriver and there you can buy snacks, water and sodas as well as minimal other supplies. After hanging out in the pleasant main plaza and taking a break, continue on to **San Lorenzo** which is situated approximately 125km from Ollantaytambo. Here in San Lorenzo there are a few basic stores to buy soft drinks or perhaps a cold beer. From here, the road begins to climb as it goes towards **Echarate**, then on to Chaullay, at an altitude of 1780m. At Echarate, take the turnoff south towards Quillabamba which is 1hr upriver.

The lack of automobile access until very recently has prevented much development from coming into this area; hopefully it will remain unspoiled.

The Occobamba valley produces excellent arabica coffee

173

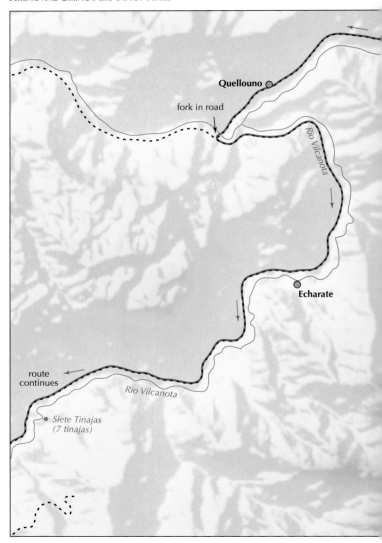

Quellouno

fork in road

Rio Vilcanota

Echarate

route
continues

Rio Vilcanota

Siete Tinajas
(7 tinajas)

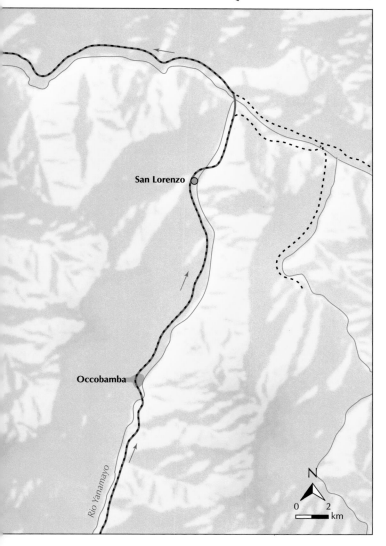

San Lorenzo

Occobamba

Rio Yanamayo

N

0   2
km

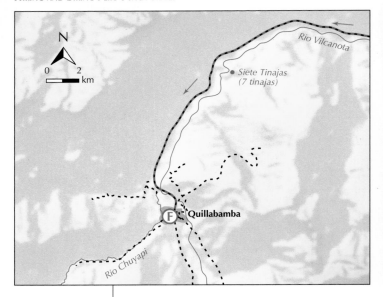

About 20 minutes outside of Quillabamba there is a natural water feature that is worth visiting called **Siete Tinajas**. Costing just a few soles to enter, it is a series of jungle waterfalls and natural pools and is very lush and beautiful. There is a rope ladder to aid in climbing up to the highest pools; the ladder is a bit dodgy so use caution – also the rocks are very slippery.

From Siete Tinajas it is a short ride further into **Quillabamba**, a boisterous jungle outpost town where supplies of just about anything can be replenished. There are several hotels and hostels, though a bit run down, but the appeal of Quillabamba is the climate and the food. If you fancy a warm climate, roasted chicken or fruit juice, you may never want to leave but if you do, you will have a choice of bus, minivan or taxi to take you back to Ollantaytambo.

ROUTE 24
To Quillabamba via Abra Malaga

Start	Ollantaytambo (2850m)
Finish	Quillabamba (1060m)
Distance	142km
Total ascent	1620m
Total descent	3410m
Difficulty	Easy to moderate
Time	3hrs by motorcycle, 8hrs by bike
Trail type	Asphalt road, rugged dirt road
High point	4320m (Abra Malaga)
Hike or bike?	bike
Agency/guide?	no

Up until 2005 this was a much tougher and more epic route, as it was passable only with a 4WD, motorcycle, or a public bus. Since then, the road has been smoothed and paved from Ollantaytambo to Abra Malaga and a third of the way down the pass. Nonetheless it remains one of the most spectacular routes in the region, as in just a few hours the climate zones change from having glacial ice on the side of the road at the pass, to include bananas and coffee plants further down the mountain.

The road goes first to St. Maria, where the majority of travellers turn off on a side road that goes to St. Theresa, then to the hydroelectric station and on to Machu Picchu (see Route 26). This route, however, continues downriver from St. Maria for a little under 1hr more to Quillabamba, a hot jungle town that is a nice place to relax and eat lots of fruit! It also makes a good jumping off spot for trips to the Pongo de Manique and further down the river into the Amazon, as well as a stopover on the long journey back from Espiritu Pampa (Vilcabamba).

This is a straightforward route, passing very few other roads along the way. It is about 8 hard hours by bicycle to Quillabamba from Ollantaytambo, or 4hrs in public bus or taxi, or about 3hrs on a motorcycle. To begin, take the road from the base of the fortress in **Ollantaytambo** towards Km 82. Go past the turnoff, located at **Phiry**,

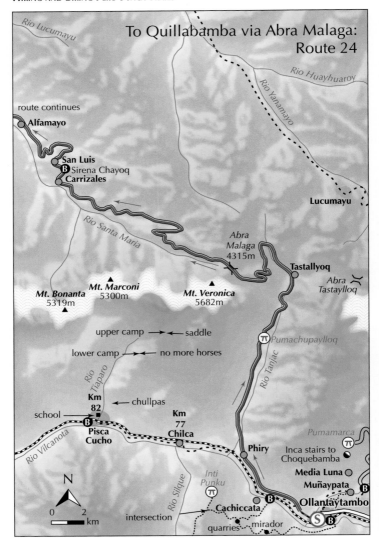

To Quillabamba via Abra Malaga:
Route 24

Rio Lucumayo

Rio Huayhuaroy

Rio Yanamayo

route continues
Alfamayo

San Luis
Sirena Chayoq
Carrizales

Rio Santa Maria

Lucumayu

*Abra
Malaga*
4315m

Tastallyoq

*Abra
Tastaylloq*

Mt. Bonanta
5319m

Mt. Marconi
5300m

Mt. Veronica
5682m

Rio Tanjac

Pumachupaylloq

upper camp → ← saddle
lower camp → ← no more horses

Rio Tiaparo

**Km
82** ← chullpas

school →

**Pisca
Cucho**

**Km
77
Chilca**

Phiry

Pumamarca

Inca stairs to
Choquebamba

Media Luna ○

Muñaypata

Rio Vilcanota

Rio Silque

*Inti
Punku*

Cachiccata

intersection

quarries   mirador

Ollantaytambo

N

0   2
km

and begin the massive climb up to the shoulder of Mt. Veronica.

There are several sets of pre-Inca ruins along the way: look for the square house built atop of a rock near the waterfall just above the site called Peñas.

> **Pumachupaylloq** is a perfect example of Inca architecture at it's best, blending the natural contours of the mountain landscape, as well as several large boulders, into a cohesive expression glorifying both mankind and nature at the same time. This description may seem a bit hyperbolic, until you see this site for the first time from the road – it is very impressive.

Continue upwards past **Tastallyoq** and after crossing over to the other side of the valley reach the pass of **Abra Malaga**, which is located at 4316m above sea level. There is a small church at the pass, at which it is customary to light a candle asking for a safe journey. It is usually quite cold at the pass so before to bring a warm hat and jacket.

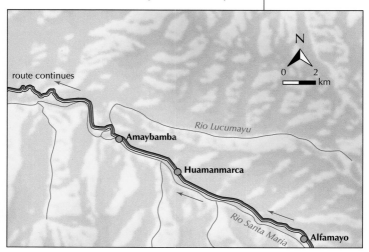

The route up to Abra Malaga, on the way to Quillabamba

The road leaves the church and begins winding down the massive glacial valley. The original Incan road (and probably a well-used trade route for hundreds of years before them) is visible off to the left, over on the other side of the valley. The scenery is gorgeous as the highway continues to drop down towards the Amazon, hugging the precipitous flanks of the mountains. Use caution as this stretch of the highway is prone to frequent landslides as well as the outer edge of the road collapsing. It first passes through a tiny settlement called Carrizales, then arrives at the first viewpoint, identified by a large white sign with the Peruvian police emblem on it. This is a former drug checkpoint, its location having been moved a few kilometres further down where the climate is more hospitable. There are excellent views from here, and more importantly it should be noted that however horrendous the weather was from the pass up to here, beyond this point it becomes progressively warmer and with clearer skies.

The road drops steeply from here, crossing the next valley at a massive, new bridge built to alleviate the many washouts of the old road due to landslides.

> The site of the bridge is called **Sirena Chayoq**, meaning 'place of the mermaid'. Legend has it that a beautiful mermaid lives here, and that leaving some flowers in the river will please her and ensure safe passage. Many passing truck drivers ritually do so, and so there are always beautiful flowers laying in the river.

A bit further down, the police checkpoint is now located at **San Luis**, a small clearing where the police stop most traffic passing by to check for shipments of cocaine. This road exits from one of the worlds' most prolific coca growing regions, thus the checkpoint. Generally, however, there appears to be little enthusiasm for any real kind of search, typically they will glance into the back and wave you on. The road keeps going down until **Alfamayo**.

From Alfamayo the road continues down towards the jungle and banana, coffee and other fruit plants begin to appear. Fifteen kilometres down the mountain is the Inca site of **Huamanmarca**. This is a classic Inca communication platform and palace site and it has sight lines closely connecting it with Ollantaytambo, Machu Picchu, Vilcabamba and Choquequirao. The site is in the process of being excavated and restored. Ten kilometres further down lies **Huyro**, which is one of the region's largest producers of tea.

The road continues down to **St. Maria**, a growing jungle outpost now serving as Grand Central Station for adventurous travellers who are taking the back door route to Machu Picchu. There is a small police checkpoint here that ostensibly registers all people entering *adentro* ('within'), as the jungle area east and downriver of here is called. After a few kilometres there is a small town called **Chaullay**, where the road forks. To continue going straight will also lead to Quillabamba, via Maranura.

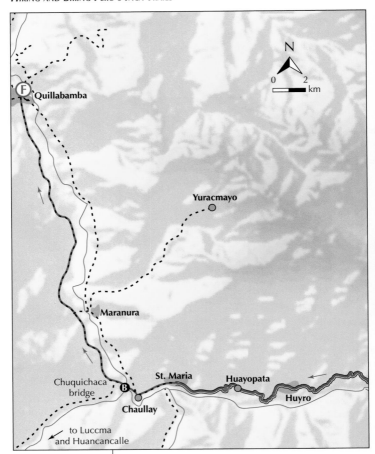

However, the left fork of the road goes to Quillabamba via a more interesting route. To take it, look for a downhill turn off to the left in what passes for the centre of this two-block town. There is a large corner store and bus stop that marks the turn, which goes down a few hundred metres and then crosses the Rio Vilcanota at the site of the historic Inca bridge **Chuquichaca**. Guarding one of the few entrances to the Inca refuge of Vilcabamba, this was the site of an important battle between the Spaniards and Incas. Just after it is the turnoff to Huancancalle and the Vilcabamba region. Instead, continue north along the river on the main road until reaching **Quillabamba**. ▶

Use caution as the road is frequently washed out and jungle drivers tend to be quite a bit more aggressive in their driving habits than their high mountain brethren.

Quillabamba is a pleasant place to arrive after a long journey. There are plenty basic hostels as well as restaurants to be found, including an astounding number of *pollerias* (restaurants serving roasted chicken). Quillabamba is a mid-sized town that serves as a focal point for all types of traffic coming from jungle towns further in. It has several banks, ATMs and internet cafes. More importantly, it has a great many ice cream shops and fresh fruit stands. From here you can venture further in towards the Amazon, via the Pongo de Manique as described in Route 25.

Biking to Quillabamba, with the Incan site of Media Luna in the background

ROUTE 25
To Ivochote and Pongo de Manique

Start	Ollantaytambo (2850m)
Finish	Ivochote (800m)
Distance	265km
Total ascent	1620m
Total descent	3670m
Difficulty	Easy except for the rigours of dusty, bumpy roads
Time	4–7 days, depending on mode of transport
Trail type	Rugged dirt road
High point	4320m (Abra Malaga)
Hike or bike?	(motor)bike
Agency/guide?	no

This is a popular route for travellers wanting to leave the local beaten path. It can be done via public or private car, motorcycle, or by masochistic mountain bikers. No matter the form of transport, this is a pretty 'challenging' trip due to the distance and the poor quality of roads. The final part of the journey from Ivochote is a white-knuckle boat ride through the rapids to the waterfall-filled canyon of Pongo de Manique – quite beautiful and well worth the journey, and there are recent reports of Incan ruins there. (Thanks to traveller Justin Kleiter for his contribution to this section.)

If not travelling by bicycle or motorcycle there are two other choices: private car or public transport. Public transport is plentiful and inexpensive up to Quillabamba. To travel onwards from Quillabamba to Ivochote you should be able to find trucks leaving every few hours during daylight hours. Limited bus transport does exist as well but can be very slow. It is a long and gruelling road to Ivochote, approximately 7hrs from Quillabamba, and is not recommended during the rainy season.

If you are travelling by motorcycle or bike you will need to make an overnight stop. Unless you are camping, the only places to stay are Quillabamba (which has a range of hostels and hotels) or Kiteni (two basic hostels

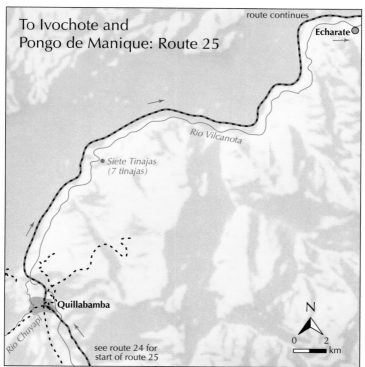

To Ivochote and
Pongo de Manique: Route 25

route continues

Echarate

Rio Vilcanota

• Siete Tinajas
(7 tinajas)

Quillabamba

Rio Chuyapi

N

0   2
km

see route 24 for
start of route 25

and nothing more). Cyclists will have to stay in Kiteni. Those who have hitched a ride from Quillabamba, would probably go the full distance in one shot.

From **Ollantaytambo** follow the directions given in Route 24 to arrive at **Quillabamba**. From there, there is only one other road leaving Quillabamba and this is the road to take. If there are any doubts, just ask a local to point the direction to 'Siete Tinajas'. ▶

The road continues towards Quellouno, first passing **Echarate** which is a little less than 30km from Quillabamba. At the time of writing the road was under construction and very rough – even during the dry

Siete Tinajas is a group of cascading waterfalls worth a stop if travelling by private transport.

185

The lush waterfall complex known as 'Siete tinajas'

season, potholes and giant puddles are encountered frequently. However, the construction continues aggressively and the road continues to improve.

After travelling 41km from Quillabamba, a **fork** in the road is reached. To the right a short distance away lies Quellouno, and from there the road continues to Lares and Calca (see Route 24). For this route, take the road to the left. The massive Vilcanota River can be seen continuing towards **Rosalinda**, which is 23km from the fork. After Rosalinda, 64km of dusty potholed dirt and gravel road leads to **Kiteni**, the last village of any size before the Pongo. Stock up here on any last minute supplies. Another 10km ahead lies an interesection in the road. The left fork goes to Koshireni, however the correct direction is to the right towards Malaquiato. **Ivochote** is approximately 20km further. New roads are being constructed in this area around Malaquiato – taking a right-hand turn at any fork should bring you to Ivochote, if there is any doubt just ask any local to point out the direction. Simple cold water hostels and *hospedajes* (small, basic

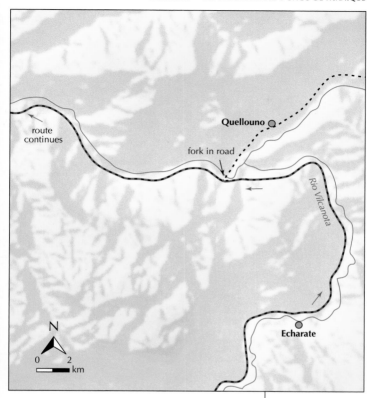

family run hostels) are located on the main street just across the bridge. Motorcycles and bicycles can cross the bridge along with pedestrians, however larger vehicles cannot. ▶

A few basic restaurants and several simple stores line the main road near the bridge.

Hiring a boat to **Pongo de Manique** can be arranged under the bridge at the river. Private express tours can be arranged (500–700 soles) or passage on a boat carrying cargo (50–75 soles per person) can often be found. The tour to the waterfall-filled

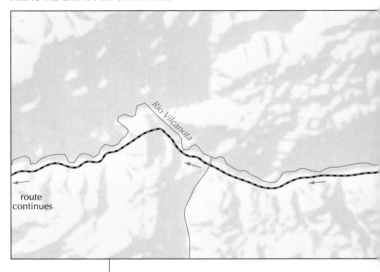

Jungle youth floating downriver near Pongo de Manique

canyon takes about 5hrs round trip with an express boat. This ride is typically in a 50-ft long wooden *lancha* (small, narrow river boat) with an outboard motor descending some amazing rapids as the

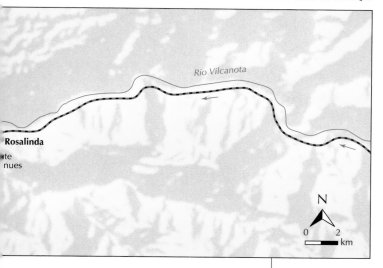

Rio Vilcanota makes its way down to the Amazon basin. There are a couple of jungle lodges further down the river, as well as the Sabeti salt lick, which draws a variety of wildlife.

Crossing a river on the route to Pongo de Manique

189

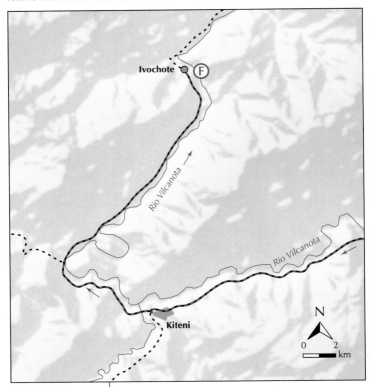

For the truly adventurous, this trip opens doors to the Amazon. River transport continues all the way to Pucallpa and beyond to Brazil and eventually the Atlantic Ocean. Or, return the same way back to the amazing mountains of the Andes.

ROUTE 26
Machu Picchu 'back door' route

Start	Ollantaytambo (2850m)
Finish	Aguas Calientes (2040m)
Distance	155km
Total ascent	2100m
Total descent	2910m
Difficulty	Easy to moderate
Time	1–3 days, depending on mode of transport
Trail type	Paved road, rugged dirt road, train track
High point	4320m (Abra Malaga)
Hike or bike?	bike
Agency/guide?	no

This route had always been popular with in-the-know guides and alternative tourism companies, but it wasn't until the disasters of constant train strikes, difficult schedules and price gouging by Peru Rail, starting around 2005, that local companies began bringing mountain bikers to Machu Picchu via Abra Malaga and St. Theresa. Now, the 'back door' route to Machu Picchu is a favourite among backpackers and independent travellers.

Most common is to ride a mountain bike from the pass of Abra Malaga, from where it is over 70km of nearly all downhill to the jungle town of St. Maria. Only part of this ride is usually done on bike – most people opt to cycle only down to St. Maria, as from there the road is very hot, dusty and full of speeding traffic. The rest is done via a combination of taxis, buses, optional train and on foot. It is included here in the book because it is such a popular route with ever-changing conditions and is the subject of a great deal of uncertainty and confusion among travellers. Nonetheless, it is an outstanding route.

It is not possible to take motorized transport all way to Aguas Calientes. However, you can get as far as the hydroelectric station, which is about 20mins by car further upriver than St. Theresa. In 1998 a landslide destroyed the train tracks between the hydroelectric station and St. Theresa, so now the train only goes as far as the hydroelectric station. From here there is a tourist train that departs once daily in the afternoon (tourists are not allowed on the other local train departures), but most travellers elect to walk the 3hrs along the train tracks to Aguas Calientes.

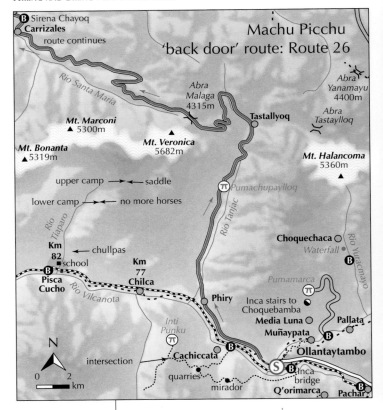

Machu Picchu
'back door' route: Route 26

B Sirena Chayoq
Carrizales
route continues

Rio Santa Maria

*Abra
Malaga
4315m*

*Abra
Yanamayu
4400m*

Tastallyoq

*Abra
Tastaylloq*

Mt. Marconi
▲ 5300m

Mt. Veronica
5682m

Mt. Halancoma
5360m
▲

Mt. Bonanta
▲5319m

π *Pumachupaylloq*

upper camp → saddle

Rio Tarjac

Choquechaca ○
Waterfall ●

lower camp → no more horses

Rio Tiaparo

B

Rio Yucramayo

**Km
82** ← chullpas

π *Pumamarca*

**Km
77**

Pallata

B school

Chilca

Phiry

Inca stairs to
Choquebamba

**Pisca
Cucho**

Rio Vilcanota

Media Luna ○

Muñaypata
B

Ollantaytambo

*Inti
Punku*
π

N

Cachiccata B

S B

intersection

0   2

quarries •
mirador

Inca
bridge

Q'orimarca ○

B

Pachar

km

Start from **Ollantaytambo** and take the main road up to
the pass of **Abra Malaga**. There are several new Inca sites
that have recently been uncovered and cleaned and the
whole way up is very scenic. Cross the pass and begin the
massive downhill to St. Maria. The road is paved as far as
Alfa Mayo but there are plans to continue paving it all the
way to Quillabamba.

There is a police checkpoint at **San Luis**. Use caution
as the traffic on this side of the pass tends do be more

frequent and also more aggressive. During rainy season this route needs to be classified as dangerous, as there are frequent landslides. Nonetheless this is one of the most scenic routes in all of South America and it passes through many different climatic and ecological zones as it goes down towards the Amazon jungle.

Incan lookout platform of Huamanmarca, along the Inca road to Machu Picchu

Some 55km below the pass of Abra Malaga, a few kilometres after the town of Inca Tambo, lies an Inca site called **Huamanmarca**. This is yet another one of their many 'signalling stations' that are strung throughout the Andes. As noted by explorer and author Vincent Lee, this particular one was an important link in the communication line between Choquequirao and Machu Picchu, as designed and built by the Incas. Using smoke signals or flags, they could send a message in just a few minutes across terrain that represented several days walking, even by a fleet chasqui (Inca foot messenger).

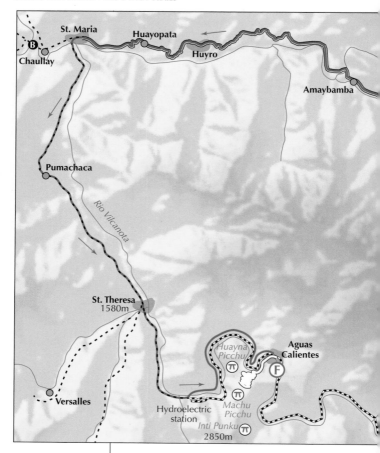

Keep going down, past the town of **Huyro**, which is very well known for the tea it produces and sells under a brand by the same name. Continue down the road and by now there are banana and coffee plants growing along the roadside, as well as oranges, papayas, avocados and numerous other delicious gifts from the jungle. The road

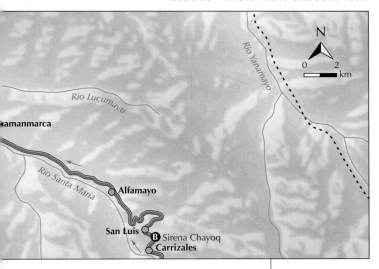

becomes quite hot from here all the way down to **St. Maria**, which is a good place to stop and rest and enjoy something cold to drink. There are a few restaurants in town and several stores here that cater to the backpackers taking this route, as well as several small roadside stands selling fresh fruit to the buses passing to Quillabamba.

It is here at St. Maria that you must take the turnoff to St. Theresa. The turnoff is located right in the middle of this small village, turning left off of the main road. It is not well marked and looks more like a driveway, but anyone can point you in the right direction. The road from St. Maria to St. Theresa is always an adventure. This area is highly prone to landslides during the rainy season, so the road is in a constant state of disrepair. There are two routes, a lower and an upper route. The upper route is used in times when the lower road, which runs near the river below, is flooded or blocked by landslides, which happens quite frequently. The upper road takes approximately 2–3hrs while the lower road takes about half that time to reach St. Theresa. Ask a local for current

Descending the trail towards St. Theresa

conditions. The road along the river is mostly flat, passing **Pumachaca** at about the halfway point before continuing upriver and finally arriving at **St. Theresa**.

The town of **St. Theresa** lies at 1580m and has a jungle feel, and although small it is a bit chaotic. New hotels are sprouting up everywhere and there are several new pizza restaurants for the tourists. There is a quite decent hostel ran by the municipality, they charge 30 soles per person for a room with private bath. At this time they have neither a phone nor email address; instead ask around upon arriving town. Another good alternative is Hostel Orquideas just off the main street. The central plaza has recently been redone and is quite a pleasant place to pass some time in the afternoon or evenings. Also, a brand new place called Eco Quechua Lodge has opened and is highly recommended.

From St. Theresa it is approximately 7km to the hydroelectric station. Currently, you can take a taxi up to this point but no further. There is an INC booth here where each traveller will need to register. The walking path to Aguas Calientes begins here, to the left of the booth. It is illegal to walk on the train tracks themselves.

The walk takes 3hrs and is very pleasant. The path goes directly alongside the Urubamba River, and there is a wide variety of plant and animal life along the way. Just before arriving at **Aguas Calientes**, a small pathway off to the right connects the railroad path with the main road that goes up to Machu Picchu. Better to take the road into town, as the last kilometre of train track features two different tunnels that are a bit dangerous to enter.

ROUTE 27

To Huayllabamba and the start of the Inca Trail

Start	Ollantaytambo (2850m)
Finish	Huayllabamba (3000m)
Distance	50km
Total ascent	2600m
Total descent	2450m
Difficulty	Moderate to strenuous
Time	2–3 days hiking
Trail type	Incan road, singletrack
High point	4650m (Abra Huayanay)
Hike or bike?	hike
Agency/guide?	yes

An excellent way to tack on two or three days to the beginning of the classic Inca Trail, in order to acclimatize. This trek passes gorgeous glacial scenery, authentic Andean high mountain villages, and a few impressive Inca sites. A final advantage is the opportunity to spend some solitary time trekking, as this trail sees very few visitors. This route is not suitable for biking.

All supplies need to be obtained in Ollantaytambo before beginning this trek, as there are no places along the way to buy food or drinks. This route can be done either with horse support or without. If horses are desired, they should be arranged in Ollantaytambo beforehand.

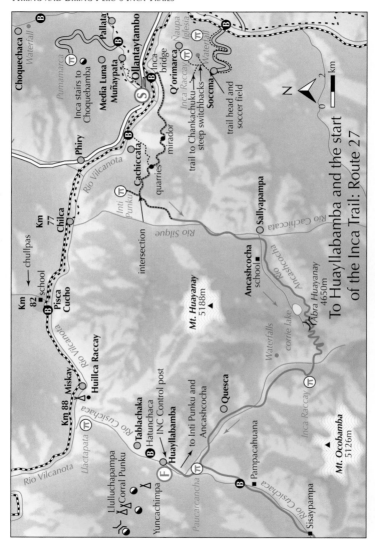

To Huayllabamba and the start of the Inca Trail: Route 27

Begin in **Ollantaytambo** and follow the directions for **Inti Punku**, as given in Route 20. After leaving Inti Punku you will be heading into, and then climbing, the massive valley below Silque, known locally as Ancashcocha, which means 'blue lake' in Quechua. This valley lies southwest of the site of Inti Punku, in the opposite direction from Mt. Veronica. ▶ Take the trail from Inti Punku down 0.5km, to the saddle below it. There is an intersection and a trail goes off to the right, to the saddle that is clearly visible before the next valley (the Ancashcocha valley, where the trail is going).

If the weather allows, a clear view of the valley and its distinct red mountains is visible.

Upon arriving to the high point of the saddle, there is an outstanding view to the west, both of the Ancashcocha valley and especially the mountains and glaciers that lie between here and Machu Picchu. The entire Veronica chain, which includes the glaciers of j and Wacay Wilka, can be seen, as well as Salkantay to the west on a clear day. Also visible is a massive black mountain directly on the other side of the Silque valley that is called Yana Orqo, or 'black mountain' in Quechua.

Wacay Wilka in Quechua means 'sacred tears' and is believed to refer to the glacier peaks of these mountains. One story behind the name is that the locals believe that before the Spanish Conquest the mountains were bare rock. After the tragic loss of their entire society and way of life, the story goes, the sacred mountains that overlook Machu Picchu (such as Mt. Veronica) cried sacred tears upon their flanks, which then turned to ice.

After this spectacular vista, take the trail south as it traverses the ridge a bit while gradually descending to the river valley below. Between 2km and 3km later, the trail starts climbing back up the mountain to the left. Shortly after this, there is a trail that splits off from the main trail and goes down to the right, southwest towards the river. This is the way to Ancashcocha. Take the trail all the way down to the Rio Silque, where it meets up with the main trail that is coming from Chilca below, at Km 77. ▶

This is a lovely trail, that heads south up the Silque valley along the river of the same name.

199

The trail crosses back and forth several times over the next 5km but eventually takes the western side of the valley, the right-hand side. Shortly after passing by a river valley that brings the Cachiccata River in from the left, comes the small community of **Sallyapampa**. There are a few scattered thatched roof buildings around that are mostly seasonal huts for the locals. This is a good place to camp if it is getting late. The village of Ancashcocha, sometimes referred to as Silque, is 2hrs 30mins of walking further up. Camping is possible virtually anywhere suitable on this stretch. Ask for permission if camping near a village, but a low-key campsite anywhere on this stretch, left clean the next day, isn't really going to bother any of the locals.

Up the valley lies **Ancashcocha**. There is a small school and at least 30 houses scattered across the large, flat pampa at the confluence of three glacial rivers. It makes a good place to have lunch or camp. From here, follow the valley up and stay on the left-hand side,

Walking above Ancashcocha

climbing up the left (western) ridge. The river to the right below is the Río Huayanay. Climb for 1–2hrs to arrive at the top of the ridge, with excellent views back down of the Ancashcocha pampa 2km below.

The next destination is Abra Huayanay, the pass leading over into the Pucamayu valley. Continue walking uphill and after just a bit the glacial **corrie lake** will appear ahead. Lying at the base of the pass and at an altitude of 4270m, it is the last place to camp before ascending the pass. Otherwise, if there is still plenty of daylight left, climb the loose scree slope up to the pass, **Abra Huayanay**, which has beautiful views in all directions and lies at an altitude of 4650m.

From the pass the trail is a bit difficult to follow, especially when the cloud and fog roll in, which is often. Use a compass or GPS and go north-northwest. Do not go too far to the north, or right, from the pass as it descends into a narrow, separate canyon. Walk more or less straight ahead, staying left at any juncture and keep on the largest trail. This will bring you perfectly down the mountain and across a small stream to **Inca Raccay**, a set of Inca buildings built at the head of the valley below the glacier. It takes a little under 1hr to get from the pass down to Inca Raccay.

The path from here is on the left (western) side of the river, as it enters the valley of Pucamayu, or 'red river' in Quechua. It continues downstream for the next 5km. After passing the **waterfalls** visible across the valley on the right-hand side, gradually work your way down to the valley floor. There are many, many intersecting cattle trails in the next few kilometres which can make the route seem confusing. However, there really is no wrong way downstream; just stay on the highest and driest path available and use a general sense of direction to continue going down the valley to reach **Quesca**, which is 8km below Inca Raccay or 9km from the pass.

From Quesca it is 2hrs hiking to the confluence of the Río Pucamayu with the Río Cusichaca, and the Inca tambo of **Paucarcancha**. The Río Cusichaca flows down from the left, coming from the glacier of Mt. Salkantay.

In that direction, after going up and over the pass of Sisaypampa, lies Mollepata in one direction and over another pass to Collpapampa and St. Theresa in the other direction. For this route, however, go right and downhill after visiting the site of Paucarcancha.

> **Paucarcancha** is well worth the visit and is worth an hour of time exploring and checking out its excellent vantage point. This site, occupying an important and strategic position, was likely a classic Inca combination of several functions: housing, lookout site and signal station.

From Paucarcancha, take the trail on the near (east) side of the river and go about 45mins downhill, to where there is a bridge that crosses over to the western side of the river. There is an INC building here, built primarily to serve as a control post for the many mules and horses that come down from Salkantay. This is not yet the official Inca Trail, but it is possible independent travellers will be questioned here all the same. Horses and mules are not permitted beyond this point.

Huayllabamba is 15mins further downhill, and is at the entrance to the valley of Llulluchayoc. This is the official entrance to the Inca Trail. ◄ At the time of writing, independent trekkers who are not doing the Inca Trail to Machu Picchu are allowed to continue downhill past Huayllabamba on to Patallacta and Huillca Raccay, which both lie down on the Rio Vilcanota 5km below at Km 88, and then up the southern, right-hand side of the river up to Km 82.

If continuing on to do the Inca Trail, the group should meet up here in the village of Huayllabamba.

However, this section is technically part of the Inca Trail and it is likely trekkers will be questioned repeatedly about where they are going and with whom. (The author was once escorted out to the park entrance by several park officers!) It is not a problem, just politely explain where you came from and then continue on out to Km 82, where it is possible to find a combi out to Ollantaytambo, or else it is a pleasant 3hr walk back to Ollantaytambo along the southern (right-hand) side of the river.

ROUTE 28
Ollantaytambo to Soraypampa via Salkantay

Start	Ollantaytambo (2850m)
Finish	Soraypampa (3750m)
Distance	64km
Total ascent	4450m
Total descent	3550m
Difficulty	Moderate to high
Time	4–5 days hiking, depending on pace
Trail type	Inca Trail, mountain trail
High point	4970m (Abra Incachiriaska)
Hike or bike?	hike
Agency/guide?	no

This can either be an alternative to the Inca Trail or an extension to it. If you are intending to hike the Inca Trail and wish to acclimatize, you can start two days early and arrive at the beginning of the Inca Trail at Huayllabamba to meet your group by following the first part of this route. Another option is to pick up the Salkantay route to St. Theresa and on to Agua Calientes described in Route 30. This makes an epic, adventurous route to Machu Picchu and one that is (currently) unregulated by the INC, meaning you don't need an official guide or to pay any fees. It passes by several Incan sites and also the majestic glacier of Salkantay.

Follow the directions given in Route 20 from **Ollantaytambo** to **Inti Punku**. Then follow the directions from Inti Punku to **Paucarcancha**, given in Route 27. At Paucarcancha, take a right and go down the mountain towards Huayllabamba and the Inca Trail, but our route instead takes the trail south going up the mountain towards Mt. Salkantay. The trail leaves from Paucarcancha on the same side of the river (left) and can be clearly seen from the plaza.

Take this trail and begin the long, but beautiful, climb upwards towards the Salkantay glacier. The river being followed is known as the Rio Cusichaca. The gradient is

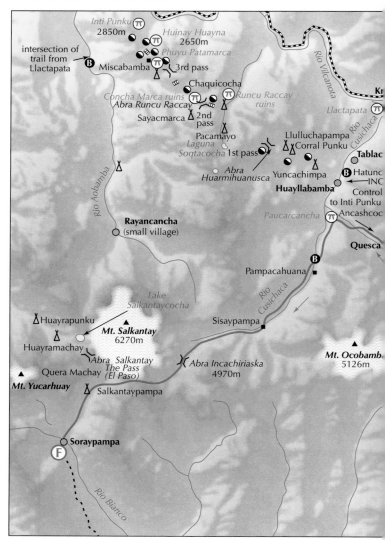

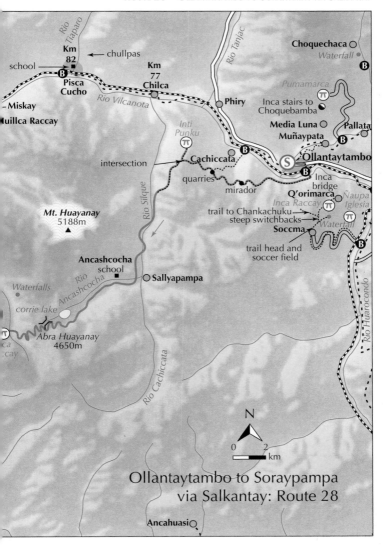

Ollantaytambo to Soraypampa
via Salkantay: Route 28

The canyon between Inti Punku and Ancashcocha

This route is often done on bicycle by some of the crazier locals – but most of this uphill section is unrideable and so the bike would have to be pushed or carried.

gentle but the sheer size of the valley is impressive. You can really sense the scale of these mountains. ◄

It takes about 3hrs to reach the best spot to camp, a small settlement just below the larger village of **Pampacahuana**. However, most of this section has places suitable to camp. Just before arriving at Pampacahuana the trail climbs through a narrow gorge and there is a bridge that goes over to the right (western) side of the river. Here there is a large flat area that has a few houses and a football pitch. This is also a good place to camp. There also can be seen here the still functioning remains of an Incan canal, built hundreds of years ago to turn the swamps above it into usable land.

The trail continues upward from Pampacahuana, back across the bridge and up the trail on the left (northern) side of the river. The climb gets much steeper here, and it takes about 1hr of climbing from Pampacahuana to reach **Quebrada Sisaypampa**, which is merely a large flat area that is suitable for camping or lunch. Here the vegetation starts to change to the short, scrub grass of the high Andean plains called puna. This can make the trail difficult to find but if you are climbing upwards then you are going the right direction. There are a few more campsites 1hr ahead, after which the trail is on the rocky, glacial moraine and there are no good campsites until the other side of the pass Abra Incachiriaska.

There still remains a solid 3–4hrs of stiff climbing to reach **Abra Incachiriaska**, so it is imperative not to leave the area of Quebrada Sisaypampa any later than midday, preferably earlier. The pass sits at an altitude of approximately 4970m above sea level and is not a good place to be after dark or in bad weather, so be sure to plan campsites accordingly. (Incachiriaska means 'very cold Inca' in Quechua!)

The last hour of hiking up to the pass is steep and unrelenting. The huge glacier of Salkantay, the source of the Rio Cusichaca, lies on the right (southern) side of the trail as you climb up to the pass. The pass itself is one of the most dramatic perches in the Sacred Valley and perhaps all of Peru.

> **Abra Incachiriaska** is nothing but a very narrow ledge between two precipitous drops and is truly a spectacular and exhilarating reward for the climb just endured. There are clear views in all directions, as this is the second highest point in this area besides the Mount Ausangate region on the eastern side of Cusco.

From the pass it is 1–2hrs of downhill walking, past the huge glacial moraine on the right, down to the campsite of **Salkantaypampa** on the far, western side of the pampa below. Follow the trail down below the moraine and cross the icy river and walk down and over to Salkantaypampa. This is a common spot to camp for trekkers and a new mountain lodge has also recently been built nearby. It is a very scenic campsite with views of both the Salkantay and Tuscarhuay glaciers.

Trekking in the Andes is always visually rewarding

From here you can go down valley to the left, to **Soraypampa** and then down to Soray and finally Mollepata and the main highway from Cusco. If you plan to finish your trip at Soraypampa, you will have to arrange for a driver to pick you up there, as there is no public transport and very little traffic between Soraypampa and Mollepata.

Travellers bound for Machu Picchu, however, should continue over the western pass of El Paso/Abra Salkantay towards St. Theresa by following the directions given from Soray in Route 30, and on to Machu Picchu along the train tracks, as described in Route 26.

5 SOUTH AND WEST OF MACHU PICCHU

Ascending towards the pass of Choquetecarpo (Routes 34 to 36)

INTRODUCTION

An Incan road in excellent condition (Route 34)

The area to the south and west of Machu Picchu contains most of the most impressive Inca sites in the Sacred Valley. The classics are all here: the treks aound the massive glacier and sacred Inca mountain Mt. Salkantay; Choquequirao, the 'sister site' of Machu Picchu; the spectacular but rarely visited Incan shrine of Inca Wasi; Huancancalle, the home of famed Incan rebel Manco Inca; Espiritu Pampa, the last refuge of the Incas; and many others.

This is the Peru of your dreams: Inca roads, huge mountains and glaciers, jungle vegetation, roaring rivers, and countless Incan archaeological sites. The villages here offer only the basic services. Cachora and Huancancalle are the starting points most of the routes in this section. Both have small grocery stores and a few other stores that also sell basic groceries, and they each have simple and inexpensive hostels with cold-water showers. This is a remote region without much in the way of cellular coverage or internet services. English is barely spoken by the local population, and the US dollar and Euro will not be accepted. In Huancancalle, try the hostel SixPac Manco Inca (tel 984 455364).

Many new archaeological sites are still being explored and uncovered, and the region known as 'Vilcabamba', a large area roughly centered around Huancancalle, almost certainly contains undiscovered Incan sites. There are also several different trekking routes from here that end up near Machu Picchu, which means you can trek to the site without taking the classic Inca Trail trek, which can sometimes be difficult to book onto. These routes are best done with a local guiding company but most can also be tackled independently. If you opt for the latter be sure to come completely prepared with all the clothing and food needed for a rigorous expedition – these are very remote and rugged mountains!

ROUTE 29
Mollepata to Huayllabamba

Start	Mollepata (2800m)
Finish	Huayllabamba (3000m)
Distance	52km
Total ascent	3300m
Total descent	3100m
Difficulty	Strenuous, lots of climbing at high altitude
Time	3–4 days hiking, 2–3 days biking
Trail type	Mountain trail
High point	4970m (Abra Incachiriaska)
Hike or bike?	hike
Agency/guide?	no

This trip makes another excellent extension to the Inca Trail, as it ends in Huayllabamba where most Inca Trail trips begin. By then you will be fully acclimatized and fit. This route features a dramatic, high-altitude pass over the shoulder of Mt. Salkantay, at nearly 5000m. The trail drops from this preposterously narrow spit of rock between two glacial drainages all the way down to the Incan site of Paucarcancha (at the intersection of an Inca route to Ollantaytambo, Route 27) before arriving at Huayllabamba and finally Cusichaca (Km 82) on the Vilcanota River and also the site of Llactapata. This is an world-class trek through a wide variety of climactic zones and ecosystems. It also is outstanding mountain bike ride for expert riders in good physical condition.

▶ To begin, go from either Ollantaytambo or Cusco to **Mollepata** and then **Soraypampa** as described in Route 30. Continue upward to **Salkantaypampa**. It takes about 1hr to trek from Soraypampa to Salkantaypampa. This is a common place to camp for trekkers, and there are gorgeous views of the surrounding glaciers here. Upon leaving Salkantaypampa, follow the trail out of camp and go east as it goes around the right-hand side of the base of the moraine. The views of the moraine keep getting better as the trail goes up and begins to ascend the steep ridge.

From Mollepata up to the pass involves a very steep ascent to nearly 5000m. Careful preparation (well rested and hydrated) is essential as is a slow, steady pace to avoid altitude sickness.

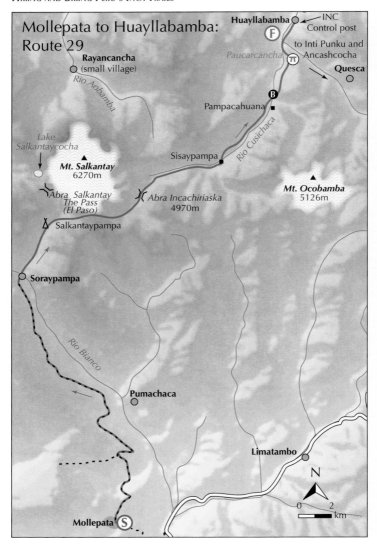

Mollepata to Huayllabamba:
Route 29

Huayllabamba — INC Control post
(F)

to Inti Punku and Ancashcocha

Paucarcancha (π)

Quesca

Rayancancha
(small village)

Rio Aobamba

(B)

Pampacahuana

Rio Cusichaca

Lake Salkantaycocha

▲ **Mt. Salkantay**
6270m

Sisaypampa

Abra Salkantay The Pass (El Paso)

Abra Incachiriaska
4970m

▲ **Mt. Ocobamba**
5126m

Salkantaypampa

Soraypampa

Rio Blanco

Pumachaca

Limatambo

N

0   2
▬▬▬ km

Mollepata (S)

Continue climbing but do not go down toward the river and glacial moraine below, but rather up the steep and narrow gully ahead. After it crests a small ridge the trail sort of disappears a bit, but keep climbing straight and soon the monstrous pass of **Abra Incachiriaska** is visible, as is the brutal climb leading up to it. The path goes straight up seemingly forever through the red and orange landscape until finally reaching the pass, 3km from Salkantaypampa.

A great perspective on the pass of Abra Incachiriaska

> **Abra Incachiriaska** (4970m) is one of the most impressive passes in the Andes. The views of the huge Salkantay glacier and its glacial moraine below are seen, in addition to the steep drop over the other side of the pass down into the Cusichaca valley.

From here, the trail drops down the valley for several kilometres of rugged puna and high alpine terrain. The first kilometre or two down from the pass is a rocky trail descending down the valley, after which the next 3–4km are a bit swampy and wet, and the trail goes all over the place trying to find high ground. There are numerous small streams flowing all through this area, and the route finding can be a bit difficult. However, there are no other valleys leaving this one yet, so the main thing is to keep going down and try to stay as dry as possible. The trail continues down and arrives first at a large, flat space the locals call 'Sisaypampa'. This can be a good place to camp, although it is often wet from glacial runoff depending on the time of the year.

It continues descending, going past Pampacahuana, where there is good camping, and then **Paucarcancha** before arriving at **Huayllabamba**, the official entrance to the Inca Trail. Two hours below Huayllabamba is the Vilcanota River and Km 88 of the Inca Trail. From here it is a 30min walk to Km 82 (Pisca Cucho) or 3hrs to Ollantaytambo.

ROUTE 30
Soraypampa to Machu Picchu via Salkantay

Start	Soraypampa (3750m)
Finish	Aguas Calientes (2040m)
Distance	66km
Total ascent	1390m
Total descent	3100m
Difficulty	Strenuous hiking, strenuous and difficult biking
Time	3–4 days hiking, 2–3 days biking
Trail type	Mountain trail
High point	4740m (Abra El Paso/Abra Salkantay)
Hike or bike?	both
Agency/guide?	no

A popular alternative to the Inca Trail, and with good reason, this trek passes by some of the best scenery in the entire Sacred Valley, including the sheer, snow-capped peaks of Salkantay, Tucarhuay and Huamantay. This is the classic Salkantay trek and is probably the most popular in the Sacred Valley, thus do not expect solitary campsites with no one around. However, the term 'crowded' is relative and it remains one of the best treks in the world due to the surrounding terrain and friendly people along the way.

From either Cusco or Ollantaytambo, take transport to Mollepata. If travelling by bus, buy a ticket for Abancay and then ask to be let out at Mollepata. Not long ago, the road went no further than Mollepata, and the trek began here. Recently, however, a new road has been constructed from Mollepata up to Soraypampa. Although in rough condition, it has allowed trekkers to skip the walk between the two villages and take auto transport instead – bit of a shame, really, as the walk is lovely. Trekkers can opt to walk the section from Mollepata up to Soraypampa by adding one extra day to the trip; there is a very nice trail that leaves Mollepata and ascends the other side of the valley, away from the road, up to Soraypampa. Otherwise it is a 1–2hr drive from Mollepata to Soraypampa depending on road conditions. The road is frequently impassble during the rainy season of December to April.

Frequent landslides can make for challenging trails

Upon arriving at **Soraypampa**, you will notice a new mountain lodge that has been constructed in the middle of the alpine meadow to cater to high end trekkers.

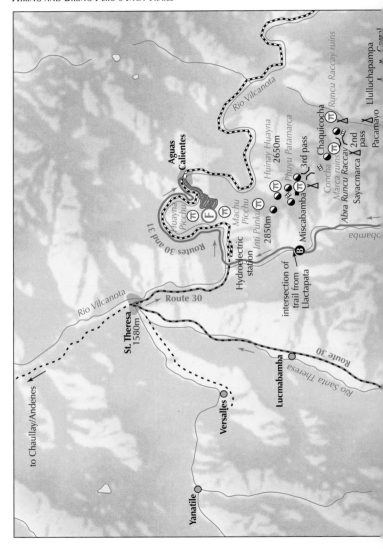

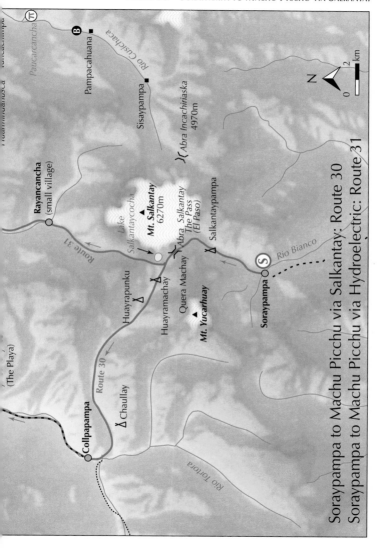

Soraypampa to Machu Picchu via Salkantay: Route 30
Soraypampa to Machu Picchu via Hydroelectric: Route 31

The other thing that will be noticed are the views of the glacier Huamantay that will leave any traveller breathless – when the views are clear, this is one of the most majestic meadows in the entire Andean chain. There is a campsite here, but given that it is practically in the front yard of the lodge, it is worth hiking 1hr further up valley to the remote and beautiful field of **Salkantaypampa**. There are spectacular views of the glaciers from here, but it is quite chilly during the winter months of June to August. ◄

At this altitude, remember to have a warm hat.

Mt. Salkantay is directly north of this campsite. Interestingly, looking at a map you can see that Machu Picchu is located on the other side of Salkantay, in an exact line going north. Given what we know of the Incas, this is almost certainly not a coincidence. The next day features a nice climb up to the pass, ascending via a series of steep switchbacks over the southwest shoulder of the massive 6270m summit of Mt. Salkantay. The mountain takes its name from the Quechuan word *salqa*, which means 'wild' or 'savage'. That is a good name for this area, as it passes through some of the wildest mountain terrain in all of Peru. The trail leaves Salkantaypampa heading straight north and splits into two. The right-hand side crosses the bottom of a massive moray coming off of the southeastern flank of Mt. Salkantay in the direction of Ollantaytambo and Km 82, as described in Route 29.

The left trail stays on the western side of the glacial debris and ascends the western side of Mt. Salkantay. It takes 3–4hrs to climb the 8km up to the pass of **Abra Salkantay**, passing a false summit before arriving at the real thing.

The pass is referred to by various names, primarily **El Paso** (The Pass) as well as **Abra Salkantay**, and is located at an altitude of 4740m. There are fantastic views of the terminal glacial moraine below Mt. Salkantay, and the trail going up over the pass of Abra Sisaypampa is also visible. Straight to the west is Choquequirao, and to the east Cusco.

Cross over the pass and descend the trail down the other side, passing by the small Lake Salkantaycocha. The next few kilometres are through high-altitude marsh-lands, or puna. It is often wet here so try to seek higher ground – the left-hand (west) side of the valley is the better place to walk and it is also where the trail solidifies and is easier to follow as it continues down. The next destination is **Huayramachay**, a Quechuan name.

> With huayra meaning 'wind' and machay meaning 'place', **Huayramachay** is the 'place of the wind'. Which sounds maybe like not such a pleasant place to camp, but in reality it is a nice little spot: level, and with good views of the glacier of Mt. Huamantay.

It is 3.5km from the pass down to Huayramachay. There is a second village, **Huayrapunku**, which means 'wind gate' in Quechua, just a short distance downriver, which also has good places to camp.

The next stop is **Chaullay**, a popular campsite for trekking groups. This area is often also called the Andenes. Three hours and 9km below Huayrapunku, it is a nice place to spend the night or have some lunch by the river. ▶ Cross the bridge and the trail continues to drop, first below treeline and then even further into this land the locals call *adentro*, or 'within'. The vegetation changes, the landscape changes and even the air itself becomes thicker, warmer, and carries the smells of the high jungle. The contrast, from the icy blasts of the high glacial mountains of a day ago to this jungle of chirping parakeets and bright flowers, is very pleasant.

The altitude here is 2920m and by now it is quite warm.

Two kilometres further down is the confluence of the Tortora River, entering from left and coming down from the pass above Yanama. Here there is a junction of two trails. The trail to the left climbs up the Tortora valley to the pass and then down to Yanama. However, this route is going to St. Theresa, and so the trail to take is the one to the right, which goes down in a northeasterly direction another 1km to **Collpapampa**. This is a small settlement

On the trail to Collpapampa

with some excellent hot springs just outside of it, and there are also places to camp.

From Collpapampa, it is 8km and 3–4hrs of walking downhill to the **Playa Sahuayaco**, usually just referred to as The Playa. This stretch is very beautiful, with an astounding variety of plants, waterfalls, and exotic jungle birds such as the famous cock-of-the-rock (*Rupicola peruviana*). The road used to go only as far up as Paltachayoc. However, the road has recently been extended up to the Playa, and so from here you can take a public combi all the way down the 14km down to **St. Theresa**. Halfway, at the village of **Lucmabamba**, there is a new trail cut that ascends the ridge above the Aobamba River and to the site Llactapata, 'rediscovered' by explorer Hugh Thompson, as detailed in his fantastic book on this area, called The White Rock. This is an option if another day of trekking is desired. Otherwise, continue down to St. Theresa where transport can be arranged for the short trip upriver to the hydroelectric station, from where it is a 3hr walk along the train tracks to **Aguas Calientes**, as described in Route 26, and **Machu Picchu**.

ROUTE 31

Soraypampa to Machu Picchu via Hydroelectric

Start	Soraypampa (3750m)
Finish	Aguas Calientes (2040m)
Distance	55km
Total ascent	1950m
Total descent	3660m
Difficulty	Severe, due to altitude and poor trail conditions
Time	3–4 days hiking
Trail type	Mountain trail
High point	4750m
Hike or bike?	hike
Agency/guide?	yes
Route map	see Route 30

This route is much less travelled than other routes in the Salkantay region, due to the more rugged terrain of the narrow Aobamba canyon through which it travels before finally arriving at the hydroelectric plant down on the Rio Vilcanota, just a few hours' walk from Aguas Calientes and Machu Picchu.

At the time of writing the trail was only barely passable due to landslides. Inquire locally about conditions before setting out on this trek. It is not suitable for biking. In the event the primary route is closed due to landsides, the majority of this route can also be accessed from the other side of Salkantay (the route that comes up from Ollantaytambo and Huayllabamba) by entering the valley at Pampacahuana and heading west.

The road from Mollepata goes as far as Soraypampa. From here follow the trail along the river to **Salkantaypampa**. From Salkantaypampa, go up to the pass of El Paso/Abra Salkantay, as described in Route 30, and then up and over the other side and down to **Lake Salkantaycocha**, which lies below the southwestern flank of Mt. Salkantay. From here, turn directly north to follow an obscure and difficult route directly north, over a very rugged 5000m pass between Mt. Salkantay on the east and Mt. Huamantay

Crossing over the Aobamba river, below the pass

on the west. This pass can often be covered with snow, and is treacherous at any time of the year. For this reason (not to mention the frequent landslides that cover the trails below on a regular basis) the trek is rated as severely difficult.

Go down off the pass in a northerly direction down the quebrada (canyon) known as Rayancancha down towards the village of the same name, which lies 5km downstream at the intersection of the Rio Aobamba, which flows from the eastern drainage of Mt. Salkantay in the direction of Sisaypampa, Ollantaytambo and Pisca Cucho (the start of the Inca Trail). The walk through this canyon is stunning; there are great views behind you of Mt. Salkantay and also Mt. Huamantay. The hydroelectric station lies directly ahead, about 20km as the crow flies. First, though, there is some serious trekking yet to be done through this high jungle terrain known in Spanish as the Ceja del Ojo, or 'eyebrow of the jungle'.

Rayancancha lies at the confluence of the Rio Rayancancha and the Rio Aobamba rivers. There are a several families living in this area, but there are no stores of any kind. Instead, try to bring a few items of food to leave behind rather than purchase from the local families. Eggs, sugar and rice are always welcome and appreciated. It is a good idea to camp here.

From here, the trail makes a left-hand turn in the valley and goes northwest for a bit before it finally settles on a more or less direct course north, plunging successively down the ecosystem ladder until soon fruit plantations begin to appear. There are not many places to camp on this descent, and there are no established campgrounds of any kind, a bit surprising given its proximity to Machu Picchu. Walking through the harsh terrain, however, it is easy to see why the route has not been further developed. Three kilometres below Rayancancha, the Rio Mamamayo ('mother river' in Quechua) enters from the right-hand side, a drainage of the glacier Mt. Paljay which lies directly to the east. This is a suitable place to make a camp for the night – there is not a lot of flat terrain but there is enough. The trail then crosses the river two more times on pretty sketchy footbridges made of a few logs lashed together with vines, until it arrives near the valley floor and the bridge and intersection of the trail from Llactapata, reaching the **hydroelectric station** which is 9km below the confluence of the Rio Aobamba with the Rio Mamamayo. From the hydroelectric station, you can walk on to **Aguas Calientes** and then **Machu Picchu**, 3hrs on a small trail along the train tracks, as described in Route 26. Alternatively, you can go west downriver to St. Theresa.

ROUTE 32
Choquequirao from Cachora

Start/Finish	Cachora (2920m)
Distance	64km round trip
Total ascent/descent	3130m
Difficulty	Very strenuous due to steepness, length and heat
Time	4–5 days hiking
Trail type	Mountain trail
High point	3100m (Choquequirao)
Hike or bike?	hike
Agency/guide?	recommended, but not required

This is the most popular route to Choquequirao, as the trail is well maintained and it is the shortest way in and out. Choquequirao is known as a 'sister site' to Machu Picchu due to its mountaintop location, extensive terracing and Inca architecture. While lacking perhaps in the fine stonework and grandeur of Machu Picchu, the site of Choquequirao contains many surprises of its own and is only now being fully uncovered. At the time of writing, no trail permit (or even a guide) is required by the INC, but unfortunately that is likely to change soon.

The quality of the trail is good and has been improved in recent years, allowing you to walk and fully appreciate the beauty of the area and the canyon of the Apurimac River as it passes through this range. Biking is not permitted.

This is a difficult hike and most choose to go with horses to carry their gear. It is possible to carry your own gear, however, and there are even a few small stores along the way to replenish supplies. Cachora, too, has stores catering to hikers, selling food, gas and other necessary items. It is still preferable to buy your supplies in Cusco or Ollantaytambo. A water filter is highly recommended unless you want to spend a small fortune on bottled water along the way. There is regular transport from Cusco to Cachora, and every day more and more taxis are plying the route. The two best options are to leave either Cusco

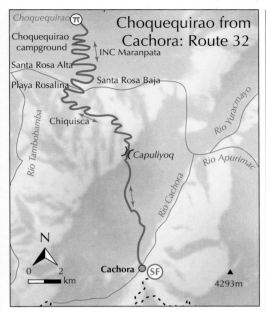

or Ollantaytambo very early in the morning for the 4hr drive to Cachora, or otherwise spend the night in Cachora for an early start the next day. There are limited campsites on the trail, so you need to start on the right rhythm or it will throw the whole trip off.

Starting from the main plaza in **Cachora**, follow the road downhill from the right (east) side of the plaza. There is now a rough road that goes as far as Capuliyoc, which is 12km from Cachora. This road is marked with signage posts indicating the route to Choquequirao, listing the kilometres as well, starting with 0 at Cachora. There is also a foot trail which shortcuts the road several times and if walking the route this is the shorter and thus more preferable way to go. This trail is not as well marked as the road and can be a bit confusing. Ask a local for directions or use your sense of direction; as long as you

Most treks to Choquequirao depart from the scenic town of Cachora

The pass isn't a great place to camp due to high winds and lack of water, but if late in the day it is an option.

are walking downhill and towards the left and not the right, there shouldn't be any problems.

The foot trail rejoins the road after about 5km and from there to **Capuliyoc** (a further 7km) the road and the trail are one and the same. This section is a fairly flat route with spectacular views of the Salkantay range, and after 12km reaches the pass of Capuliyoc, from where the trail drops steeply down to the Apurimac River nearly 2000m below. ◄ You can actually see Choquequirao from the Capuliyoc pass by looking straight north to the upper saddles of the mountains on the other side of the river. Occasionally, a señora from Cachora will be out here selling water and soft drinks at a reasonable price.

Continue to drop down into the canyon for several more kilometres, stopping for the night to camp at either Cocamasana (Km 15) or **Chiquisca** (Km 17). Given the tough climb up the other side of the canyon the following day, the lower spot at Chiquisca is preferable. Both have campsites, basic bathrooms and cold showers for trekkers, free of charge. They also have small stores on site selling sodas, beer and snacks, doing brisk business. Bring change and small bills.

It is very important to leave either of these camp-sites early in the morning due to the length, steepness and especially the heat of the climb up the other side. Do drink as much water as possible before leaving camp, as well as the night before. Once on the trail, the next stop is the Apurimac River itself and a rest area, referred to as **Playa Rosalina**. The altitude at here is only about 1230m and it is very hot. There is a new building which has excellent bathrooms and also showers. As of the time of writing there was no charge to use either. Here, also, is an INC control post where they are registering trekkers but not yet collecting the entrance fee.

> Drink as much **water** as is possible while resting at the Playa, swatting at the gnats between gulps. (Remember, the best and perhaps only protection against these relentless biting insects is long cloth-ing. Exposing so much as an ankle or a wrist can lead to weeks of itching.) The upcoming climb is a serious one, so much so that the Peruvian guides can be heard telling their clients, only half jokingly, that the climb 'makes even a grown man cry'. Be as hydrated as possible before setting out on the climb, and be sure to begin the climb with a mini-mum of two litres of water. No water can be found until Santa Rosa, which is over 3km and 700m higher up the trail.

At **Santa Rosa Baja** (Lower Santa Rosa) there is a much-needed shaded rest stop and a bamboo bench to relax on. The owner, Juan, is a colourful character and sells soft drinks, sodas and beer. He also has several camping sites, showers and crude bathroom facilities. There is even a sugar cane press on site. A little further up is **Santa Rosa Alta** (Upper Santa Rosa), also with serv-ices. From here the climb continues relentlessly upward, culminating in a succession of brutally steep switchbacks

(14 of them in all) through loose, rocky dirt before finally arriving at **Maranpata**. Maranpata (located just past Km 28) is a beautiful site to camp, with small stores that sell snacks. Best of all, the majority of the climb is over. If early in the day, it is best to push on the last 4km to Choquequirao itself, but otherwise this is an excellent place to stay the night.

The final part of the trail follows a gentle up-and-down gradient, passing a few small waterfalls, an **INC registration post**, as well as the first good views of Choquequirao. The spectacular terraces of the lower agricultural section of the site are visible along this part of the route. Although it looks very close, it is still a solid 2hrs more of trekking to reach Choquequirao. There are signs upon entering the park highlighting the choice of going to the campground or else to **Choquequirao**. If it is early in the day it is best to proceed directly to the site, 30mins further up the trail, but if it is late in the day go straight to the campground. ◄ There are showers and bathroom facilities here. It is still another 30min walk up into the main part of the site from the campground – look for the sign at the bathrooms. There are a few different trails leaving camp and it can be a bit confusing. Most of them

The campground is quite small and usually crowded, so get there early to stake out a prime spot.

The trail to Choquequirao, seen in the background among the clouds

The spectacular 'Llamitas' of Choquequirao

arrive at the park up the mountain anyway, but if in doubt look for the blue signs or ask around.

Up at the site of **Choquequirao**, there is a park attendant who will check your entrance ticket, which is to be purchased at a small INC booth just outside of the park. It costs 38 soles for adults, or 18 soles for children or students. Be sure to allow the better part of a day to fully explore the site; many people find that to see everything a full day and a half is needed. This is a good reason to allot five days for the trek instead of four. Be sure to check out the amazing 'llamitas' section which is only now being fully excavated and uncovered. Ask the attendant to point out the entrance to this truly one-of-a-kind attraction.

Where and when to return will depend on the preference of the group. If late in the day it is best to spend another night at the campground of Choquequirao, otherwise press on back to Maranpata or even to Chiquisca on the other side of the river and return to Cachora the next day.

ROUTE 33
Inca Wasi from Yupunqua

Start/Finish	Yupanqua (2850m)
Distance	26km round trip
Total ascent/descent	1450m
Difficulty	Moderate
Time	1–3 days hiking
Trail type	Incan road, mountain trail
High point	4000m
Hike or bike?	hike
Agency/guide?	recommended, site is very remote

An epic trek to the well-preserved and dramatically placed Inca site of Inca Wasi, which has become popular only in recent years. There are very good views of the Pumasillo and Vilcabamba mountain ranges, some fine sections of Incan trail, a waterfall and more. This is one of the best short treks in the region for combining scenery, Inca architecture and relative isolation.

At the time of writing there is a road being constructed from the town of Yupanqua up to the pass of Abra Huarina, sometimes referred to as Abra San Miguel. Assuming it is completed, it will change the options for this trip considerably, as it will soon be possible to drive from Yupanqua to Abra Huarina. Until then, you face over 1000m of climb from Yupanqua up to the pass. Horses or mules cannot go much further up than the pass so it is best to camp nearby and depart for Inca Wasi in the morning. It is not permitted to camp at the ruins themselves, nor is there space anyway. The pampa below it is quite soggy and not ideal for camping either.

Leave from the bridge over the river at **Yupanqua**. There is a singletrack trail that climbs from the bridge or ask any local. From here it is about 8km of climbing up to a large, flat open area with a lake. There is no other good water source, but if you have a good filter it is possible to camp here. As mentioned, there is a road under

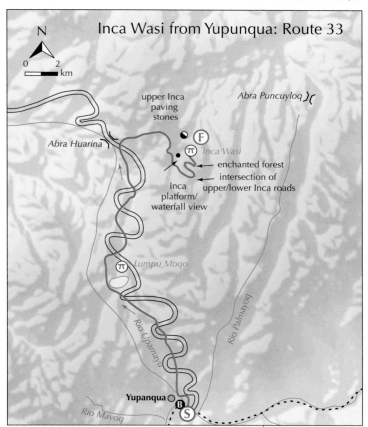

Inca Wasi from Yupunqua: Route 33

N

0   2
km

upper Inca
paving
stones

Abra Puncuyloq)(

Abra Huarina)(

F

π Inca Wasi

← enchanted forest

← intersection of
upper/lower Inca roads

Inca
platform/
waterfall view

π Lumpu Moqo

Rio Upamayu

Rio Palmayoq

Yupanqua ○ B
S

Rio Mayoq

construction and the trail and road converge here at the
lake. From here take the new road up to the pass of Abra
Huarina; it is rugged and unfinished, but quite possible to
walk on, though not yet possible to drive on). There are
remnants of an old Incan road that the new road occasionally crosses or passes near to – stay on the road so as
to not get lost.

231

*Looking towards
Mt. Pumasillo from
Inca Wasi*

Along the way are a small, basic set of stone building remains called **Lumpu Moqo**. First described by Stuart White, they most likely predate the Incas and were left by one of the tribes that lived in this area before. From here the trail and old Incan road continues to the pass – as mentioned there is a new road being built alongside the Inca one.

From the pass, finding and staying on the correct route can be difficult. Visibility is often quite poor in this area all year round due to unique weather conditions caused by these massive, jagged mountains that rise seemingly straight up from the jungle. There are no houses or signage of any kind, and in times of poor visibility it may be better to wait for better weather, as much of the navigation of this route requires a good sight line.

From the pass of **Abra Huarina**, head east and follow the contour of the mountain while maintaining a high position on the ridge. The trail here is not easy to find, but just continue going east and stay on a level course and do not climb up or down. The trail will skirt the head of the Rio Upamayu. After 1km the trail becomes more apparent and can be seen up on the slope. From here, it becomes more easy to follow, although it should be noted that in general this route is not heavily travelled and the path is frequently overgrown. ▸ Keep walking and you will arrive at a rest point with an unobstructed view of a waterfall. Continue along the trail and you will pass over the waterfall and reach an intersection of two trails. The lower, southern fork drops down and to the right and follows the north side of the river down to Yupanqua. This is a primary Inca road as described by Vince Lee and was probably the main access to Inca Wasi, coming from across the valley from Vitcos. Currently it is overgrown but there are plans to restore it.

This is a paved Incan trail, and underneath the vegetation is an excellent paved road.

Take instead the high, northern fork to the left and the trail quickly becomes a very fine Incan road and the importance of the site is readily apparent. After a short section through a very beautiful, moist, enchanted forest comes the final stretch, consisting of nearly 1km of

Stone building pegs near Inca Wasi, still waiting for the workers' return

well-engineered and preserved Inca stairway ascending nearly vertically up to the site of **Inca Wasi**.

> **Inca Wasi**, which is also called Puncuyoc, was most likely a highly ceremonial and spiritual retreat for only the most important of the Incan royalty and was certainly not for the common man. There are sight lines in all directions here, including towards Espiritu Pampa, Choquequirao, Vitcos and Machu Picchu. The place is wonderfully undisturbed and its physical location, straddling a high Andean ridge line at over 13,000ft of altitude, was perhaps the finest in the entire Inca empire.

Return down to Yupanqua the same way.

ROUTE 34
Huancancalle to Choquequirao

Start	Huancancalle (2950m)
Finish	Choquequirao (3100m)
Distance	71km
Total ascent	6500m
Total descent	6350m
Difficulty	Strenuous, due to steepness and high altitudes
Time	6–9 days hiking
Trail type	Incan road, mountain trail
High point	4650m (Abra Choquetecarpo)
Hike or bike?	hike
Agency/guide?	yes

A classic route from the heart of Vilcabamba to Choquequirao, which passes through some of the best scenery in all of Peru as well as scores of archaeological sites, via Incan roads that are in excellent condition. This is one of the premier treks in all of South America. There are excellent views during the dry season of the glaciers of Pumasillo (6070m) and Lasunayoc

(6095m). From Choquequirao, you can go back to Cusco via either Cachora or Huanipaca, or extend your trek to an epic and continue on to Machu Picchu. This route is not recommended for biking.

The logistics for this trip are complicated and so you should hire an agency. Having horses to carry food and gear is vital, as the route includes over 6000m of climbing at extreme temperatures, both high and low. Last-minute supplies can be procured in Huancancalle but it is much better to arrive with everything you need. There are very few places along this trek to replenish supplies, and you need at least two methods of filtering or purifying water. Check that the first aid kit contains electrolyte tablets in case someone in the group becomes seriously dehydrated. It is also highly advised to bring extra food and, more importantly, a backup stove in case the first one falters or breaks. Come prepared and double-check everything before setting out.

The trail begins from Hostel SixPac Manco in **Huancancalle**.

This hostel was built by the Cobos family as a base for the many exploratory expeditions that came to the Vilcabamba area in the 1980s and 1990s. Generously supporting their efforts, as well as coming up with the hostel's name, was explorer **Vince Lee** and his lovely wife Nancy, from Jackson Hole Wyoming in the US. With his many explorations, Lee filled in several missing pieces of the archaeological puzzle of the Vilcabamba, and published the definitive piece of literature for this region in his book *Forgotten Vilcabamba: Final Stronghold of the Incas*. A hardened mountain man from the old school of exploring, he named the hostel in memory of Manco Inca and his followers, who according to Lee might have had more success fighting off the Spanish Conquest if only they had drunk a little less beer!

From the front door of SixPac cross the river via the new pedestrian bridge and go left on the other side, passing by the local cemetery. One kilometre further up is a

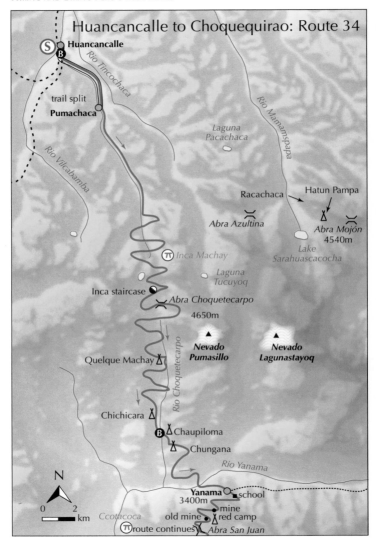

Huancancalle to Choquequirao: Route 34

(S) (B) **Huancancalle**

Río Tincochaca

trail split
Pumachaca

Río Vilcabamba

Río Mamanspapa

*Laguna
Pacachaca*

Racachaca → Hatun Pampa

Abra Azultina

Abra Mojón
4540m

*Lake
Sarahuascacocha*

(π) *Inca Machay*

*Laguna
Tucuyoq*

Inca staircase ● *Abra Choquetecarpo*
4650m

▲
*Nevado
Pumasillo*

▲
*Nevado
Lagunastayoq*

Río Choquetecarpo

Quelque Machay ⋏

Chichicara ⋏

(B) ⋏ Chaupiloma

⋏ Chungana

Río Yanama

Yanama ○ ■ school
3400m
● mine
old mine ⋏ red camp

N

0   2
         km

Ccotacoca

(π) route continues ⋏ *Abra San Juan*

giant INC sign marking the boundary to the park of Vitcos and Yurac Rumi ('white rock' in Quechua). That trail goes to the left, instead take the right fork which climbs up the valley ahead. The trail will split off into various smaller paths over the next kilometre or two; the idea is to try to stay on the biggest one and to continue climbing up and to the right. Eventually, the trail will spill onto the old Incan road, which has been bulldozed into a vehicle access road for the small mountain communities further up the valley.

Continue along this road until it reaches a good sized creek, where it makes a sharp U-turn and climbs up the other side of the valley. This area is known as **Pumachaca** ('bridge of the Puma') Here, leave the main road and begin climbing up the foot trail which leaves from where the river meets the road. Almost immediately, the trail connects with the old Incan road and begins ascending the mountain. The next several kilometres are hiking nirvana for anyone who appreciates walking on a well-preserved Incan trail, as from here up to the pass the road is classic Inca architecture, in perfect condition.

En route to Choquequirao, near Chungana

237

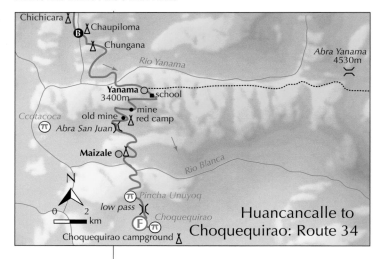

Huancancalle to
Choquequirao: Route 34

Continue up the mountain until you reach the two round walls of Misti Wachay, sometimes referred to as **Inca Machay**. These are remains from what was probably a tambo, a rest place for travellers on their way up and over the pass. Lying ahead is one of the most impressive stretches of Inca staircase in Peru. It gets steeper and steeper as it approaches the pass, undergirded by extensive Incan engineering work. Fantastic!

The pass of **Abra Choquetecarpo** finally arrives. At an altitude of 4650m it is one of the higher passes in the area and has the usual wide-open views in all directions. Do not linger too long if it is late in the day as there still are a couple of hours of downhill hiking to reach the next campsite. This is high-altitude terrain and during the dry season of June to September it is quite cold. The other months of the year it gets a lot of precipitation. Be sure to keep the group together and properly clothed during this stretch. As for all high mountain passes in the Andes, caution and common sense are required. The next camp to be found is at a site the locals call **Quelque Machay**, 2hrs walking down from the pass. There are a few flat spots before it, but Quelque Machay will be recognized by its very large boulders strewn about in the meadow. These make excellent wind and rain shelters and a good place to camp.

The next stretch of walking is typically as far as Yanama. It is, however, a long stretch of over 20km from Quelque Machay. This is one of the few sections of trail that is not straight up or straight down. Instead, it is very pleasant walking at relatively gentle gradients until reaching the bridge of Puente Toroyoqpata located in the clearing known as **Chaupiloma**. It is possible to camp here, but there are better places above and below it. After crossing the bridge, there is a short 2km climb up to the high point of **Chichicara**, where there is a small clearing suitable for either camping or a lunch break. Now the trail begins its descent around the lower part of the mountain Choquetecarpo, which rises off to the left. This is a very nice stretch of trail, with lots of unbroken forests covering the lower halves of the glaciers that lie in every direction. Continue down to the small hamlet of **Chungana**, which is a suitable place to have a snack or camp. From here it is a steep 4km descent down loose rubble to the Rio Yanama. At 2900m it is at the same altitude as Huancancalle, where this route started.

Upon arriving at the river, the trail goes upstream along the left (north) side for 1km before arriving at a small footbridge which recrosses the Rio Yanama and begins the steep climb up the other side.

Here lies one of the more harmonious villages in the Andes, and one of the author's favorite places in Peru. Unspoilt by the pressures of the 'outside world' (at least so far), thanks to the rare occurrence that no road arrives there, **Yanama** lies at a brisk 3400m in the middle of a lush valley fed by several glaciers upstream. It was an important hub for several Inca routes. Because of this, it does see a fair number of trekkers coming through, as routes from Choquequirao pass through here on their way to either Huancancalle (for Vilcabamba) or Machu Picchu or sometimes Mt. Salkantay. There are a few houses selling basic supplies here, and there is even a solar-powered satellite phone for making phone calls. This is a great place to rest up for a day if there is a rest day in the schedule. The arriero will know where to camp or ask any local family.

To continue on from **Yanama** towards Choquequirao, take the trail which goes south away from the school, heading uphill and towards the right (western) side of the mountain. There are many different foot trails here and it is easy to get a bit lost. Keep heading up and southwest and the trails will eventually merge into one. Or better yet, keep asking the locals along the way to point the way to Abra San Juan.

There are a few **old mines** on the trail just before the pass, and in fact this pass is often referred to as Abra Victoria, after the Victoria Mine it was built to service. ◄ It seems likely that this mine was a principal source for the mineral wealth of the Inca empire. In fact *Choquequirao* is a word from Aymara, the language of the Bolivian highlands, and it means 'cradle of gold'. The pass is very scenic, with views in all directions and you may see condors flying above. Looking straight west you can see the Inca mirador (lookout platform) Q'ori Huayracachina. Also behind from where you came is the Pumasillo massif as well as several other peaks.

This mine has been exploited by both the Spanish and Incas before them.

From the pass, the trail begins descending towards the canyon of the Rio Blanco. The trail is classic Incan for a while, zigzagging its way down the mountain in typical fashion. It passes a small campsite and mine entrance known as Puka Mina ('red mine'), then abruptly enters a unique microclimate, a very moist one that provides some of the most interesting vegetation of the entire trek. The trail gets quite steep and rocky here – if it is raining (which it often is) it can be quite treacherous and slippery. Continue descending until reaching the next available spot to rest, a lovely clearing known as **Maizale**.

Maizale is about halfway down the huge descent from Abra San Juan down to the Rio Blanco, so it makes a good spot to camp. The family that lives here sells basic supplies including beer, sodas and snacks and also offers free use of their land for camping. Try to leave something of value for their hospitality, but it doesn't have to be money. Food staples, in the unlikely event your expedition has an excess amount, are a great gift to this family, who live many days from the nearest road.

The trail to Choquequirao between Yanama and the pass of San Juan

The trail leaves Maizale and continues down for what seems like a very long time until finally reaching the Rio Blanco. The river isn't always a pleasant place to be. For starters, there are the same fierce biting gnats down here that are found at the Apurimac campsite known as The Playa, on the route from Cachora to Choquequirao. They are known locally as *pumahuacaychi*, which translates from Quechua as 'that which makes the Puma cry'.

241

The terraces of Pincha Unuyoc, near Choquequirao

The only real protection is to cover as much of the body as possible, which is tough to do in these temperatures. The heat in this part of the canyon is quite stifling and dangerous, so it is important the whole group is drinking plenty of water, especially as there is a killer stretch of climbing up the other side, where it is also very hot. There is plenty of fresh glacier run-off here to filter or treat. There are campsites here at the river but it is not particularly recommended to camp here because of the heat and insects.

The next stretch of trail climbs up the other side of the canyon of the Rio Blanco. This is the last climb before Choquequirao, which will probably be welcome news by this point in the trek. Depending on timing, it is possible to camp at Choquequirao itself after spending the previous night at Maizale but that makes for a very long day of hiking. Perhaps a better option is to camp half-way up at a site called **Pincha Unuyoc**. This is an interesting place and probably served as worker and servant housing for the royal Inca estate of Choquequirao, which lies just on the other side of the mountain. ◄ The ruins

There is fresh water here and some nice flat places to camp.

here were excavated and cleaned up recently, but have already grown back extensively in just one year. It makes you realize just how hard a task it is to keep all these sites maintained.

After leaving Pincha Unuyoc, continue climbing up the hill. The walking is a bit steep but otherwise quite pleasant. The trail finally gains the shoulder summit of the ridge, although there is no sign marking it. First it winds around the top a bit to the other side, then crosses a low pass and starts going down towards **Choquequirao**. After 1km the first view of Choquequirao itself is visible. A large, round flat spot on top of a mountain appears, looking a lot like a helicopter landing pad. This was a part of the Inca system of lookout points, and from here you can see clear all the way to the pass of Chaupiloma, above Arma. Continue down the trail for another 4km to reach the main entrance trail of Choquequirao.

From here, take a right and walk 2km up a gentle hill to the main entrance to Choquequirao and its

Typical Incan 'eye bonder' construction examples at Choquechirau

accompanying terraces. Alternatively, if it is late go directly to the campground which is located a bit below the main trail. To get there, take a left instead of a right and after 1.5km a sign will appear, indicating the campground down and to the right.

From Choquequirao return the same way back to Yanama and from there to Huancancalle. Alternatively, you could go on to Cusco using the traditional route via Cachora, described in Route 32.

ROUTE 35
Huancancalle to St. Theresa via Yanama

Start	Huancancalle (2950m)
Finish	St. Theresa (1580m)
Distance	87km
Total ascent	2830m
Total descent	4200m
Difficulty	High due to length and altitude of passes
Time	4–6 days hiking
Trail type	Incan road, mountain trail, dirt road
High point	4650m (Abra Choquetecarpo)
Hike or bike?	hike
Agency/guide?	no

Hike to Machu Picchu without a guide or fee. This route goes up and over the spectacular Inca-paved pass of Choquetecarpo and onwards to the gorgeous Andean mountain village of Yanama, then down to St. Theresa. From there it is just a few hours of walking along the railroad tracks to Agua Calientes and Machu Picchu. Hiring horses or mules to carry gear is highly advisable – this is a long and remote trek and there are very few services or places to buy food along the way. This route is not recommended for biking.

Follow the directions from **Huancancalle** to **Yanama** as detailed in Route 34.

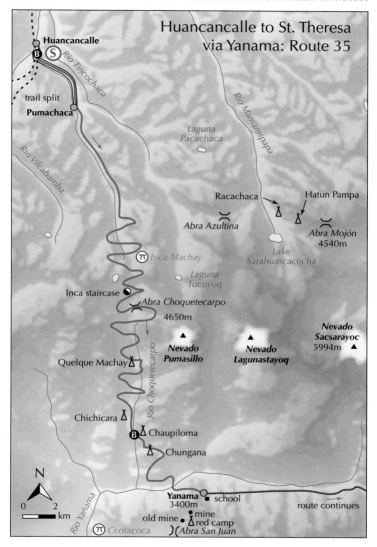

Huancancalle to St. Theresa
via Yanama: Route 35

Huancancalle

Río Tincochaca

trail split

Pumachaca

Río Vilcabamba

Río Mamanspapa

Laguna
Pacachaca

Racachaca

Hatun Pampa

Abra Azultina

Abra Mojón
4540m

Inca Machay

Lake
Sarahuascacocha

Laguna
Tucuyoq

Inca staircase

Abra Choquetecarpo
4650m

Nevado
Sacsarayoc
5994m

Nevado
Pumasillo

Nevado
Lagunastayoq

Río Choquetecarpo

Quelque Machay

Chichicara

Chaupiloma

Chungana

N

0   2
km

Río Yanama

Yanama
3400m

school

route continues

old mine

mine
red camp

Ccotacoca

Abra San Juan

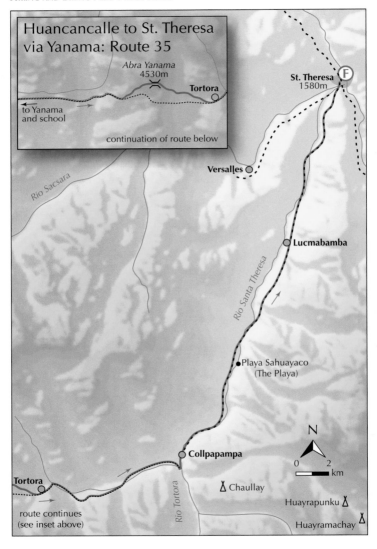

Huancancalle to St. Theresa
via Yanama: Route 35

Abra Yanama
4530m

Tortora

to Yanama
and school

continuation of route below

St. Theresa
1580m
Ⓕ

Rio Sacsara

Versalles

Lucmabamba

Rio Santa Theresa

● Playa Sahuayaco
(The Playa)

N

0   2
▬▬▬ km

Tortora

route continues
(see inset above)

Rio Tortora

Collpapampa

⛺ Chaullay

Huayrapunku ⛺

Huayramachay ⛺

Trekking above Yanama towards the pass

From Yanama, instead of going south towards Abra San Juan and Choquequirao, instead go east, directly up the scenic valley of Yanama 10km to the **Abra Yanama**, at 4530m. Cross the pass and begin descending down to **Tortora**, which is 6km below the pass. ▶ Seven kilometres below Tortora lies **Collpapampa**, an important intersection with the trail and river that comes down from the high pass over Mt. Salkantay, a popular route with trekkers. Another 7km down the trail is a small but growing village called La Playa.

In recent years a road has been bulldozed to here from down below, and it is now possible (perhaps preferable, given the traffic) to finish the last section down to **St. Theresa** in a taxi or combi. It is about 25km down the valley to St. Theresa. As described in Route 30, before arriving in St. Theresa the road passes by Lucmabamba, from where as an alternative route it is possible to hike up to the Incan site of Llactapata and then down to the hydroelectric station; or else from St. Theresa follow the directions given in Route 26 to Machu Picchu.

There are excellent views of Mt. Salkantay on this descent.

247

ROUTE 36
Huancancalle to St. Theresa via Abra Mojón

Start	Huancancalle (2950m)
Finish	St. Theresa (1580m)
Distance	40km
Total ascent	1800m
Total descent	2950m
Difficulty	Moderate
Time	3–5 days hiking
Trail type	Incan road, mountain trail
High point	4540m
Hike or bike?	hike
Agency/guide?	no

A shorter version of the previous trek, this is one of the shortest possible treks to Machu Picchu and thus is recommended if time is short. It features some outstanding scenery, including close views of the Pumasillo glacier as well as some isolated Incan ruins.

From **Huancancalle**, cross the bridge in front of Hostel SixPac and head south, up the main valley, up the Tincochaca River towards Choquetecarpo pass. Five kilometres up valley the trail splits – the correct way is to the left or east. The trail now climbs up the drainage of a smaller tributary of the Pumasillo glacier. There are some suitable places to camp here, and it is recommended to do so if it is getting late.

The first pass is **Abra Azultina**, which is 12km from Huancancalle. This is pretty impressive terrain and there are great views in all directions. The trail then drops down to the next valley and ascends to the small community of **Racachaca**, which is a nice place to camp. An even better choice is **Hatun Pampa** ('big plain'), 2km further up. From here, there is one more climb before finally reaching the pass of **Abra Mojón** at 4540m on the northern

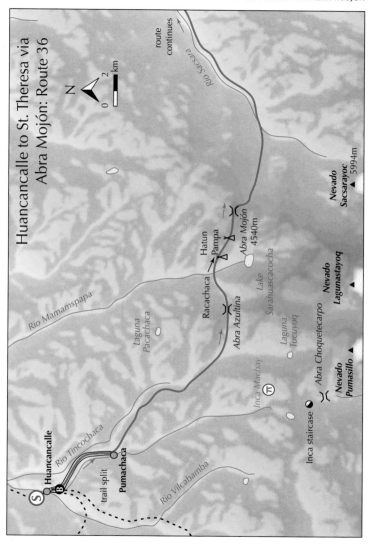

Huancancalle to St. Theresa via
Abra Mojón: Route 36

N

0   2
km

route
continues

Río Sacsara

Nevado
Sacsarayoc
▲ 5994m

Hatun
Pampa

Abra Mojón
4540m

Lake
Sarahuascacocha

Racachaca

Nevado
Lagunastayoq
▲

Abra Azultina

Laguna
Tucuyoq

Abra Choquetecarpo

Nevado
Pumasillo
▲

Río Mamamspapa

Laguna
Pacachaca

Inca Machay

Inca staircase

Huancancalle

Río Tincochaca

trail split   Pumachaca

Río Vilcabamba

S
B

249

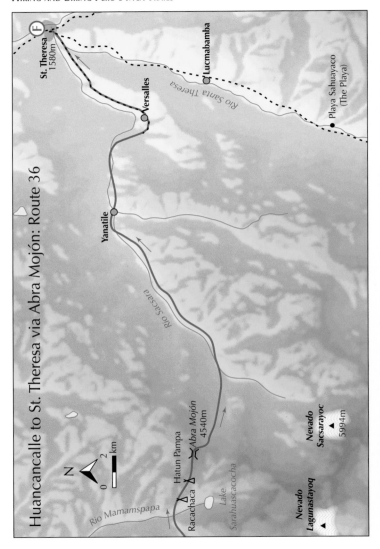

Huancancalle to St. Theresa via Abra Mojón: Route 36

St. Theresa 1580m

F

Versalles

Lucmabamba

Río Santa Theresa

Playa Sahuayaco (The Playa)

Yanatile

Río Sácsara

Abra Mojón 4540m

Hatun Pampa

Racachaca

Río Mamamspapa

N

0   2
km

Lake Sarahuascacocha

Nevado Saesarayoc 5994m

Nevado Lagunastayoq

Trekking a stretch of Inca road below Abra Mojón

edge of the Pumasillo glacier. There is also a nice mountain lake near the pass.

Cross the pass and descend down to the Sacsara River, which lies 5km below. Here is another good place to camp if it is late in the day. The next day, it is a 15km pleasant downhill walk, past **Yanatile** and into **St. Theresa**. There is now a road as far up valley as Yanatile, so this section of hiking is along a rough dirt road and there may be transport available down if you are tired. Just before entering St. Theresa the road passes by a zip-wire operation called Cola de Mono ('monkey's tail') that offers a thrilling ride above the canopy on a steel cable. For reservations contact info@canopyperu.com. From St. Theresa, follow the instructions as given in Route 26 to Aguas Calientes and Machu Picchu.

ROUTE 37
Mollepata to Choquequirao

Start	Mollepata (2800)
Finish	Choquequirao (3100m)
Distance	101km (one way)
Total ascent	6350m
Total descent	6050m
Difficulty	Moderate to difficult, due to length and remoteness
Time	5–8 days hiking, 4–6 days biking (one way)
Trail type	Mountain trail
High point	4750m (Abra Salkantay)
Hike or bike?	both
Agency/guide?	yes

This is a unique twist on two of the more popular treks in the area, the Salkantay trek and the trek that goes to Choquequirao. It goes from Mollepata up to the base of the 6270m Mt. Salkantay, before visiting the gorgeous, isolated mountain village of Yanama and then on to Choquequirao. This is an epic trek, in a direction that few tour groups go in. Expect amazing scenery on this route, paid for by a lot of climbing and descending along the way.

This route can be done on mountain bike but requires full mule support as well as a quality mountain bike that can handle this type of terrain – this is as big as it gets and very demanding both physically and logistically. Getting up the ascents will require a mule or porter to carry your bike and the descents are extremely technical and for experts only. Hiring an agency is highly recommended. Note that the time given above is only for getting to Choquequirao; from there add anywhere between 2 and 4 days depending on your exit strategy.

The trip begins in Mollepata, from which a new road has eliminated what was once a half a day's hike up to **Soraypampa**, where the real hiking or biking begins. Either public or private transport can be taken to arrive

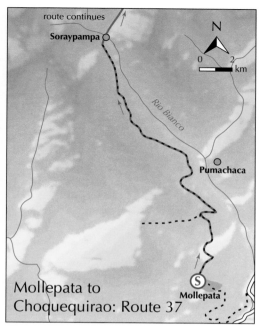

route continues

Soraypampa

N

0   2
km

Rio Bianco

Pumachaca

Mollepata to
Choquequirao: Route 37

S
Mollepata

to Mollepata, where there are generally taxis available to
take you on to Soraypampa. Supplies should be bought
in Cusco; however, there are small stores for last-minute
snacks in Mollepata. There are occasional small mountain *tiendas*, or stores, but they cannot be relied upon
and all food and means of treating water must be brought
along.

This route is a composite of several routes described
elsewhere in this book. The first section, Mollepata to
Collpapampa, is described in Route 30. Most Salkantay
trekkers turn down valley at Collpapampa and head
northeast down to St. Theresa to go to Machu Picchu.
This route, however, climbs up the to the head of the
Collpapampa valley and over the pass before descending
into the village of Yanama.

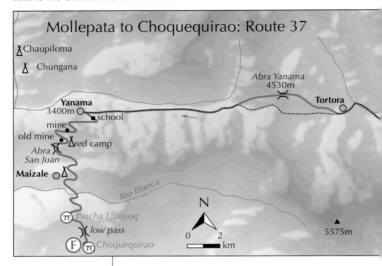

Mollepata to Choquequirao: Route 37

Chaupiloma

Chungana

Abra Yanama
4530m

Tortora

Yanama
3400m school

mine

old mine *red camp*

Abra
San Juan

Maizale

Rio Blanca

N

Pincha Unuyoq

low pass

Choquequirao

0   2 km

5575m

Horses or mules are a
common way to carry
the load in the high
Andes

Thus, 3km below **Chaullay**, and 1km before Collpapampa the trail briefly heads up into the quebrada of **Tortora**. Here there is an intersection, with trails leading to both the left and the right. The trail to the right goes down toward Collpapampa and St. Theresa. The trail

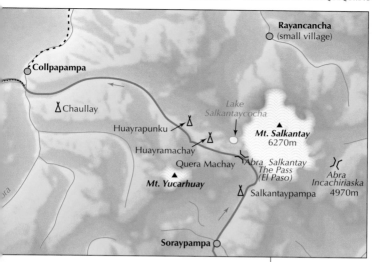

Rayancancha
(small village)

Collpapampa

Chaullay

Huayrapunku

Huayramachay

Quera Machay

Mt. Yucarhuay

Lake Salkantaycocha

Mt. Salkantay
6270m

Abra Salkantay
The Pass
(El Paso)

Salkantaypampa

Abra Incachiriaska
4970m

Soraypampa

to the left goes up to the pass, then down to **Yanama**. This route is described in detail in Route 35. Once in Yanama, there are trails to both Huancancalle as well as to Choquequirao (as described in Route 34) and on to Cachora, shown in Route 32).

Extreme mountain biking, a favourite sport of the locals

ROUTE 38
Huancancalle to Espiritu Pampa (Vilcabamba)

Start	Huancancalle (2950m)
Finish	Espiritu Pampa (1020m)
Distance	61km
Total ascent	1000m
Total descent	2930m
Difficulty	Moderate
Time	4–7 days hiking, depending on pace
Trail type	Incan road, mountain trail
High point	3860m
Hike or bike?	hike
Agency/guide?	yes

The classic trek to the famous Vilcabamba, 'Last City of the Incas', located deep into the edge of the Amazon jungle. It is also known as Espiritu Pampa or 'plains of the ghosts'. Rich in post-Conquest history, this hike encompasses many different climate and vegetative zones as well as several other archaeological sites along the way. As an added bonus the hike starts in Huancancalle, where the excellent Inca sites of Vitcos and Yurac Rumi are located. It is not possible to bike this route.

This trek is usually done one way, with transport becoming ever more available in Chuanquiri/San Miguel (another day's hike on from Espiritu Pampa to the road end) for the return to Ollantaytambo and Cusco. It is highly recommended to hire horses and a guide, and this can be easily arranged in Huancancalle with the Cobos family or with an agency in Cusco or Ollantaytambo. At the time of writing there are no services of any kind along the way. There is nowhere at all to buy sodas, snacks, or food so be sure to bring along everything you need. Although hiring transport in Chuanquiri is becoming easier, it is still sporadic and you may have to wait an entire day or even two before obtaining a ride. If time is of importance, it would be better to prearrange to have a private taxi waiting. If going on an organized tour, this will all be taken care of ahead of time.

Up until just a few years ago, there weren't any options for leaving **Huancancalle**, save for walking up the trail that went up to the pass. The trail has since been made into a road, however, and in fact has recently been extended up over the pass and down the other side. The ascent from Huancancalle to the pass of Collpacasa is 10km or about 8km if you take the various footpaths that cut off long sections of switchbacks in the road. Some groups have even begun to start the trek at the Collpacasa pass itself, driving up from Huancancalle.

There is a small Inca mirador, or lookout post, located at the top of the **Abra Collpacasa**. It has outstanding sight lines in all directions, but particularly southwest towards Machu Picchu and Choquequirao. This pass was a very important and strategic checkpoint in the Inca empire. It was

Trekkers enjoying the views near Abra Collpaccasa

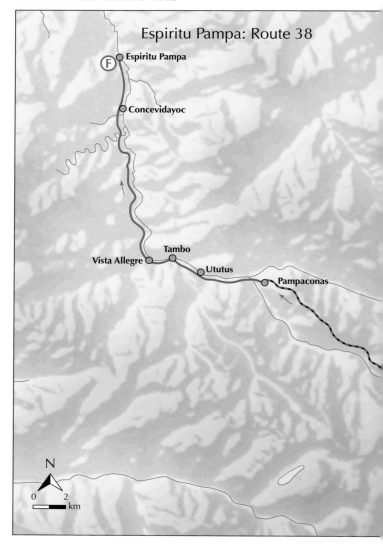

Espiritu Pampa: Route 38

F — Espiritu Pampa

Concevidayoc

Tambo

Vista Allegre — Ututus

Pampaconas

N

0   2
├────┤ km

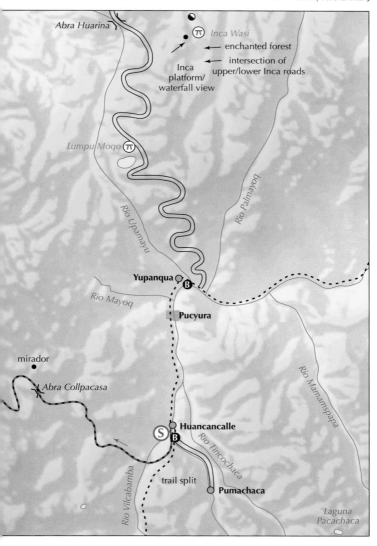

Abra Huarina

Inca Wasi

← enchanted forest

← intersection of upper/lower Inca roads

Inca platform/ waterfall view

Lumpu Moqo

Rio Uphupumayo

Rio Palmayoq

Yupanqua

Rio Mayoq

Pucyura

mirador

Abra Collpacasa

Rio Mamanspapa

Huancancalle

Rio Tincochaca

Rio Vilcabamba

trail split

Pumachaca

Laguna Pacachaca

one of the main routes down into the jungle, from where the Inca royalty used to frequently import exotic fruits for their dining table in Cusco and Ollantaytambo.

On a clear and sunny day, the 360° view from the pass is impressive and the place has a joyful feel. In times of bad weather, however, it can be another matter altogether. Be sure to have a wind jacket and hat with you, as well as a sturdy rain jacket or poncho.

Begin descending down the road from the pass. There are a few footpaths that lead down and to the right that will eventually lead to the same trail further down the canyon, but the route finding is tricky and it is better to stay on the road itself. ◀ There are a few stone houses off to the right in the valley, and there is overall a sense of peace and quiet that is somewhat rare for Peru, even in the mountains. A few more kilometres further downhill, the route emerges into the confluence of two giant valleys, the one you came down from the pass and another coming in from the left. This area is known by the name of the river that enters it from the east, the Río Challcha. The road sweeps broadly to the left here to **Pampaconas**, heading up the valley a bit in order to cross it before coming back around to the main valley of Concevidayoc. Again, there are numerous footpaths here that continue straight and downward, and it may be tempting to take them in order to cut off the detour to the left. Better to resist the temptation, as the trails below are very overgrown and full of thorns and most of them end at small farms and pastures.

Take the road to the left. Depending on the time of year the river that separates the road from the other side may be low or quite strong and it is best to continue ahead to the Mancachaca bridge. The altitude here is about 3300m and this is a good place for camping. Otherwise, cross the bridge and stay high and to the left as the road rejoins the main valley. The trail arrives at and crosses a large field called Muyoc before plunging into

The road only goes a few kilometres before degrading to a 4WD trail.

the underbrush. The route finding here is a bit tricky: the point to remember is to maintain a high position on the ridge line and not drop down and to the right towards the river.

Three kilometres after the bridge is the community of **Ututus**, located at 2900m above sea level. An excellent place to spend the night, there is a small lodge here that was constructed in the new spirit of eco-tourism, an attempt to provide a mutually respectful and beneficial relationship between the locals and the visitors. If nothing else, it serves as a landmark to mark progress along the trail. There are not many campsites along the trail from this point forward, so if it is late in the day it is best to camp here.

After Ututus, the narrow trail crosses over the Río Concevidayoc to the north side of the river and plunges into the undergrowth. Here, the trail becomes a bit more like what you imagine when thinking of trekking to an Inca site in Peru. The roads and houses have disappeared

On the trail to Espiritu Pampa, just above Ututus

There also large sections of intact Inca road here, including a few different staircases.

and it is now just you, the trail, and the thorns and mud. Actually, it is quite beautiful and this stretch has some of the best plant and vegetation viewing of the route, with moss and ferns growing everywhere as the trail continues downward. ◄ The trail continues downward to Cedrochaca ('cedar bridge' in Quechua) and re-crosses the Río Concevidayoc to its south side. Here the trail begins to climb up the ridge line steeply for about 1hr, until having come 3km from Ututus you arrive at the small community called **Tambo**.

> **Tambo** at first glance appears to contain no more than two or three small huts but, as is often the case in Peru, there is more to it than initially meets the eye, and there are quite a few houses hidden in the surrounding mountains. The views from here are spectacular, and you can finally see more than just a few feet down the trail, as the route opens up to the valleys ahead. It was here that Vincent Lee discovered and confirmed the location of Huayna Pucara ('old fort' in Quechua), which was described in several of the conquistador accounts of the conquest and subsequent Inca rebellion.

Four river valleys converge just a bit further downstream, including the Río Zapatero, and they all are visible from here. Continue on a few kilometres to T'oko Machay, meaning 'place with a hole' in Quechua. This is another good place to camp depending on the time of day – be sure to ask permission first if anyone is about.

The next good place to camp is 2km further downstream, at **Vista Allegre** (meaning 'happy viewpoint'). Here, there is a small community school and a few houses along with a good-sized field and water source. No donation is needed to camp here, but remember to practice no-trace camping ethics. The trail resumes in the dense underbrush 2km to a small clearing called San Guillermo. Your arriero may try to suggest this as a camping place, but it is not ideal – it is less than ten square metres of flat rocky ground in the middle of the dense forest and there is no water nearby. Instead, camp in Vista Allegre if it is getting late. It is about 5hrs over 7km from Ututus to Vista Allegre, walking briskly without stopping.

From here the trail continues onward. The terrain is rocky and steep, and any remaining image you may have about the 'descent' to Espiritu Pampa is quickly dispelled as the trail winds both up and down equally, in a long series of morale-challenging ravine crossings. The trail is often wet here even during the dry season, and during the rainy season it is every bit as muddy and difficult as advertised. Use caution and continue onward. Eventually, after gaining the ridge line the trail makes its final approach to the village of **Concevidayoc**, which is located at an altitude of 1495m and is 6–7hrs of walking time from Vista Allegre. ▶ From here it is 3km further to Espiritu Pampa, or about 2hrs 30mins of walking (16km from Vista Allegre).

Concevidayoc is a common campsite depending on the time of day.

Before reaching the ruins of **Vilcabamba** themselves, there is the grand entrance approach so common to Inca sites. You arrive first at a small clearing with a commanding view over the surrounding area. Here is the first obvious sign of the importance of this site, as there is a sizeable Inca

Traversing a trail section washed out by a landslide

mirador and a well-built and preserved set of stairs leading away from it towards the east. These stairs are really impressive in their size and scope, continuing downward seemingly forever on a broad swath of laid stones.

The end of the trek is, alas, a bit anticlimactic as without warning the trail wanes and you arrive at the tiny hamlet of **Espiritu Pampa**. This is currently the only place to camp in the area, and is still a kilometre or two from the actual site of the Inca city. There is a small field in which to camp, although it will have to be shared with the endless number of chickens, goats, horses, cows and other animals that use it as their pasture. Do not leave any food out as the chickens and pigs will find it quickly, and eat it all even quicker. This is not the most attractive village you will have camped in during the trek, but remember that long before this was a tourist attraction, families were living their normal lives here for generations.

Espiritu Pampa was found by Hiram Bingham during his astounding series of discoveries in the summer of 1911, but he brushed it off as a minor site and it was Gene Savoy, the legendary and flamboyant explorer, who should be given the credit as having realized and proven that this was the final city of the Incas as described by Titu Cusi in his memoirs. The ruins are a short walk further up the path from the village and are in the process of being restored and managed by the INC. At this time there is no charge to enter the ruins themselves, which are spectacular. As is so often the story these days, they are being uncovered and restored and the site is likely to grow even larger as the underbrush is removed.

After visiting the site, it is another full day to continue walking down to Azulmayo, to where the road from Chuanquiri now extends and it is possible to find transport down to Chaunquiri/San Miguel, and from there onwards to Quillabamba and Ollantaytambo.

6 AUSANGATE

The author gliding down an Ausangate singletrack (Route 39)

INTRODUCTION

Ausangate single track

Mt. Ausangate is the highest mountain in the Cusco region, at over 6300m, or just under 21,000ft. It anchors the Cordillera Vilcanota range and its massive glacier provides water for the region's inhabitants. It is also home to many herds of alpacas and llamas. The glacial ice and the lakes created from the its glacier are all a bright, turquoise which contrasts strikingly with the stark white of the glacier itself – some of the most dramatic landscape photography in Peru is taken here.

The trekking here is world class. Despite its proximity to Machu Picchu (during the clear winter months of May to October it dominates the skyline horizon of Cusco), it is little visited. This is perhaps because of its remoteness, although the recent paving of the access road has made the trip much easier than in the past. The only village of any size is Tinqui, which is a very basic Andean village

with no hostels or restaurants at the time of writing. There is cellular coverage but there are no internet cafés, and English is not spoken here. The villagers that live in this region work primarily in agriculture and llama breeding, and make up one of the world's few traditionally pastoral societies. They take pride in their heritage and the land that they live in, and there also many shamans practising here. Every year around the time of Corpus Christi a very famous religious ceremony called Qoyllur R'iti ('snow star', in Quechua) takes place on the northern side of the mountain.

You could trek round the entire mountain in seven to ten days but that trek is not described here. More accessible for those with limited time are these two routes, Route 39 and Route 40, on the southern side of the mountain. Both pass through areas of outstanding beauty.

ROUTE 39
Tinqui to Pitumarca via Ausangate

Start	Tinqui (3900m)
Finish	Pitumarca (3570m)
Distance	57km
Total ascent	1000m
Total descent	1330m
Difficulty	Moderate, due to high altitude
Time	3 days hiking, 2 days biking
Trail type	High alpine trail
High point	4590m (Abra Arapa)
Hike or bike?	both
Agency/guide?	no

Camping at the foot of the monstrous 6370m high Ausangate glacier while soaking in a hot spring – it doesn't get much better than this! There are many options for trekking Ausangate; this one is a shorter version than most of the others and is ideal if you are short on time. The scenery is truly epic, with the enormous glacier dominating the sky while the locals continue their lifestyle much the same as they have for centuries. This region holds some of the most beautiful glacial scenery in Peru. It is also remote and very rugged traveling, so take care to be completely prepared. The route is smooth in many places, but quite rocky in others and is a real expedition.

Vehicle transport must be taken up from Cusco to the town of Tinqui. The road has been significantly improved in recent years and is not the bone jarring ascent it used to be. The first destination is the town of Ocongate, where basic last-minute supplies can be found. Seventeen kilometres up the road lies Tinqui, a high-altitude Andean village with the windswept bleakness reminiscent of a western movie. This is the last chance to buy anything before beginning the trek (there are some small stores here selling basic supplies) and there is even a chance of rounding up a last-minute horse team if you haven't prearranged it.

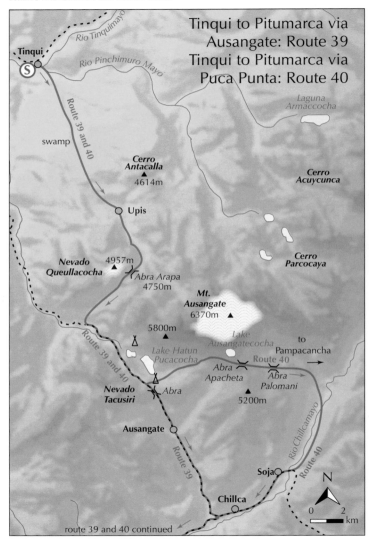

Tinqui to Pitumarca via
Ausangate: Route 39
Tinqui to Pitumarca via
Puca Punta: Route 40

Rio Tinquimayo

Tinqui

S

Rio Pinchimuro Mayo

Route 39 and 40

swamp

*Laguna
Armaccocha*

**Cerro
Antacalla**
▲
4614m

**Cerro
Acuycunca**

Upis

**Nevado
Queullacocha** ▲ 4957m

Abra Arapa
4750m

**Cerro
Parcocaya**

*Mt.
Ausangate*
6370m ▲

5800m ▲

*Lake
Ausangatecocha*

to
Pampacancha

Route 40

Route 39 and 40

*Lake Hatun
Pucacocha*

*Abra
Apacheta*

*Abra
Palomani*

**Nevado
Tacusiri**

Abra

5200m ▲

Ausangate

Route 39

Rio Chillcamayo

Soja

Route 40

Chillca

N

0   2
━━━━━
km

route 39 and 40 continued

Riding with the local kids at the base of Mt. Ausangate

From **Tinqui** the trail up to Upis lies just outside of town 0.5km on the right-hand side. ▶ There is a crude road being formed on the trail itself, and it seems likely that in the future the locals will build a more formal road up further towards Upis. Currently the road goes only 1–2km up from Tinqui before reducing to a foot trail. Upis is 17km up from Tinqui and it takes 5–6hrs to walk there. There are a few small hot springs lying just metres away from the icy cold river descending from the ice of the Ausangate glacier.

About 12km up from Tinqui, before reaching Upis, is a massive round **swamp**. It is tempting to just cross it, as particularly in the dry season it looks quite harmless. It is in fact wet nearly all year long and can be extremely swampy after any rains. Much better is to take the trail is on the left of it, curving around the high, northern side of the swamp. Keep walking on this side, until after 2km the trail returns to the valley floor again, but here it is much drier and suitable for walking. The trail is right in the centre of this narrow valley and ascends to **Upis**. The

In clear weather, the glacier of Mt. Ausangate can be seen in the distance.

269

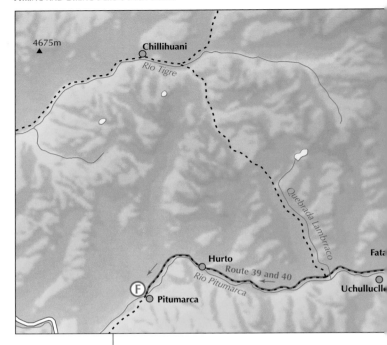

hot springs are marked with a small sign and are located on the southern side of the valley, off to the right. The views from the hot spring are as fine as anywhere in the world – enjoy!

The trail continues climbing after leaving Upis, and very soon begins veering to the right and starts to gradually climb up the western ridge line. The terrain becomes noticeably rockier as the trail winds upwards. The pass that needs to be crossed can be seen ahead, in the middle of the rugged orange and red rocks. The views of Ausangate just get better and better and the walking here is surprisingly easy, considering the altitude and the fact that the pass is approaching. The pass is called **Abra Arapa**, and is a small one that lies on the narrow spit

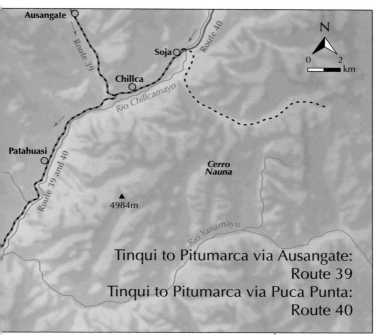

**Tinqui to Pitumarca via Ausangate:
Route 39
Tinqui to Pitumarca via Puca Punta:
Route 40**

of land between the northwestern shoulder of Ausangate and Mt. Quellacocha on the right. The terrain here is awesome, having sort of a moon-like feel to it, given the huge, barren red and grey landscape. ▸

After crossing the pass the trail descends pleasantly down this unique terrain towards a small glacial lake. The water seems to shine electric blue as the trail winds down right to the shore, where it goes past a small waterfall then traverses the right-hand (western) side of the lake before beginning a gentle climb into a giant bowl-shaped valley just below the Ausangate glacier. The trail enters the bowl on the right-hand side, then makes a sharp eastern turn and heads over the ridge towards the glacier.

This trail is a favourite of some of the local mountain bikers in the Sacred Valley, because it is fast and smooth despite the high altitude.

271

Everything here is so big in scale, you feel quite small picking along the trail with all the mountains looming overhead. Spectacular views in all directions are a real reward for the energy expended in getting here. There is ample camping anywhere in the **Ausangate valley**. In recent years the local farmers have begun charging a fee to camp in, or even pass through, this valley. Be sure to, as always, treat the locals and area customs with respect.

The area is very remote, so if a local asks you to pay it is quite likely that you are crossing their ancestral lands. A small fee of a few soles per tent and horse may be requested and you should be prepared to pay it. While it may seem a bit of a stretch of their land rights to lay claim to this wild and barren high-altitude land and charge you to walk through it, that is essentially what has happened. One sole per horse and five soles per tent is the current price. That is perhaps reasonable, but be careful not to pay more.

There are a few small glacial lakes suitable for camping as well as the larger **Lake Hatun Pucacocha**, which means 'big red lake' in Quechua. This area is a scenic camping spot. From here, the trail can clearly be seen going over the pass directly south of camp and away from the glacier of Ausangate. There is another route that goes over to Chillca, over two more passes – Abra Apacheta and Abra Palomani. The route described here, however, takes a different route to arrive at the same place, so ascend the pass above the camp. This climb takes 2–3hrs of brisk walking so it is not advised to attempt it late in the day. The pass above does not have a common name and is quite windy and cold, and there is no shelter of any kind until several kilometres below. The brisk temperatures are more than compensated for by the stupendous views from this pass, and the southern face of the Ausangate glacier feels mere metres away, so large does it loom. Below you to the south lies a huge canyon running of the slope of Mt. Tacusiri, which lies off to the west on the right-hand side. This is one of the more stunning mountain bike descents in the Sacred Valley of Peru, and it is so beautiful it is equally stunning while hiking. Continue down the canyon in a southeasterly direction as the trail descends down into the quebrada past several drainages and then the small village of **Ausangate** which lies 7km below the pass. This is a good place to camp.

It takes 2–3hrs to walk from the pass down to Ausangate, which is just a small collection of houses but, alas, no tiendas. From here, it is another 8km of trail and 3hrs more of walking to reach the intersection of the Chillcamayo River. Depending on the time of the day, any suitable spot along the section from Ausangate down to the river intersection would be a good place to camp. Despite the fact there is a road up to Chillca, if arriving there late in the day getting to Ollantaytambo or Cusco is not going to be possible anyway. So better to spend a pleasant night camping by the river above the junction rather than in some family's back yard or compost pile down in Uchullucllo.

The town of **Chillca** is just a few kilometres up this road to the north, and from there the route goes up to meet the two passes this route bypassed – that of the Apacheta and Palomani, before going on to completely circumnavigate the Ausangate glacier, or go off to the east and the huge glacial lake of Laguna Sibinacocha. Instead, this route goes downstream towards Pitumarca. There is a road up to this point, so if you are biking it is a rather pleasant descent the entire way down to Checacupe. From the junction down to the small town of **Uchullucllo** is 10km, which takes 3–4hrs walking downhill, past the small village of Patahuasi. From Uchullucllo it is a further 11km to **Pitumarca**, which will take just under 4hrs. There are many small villages lining the road virtually the whole way from Uchullucllo, so finding a soft drink or even the cold beer that you so deserve should not be too difficult. Certainly, you can reward yourself when you arrive to Pitumarca – there is a very pleasant little plaza to relax in after a long trek. It is an interesting town with an old colonial church and a laid-back feel to it.

The pre-Incan site of Pitumarca, at the base of Mt. Salkantay

If there is time in the day a visit to the ruins of Pitumarca is highly recommended. It is a 40min climb up by bike, otherwise it is best to hire a taxi in the square who would be willing to go up there for around 30 soles round trip or so. The ruins are classic pre-Inca and reminiscent of Pumamarca near Ollantaytambo. It is a fun place to walk around or maybe have a picnic lunch, and it is highly unlikely any other travellers will be there. Return to town the same way.

If you have biked the trail from Tinqui then there are still quite a few kilometres of riding down the mountain left. If trekking this route, here in Pitumarca is the place to catch a ride down the mountain to Checacupe, which lies on the main Cusco–Puno highway. Once on the main highway, there is a fairly constant stream of passing buses and taxis bound for Cusco so finding a ride won't be much of a problem. Be warned though: once it gets dark, the likelihood of passing traffic stopping to pick you up goes down significantly. Try to arrive here before late afternoon, and sit back and relax for the 2hr drive to Cusco – you earned it!

ROUTE 40
Tinqui to Pitumarca via Puca Punta

Start	Tinqui (3900m)
Finish	Pitumarca (3570m)
Distance	68km
Total ascent	1230m
Total descent	1560m
Difficulty	Moderate to strenuous
Time	3–4 days hiking
Trail type	Rugged dirt roads and high alpine trails
High point	4150m
Hike or bike?	hike
Agency/guide?	recommended
Route map	see Route 39

A variation on the trek described in Route 39, this trail crosses the same pass of Abra Arapa but then makes another ascent up and over a pass rejoining Route 39 after the high mountain village of Chillca. From there a trail/road descends down to meet up with the standard trail from Upis, and then continues downward to Pitumarca and then Checacupe. The entire route is very beautiful and classic high Andes trekking, right at the base of the giant glacier of Ausangate. It is not recommended for biking.

Follow the directions in Route 39 to arrive at Upis, then over the pass of Abra Arapa and finally the lake of Hatun Pucacocha. Here the two routes separate. For this route, leave the lake of Hatun Pucacocha and head directly east on the foot trail that leaves from the lake. The trail climbs up, but very gradually, to the lake of **Ausangatecocha**. From here, continue eastward, ascending the small mountainside to the pass that lies directly ahead, called **Abra Apacheta**. There is a nice trail here and the walking is pleasant, particularly because the enormous glacier of Ausangate looms over the entire trail and is constantly in view.

After the Abra Apacheta, there is a short descent and then ascent to a second pass called **Abra Palomani**. From

this pass, the path can be seen leading down to the next stop, the tiny hamlet of Pampacancha, which is nothing more than a collection of a few houses. However, it is a good place to camp, as is the large area below it, which is called Hatun Pampa.

From here, the route begins descending the huge southern flank of Mt. Ausangate, where after 5km the valley meets another one coming in from the east called Killimita ('little moon' in bad and spanish-ized Quechua). There is good camping here as well as a small store selling supplies. Continue down the mountain for 4.5km of easy walking until finally reaching **Chillca**. There is a road up to Chillca, so the village is growing pretty fast but is still a very pretty place and there are also places to pick up any supplies or, more likely, a beer or soda would probably hit the spot after trekking for several days.

From Chillca, the road goes down to **Pitumarca**, and on to Checacupe, as described in Route 39.

APPENDIX A

Route summary table

No	Start	Finish	Distance	Time (Hike)	Time (Bike)	Difficulty (Hike)	Difficulty (Bike)	Agency/ Guide	Page
1	Aguas Calientes (2040m)	Machu Picchu (2480m)	6km (7km with Huayana Picchu)	2hrs (4–5hrs with Huayana Picchu)	–	moderate to strenuous	–	no	69
2	Pisca Cucho (2700m)	Machu Picchu (2480m)	46km	4 days	–	moderate to strenuous	–	required	73
3	Tambo Machay, just above Cusco (3810m)	Calca (2960m)	25km	1–2 days	1 day	moderate	moderate	no	86
4	Huarocondo (3330m)	Ollantaytambo (2850m)	28km	1 day	half day	moderate	easy	no	90
5	Chinchero (3750m)	Urubamba (2880)	21km (or 10km)	2–3hrs	1–2hrs	easy	moderate	no	94
6	Chinchero (3750m)	Huayllabamba (2910m)	11km	3–4hrs	2–3hrs	moderate	difficult	no	97
7	Moray (3560m)	Pinchingoto (2890m)	14km	3–4hrs	2–3hrs	easy	moderate	no	102
8	Moray (3560m)	Paucarbamba	11km	2hrs	1hr	easy	advanced	no	107
9	Abra Azulcocha (4450m)	Calca (2960m)	26km	4–6hrs	2–3hrs	easy	moderate– difficult	no	110
10	Calca (2960m)	Lares (3200m)	49km	2 days (3–4hrs from Abra Azulcocha)	4–7hrs (1–2hrs from Abra Azulcocha)	easy to moderate	easy to moderate	no	114

No	Start	Finish	Distance	Time (Hike)	Time (Bike)	Difficulty (Hike)	Difficulty (Bike)	Agency/Guide	Page
11	Urubamba (2880m)	Urubamba (2880m)	32km round trip	2 days	—	very strenuous	—	yes (summit)	117
12	Urubamba (2880m)	Lares (3200m)	24km	9–12hrs	—	strenuous	—	no	121
13	Ollantaytambo (2850m)	Ollantaytambo (2850m)	14km	3–4hrs	2–3hrs	easy to moderate	easy to moderate	yes	131
14	Ollantaytambo (2850m)	Ollantaytambo (2850m)	26km	1 day (or overnight)	—	easy to moderate	—	no	134
15	Yanahuara (2870m)	Lares (3200m)	28km	2 days	2 days	moderate	difficult	no	136
16	Ollantaytambo (2850m) or Patacancha (3650m)	Lares (3200m)	38km from Ollantaytambo; 19km from Patacancha	2 days	2 days	moderate	difficult	no	141
17	Abra Yanamayu (4440m) or Patacancha (3650m)	Lares (3200m)	45km from Abra Yanamayu, 54km from Patacancha	2–3 days	2–3 days	moderate	difficult	no	145
18	Ollantaytambo (2850m)	Ollantaytambo (2850m)	46km from Ollantaytambo, 32km from Pachar	6–8hrs from Pachar	5–7hrs	moderate	moderate to difficult	no	150
19	Ollantaytambo (2850m)	Ollantaytambo (2850m)	24km round trip or 10km from Pachar	5–7hrs	3–5hrs	easy	easy to moderate	no	155

No	Start	Finish	Distance	Time (Hike)	Time (Bike)	Difficulty (Hike)	Difficulty (Bike)	Agency/ Guide	Page
20	Ollantaytambo (2850m)	Ollantaytambo (2850m)	16km	6-8hrs	–	strenuous	–	no	158
21	Pisca Cucho (2700m)	Pisca Cucho (2700m)	12km	3 days +		strenuous	–	yes (summit)	162
22	Tastallyoq (3860m)	Ollantaytambo (2850m)	29km	6-7hrs	5-6hrs	moderate	moderate	no	166
23	Ollantaytambo (2850m)	Quillabamba (1060m)	380km	–	3-6 days by bike or motorcycle	–	moderate	recommended	169
24	Ollantaytambo (2850m)	Quillabamba (1060m)	142km	–	6hrs bicycle; 3hrs motorcycle	–	easy to moderate	no	177
25	Ollantaytambo (2850m)	Ivochote (800m)	265km	–	4-7 days depending on mode of transport	–	easy	no	184
26	Ollantaytambo (2850m)	Aguas Calientes (2040m)	155km	–	1-3 days depending on mode of transport	easy to moderate	easy to moderate	no	191
27	Ollantaytambo (2850m)	Huayllabamba (3000m)	50km	2-3 days	–	moderate to strenuous	–	no	197
28	Ollantaytambo (2850m)	Soraypampa (3750m)	64km	4-5 days	–	moderate to strenuous	–	yes	203
29	Mollepata (2800m)	Huayllabamba (3000m)	52km	3-4 days	2-3 days	strenuous	strenuous	no	211
30	Soraypampa (3750m)	Aguas Calientes (2040m)	66km	3-4 days	2-3 days	strenuous	strenuous & difficult	no	214

No	Start	Finish	Distance	Time (Hike)	Time (Bike)	Difficulty (Hike)	Difficulty (Bike)	Agency/ Guide	Page
31	Soraypampa (3750m)	Aguas Calientes (2040m)	55km	3–4 days	–	severe	–	yes	221
32	Cachora (2920m)	Cachora (2920m)	64km	4–5 days	–	very strenuous	–	recommended	224
33	Yupanqua (2850m)	Yupanqua (2850m)	26km	1–3 days	–	moderate	–	recommended	230
34	Huancancalle (2950m)	Choquequirao (3100m)	71km	6–9 days	–	strenuous	–	yes	234
35	Huancancalle (2950m)	St. Theresa (1580m)	87km	4–6 days	–	difficult	–	no	244
36	Huancancalle (2950m)	St. Theresa (1580m)	40km	3–5 days	–	moderate	–	no	248
37	Mollepata (2800m)	Choquequirao (3100m)	101km	5–8 days	4–6 days	moderate	moderate	yes	252
38	Huancancalle (2950m)	Espiritu Pampa (1020m)	61km	4–7 days	–	moderate	–	yes	256
39	Tinqui (3900m)	Pitumarca (3570m)	57km	3 days	2 days	moderate	moderate	no	267
40	Tinqui (3900m)	Pitumarca (3570m)	68km	3–4 days	–	moderate to strenuous	–	recommended	275

APPENDIX B
Glossary of Spanish and Quechan words

abra	mountain pass
adobe	local building material made up of mud mixed with straw
aji	hot Peruvian pepper
alpaca	type of llama, known for its wool
altiplano	high mountain plateau
andene	Inca terrace, usually for agricultural purposes
anticucho	popular Peruvian street food, beef heart kebabs
apachita	rock cairn built to mark mountain pass and for good luck
apu	Quechuan name for the local mountain gods
arriero	muleteer
baños termales	hot baths/springs
calle	street
cambio	change, as in trading one currency for another
campesino	local farmer
cancha	football field, or small piece of land
ceja de la selva	high jungle (literally 'eyebrow of the jungle')
cerro	mountain, usually a non-glaciated one
cerveza	beer
ceviche	famous Peruvian dish of raw seafood marinated in lemon
chaca	bridge (Quecha)
chakra	small family farm, land holding
chasqui	Inca foot messenger (Quecha)
chicha	corn beer, a local favourite
chicharrone	fried pork rinds
chiri	cold (Quechua)
chullo	typical over the ear hat worn by the Andean mountain people (Quecha)
choclo	giant corn on the cob
Choquequirao	famous sister site to Machu Picchu
coca	native plant whose leaves are chewed for energy
collectivo	generic name for any shared public transport in Peru
cordillera	mountain range
Coya	sister-wife of the Inca king
cuy	guinea pig, a local delicacy
guanaco	relative of the alpaca, in the cameloid family

Huaca	sacred place to the Incas
huayno	Andean mountain music
huayna	young (Quechua)
inti	sun (Quechua)
llama	cameloid animal domesticated by the Incas
llipta	lime/potash mixture used in conjunction with coca leaf chewing
machay	place of (Quechua)
machu	old (Quechua)
manta	typical woven blanket used by locals as a backpack
mayu	river (Quecha)
mercado	market
mirador	lookout
nevado	snow-capped peak
Pacha mama	mother earth (Quechua)
pampa	high, flat open plain
parilla	barbeque
pisco	a type of brandy made with distilled grapes
puca	red (Quechua)
pucara	fort (Quechua)
pueblo	small town
puna	high Andean grasslands
quebrada	canyon
quinoa	high protein Andean grain
quipu	system of knotted strings used by the Incas to record information
raccay	place of (Quechua)
rio	river
rumi	stone (Quecha)
runasimi	word for the Quechuan language
selva	jungle
soroche	altitude sickness
tambo	rest house (Quechua)
tienda	store
vicuña	relative of the llama, known for its fine wool, but much more rare
Wiracocha	in Inca culture, a word for a race of tall, bearded white men prophesized to arrive in Peru

APPENDIX C
Useful contacts

Note that telephone numbers in Peru change very frequently. If you are having trouble with the numbers listed below ask for local assistance.

Health
Emergency numbers
Peru: SARA 84 229922
Cusco: 84 222600/984 708269
Sacred Valley: 84 205028/984 108958
Machu Picchu: 84 211221/984 108955

Hospitals
Regional: 84 223691/84 237661
Es Salud: 84 223030/84 237341
Clinica Pardo: 84 240997/84 249999

Consulates in Cusco
British: 84 239974
French: 84 233610
German: 84 235459
Italian: 84 228295
Spanish: 84 223031
United States: 84 245102

Police
Tourism Police (Cusco): 84 249665

In the mountain villages
Cacchin: 84 830143/84 812754
Chuanquiri: 84 812867
Huancancalle: 84 812714
Lares: 84 830009/84 812755
Pampaconas: 84 812870
Vilcabamba: 84 813800/84 813801
Yanama: 84 812575
Yupanqua: 84 830742/84 830741

Useful tourism/travel websites
www.andeantravelweb.com
www.machupicchuinformation.com

Bike rental and guides
Gravity Peru, 867 Calle Saphi, Cusco:
www.GravityPeru.com

Trekking agency
Ortiz Tours, Plaza San Francisco, Calle Garcilaso 244, Cusco:
www.OrtizTours.com

APPENDIX D
Further reading

Forgotten Vilcabamba: Final Stronghold of the Incas Vincent Lee (Six Pac Manco Publications, 2000)

The White Rock Hugh Thompson (Phoenix, 2002)

Apus and Incas Charles Brod (Inca Expeditions, 1989)

The Secret of the Incas William Sullivan (Crown Publications, 1998)

The Conquest of the Incas John Hemming (Pan, 2004)

Antisuyo Gene Savoy (Simon & Schuster, 1970)

The Shape of Inca History Susan A Niles (University of Iowa Press, 1999)

The Ancient Kingdoms of Peru Nigel Davies (Penguin, 1997)

Exploring Cusco Peter Frost (Nuevas Imágenes; 4th edition, 1989)

The Lost City of Z: A Tale of Deadly Obsession in the Amazon David Grann (Vintage Departures, 2010)

LISTING OF CICERONE GUIDES

EUROPEAN CYCLING
Cycle Touring in France
Cycle Touring in Ireland
Cycle Touring in Spain
Cycle Touring in
  Switzerland
Cycling in the French Alps
Cycling the Canal du Midi
Cycling the River Loire
The Danube Cycleway
The Grand Traverse of the
  Massif Central
The Rhine Cycle Route
The Way of St James

AFRICA
Climbing in the Moroccan
  Anti-Atlas
Kilimanjaro
Mountaineering in the
  Moroccan High Atlas
The High Atlas
Trekking in the Atlas
  Mountains
Walking in the
  Drakensberg

ALPS – CROSS-BORDER ROUTES
100 Hut Walks in the Alps
Across the Eastern Alps: E5
Alpine Points of View
Alpine Ski Mountaineering
  1 Western Alps
  2 Central and Eastern
    Alps
Chamonix to Zermatt
Snowshoeing
Tour of Mont Blanc
Tour of Monte Rosa
Tour of the Matterhorn
Trekking in the Alps
Walking in the Alps
Walks and Treks in the
  Maritime Alps

PYRENEES AND FRANCE/SPAIN CROSS-BORDER ROUTES
Rock Climbs in The
  Pyrenees
The GR10 Trail
The Mountains of Andorra
The Pyrenean Haute Route
The Pyrenees
The Way of St James
  France & Spain
Through the Spanish
  Pyrenees: GR11
Walks and Climbs in the
  Pyrenees

AUSTRIA
The Adlerweg
Trekking in Austria's Hohe
  Tauern
Trekking in the Stubai Alps
Trekking in the Zillertal
  Alps
Walking in Austria

EASTERN EUROPE
The High Tatras
The Mountains of Romania
Walking in Bulgaria's
  National Parks
Walking in Hungary

FRANCE
Chamonix Mountain
  Adventures
Ecrins National Park
GR20: Corsica
Mont Blanc Walks
Mountain Adventures in
  the Maurienne
The Cathar Way
The GR5 Trail
The Robert Louis Stevenson
  Trail
Tour of the Oisans: The
  GR54
Tour of the Queyras
Tour of the Vanoise
Trekking in the Vosges
  and Jura
Vanoise Ski Touring
Walking in the Auvergne
Walking in the Cathar
  Region
Walking in the Cevennes
Walking in the Dordogne
Walking in the Haute
  Savoie
  North & South
Walking in the Languedoc
Walking in the Tarentaise
  and Beaufortain Alps
Walking on Corsica

GERMANY
Germany's Romantic Road
Walking in the Bavarian
  Alps
Walking the River Rhine
  Trail

HIMALAYA
8000m
Annapurna
Bhutan: A Trekker's Guide
Everest: A Trekker's Guide
Garhwal and Kumaon: A
  Trekker's and Visitor's
  Guide
Kangchenjunga: A
  Trekker's Guide
Langtang with Gosainkund
  and Helambu: A
  Trekker's Guide
Manaslu: A Trekker's
  Guide
The Mount Kailash Trek
Trekking in Ladakh
Trekking in the Himalaya

ICELAND & GREENLAND
Trekking in Greenland
Walking and Trekking in
  Iceland

IRELAND
Irish Coastal Walks
The Irish Coast to Coast
  Walk
The Mountains of Ireland

ITALY
Gran Paradiso
Sibillini National Park
Stelvio National Park
Shorter Walks in the
  Dolomites
Through the Italian Alps
Trekking in the Apennines
Trekking in the Dolomites
Via Ferratas of the Italian
  Dolomites: Vols 1 & 2
Walking in Abruzzo
Walking in Stelvio National
  Park
Walking in Sardinia
Walking in Sicily
Walking in the Central
  Italian Alps
Walking in the Dolomites
Walking in Tuscany
Walking on the Amalfi
  Coast
Walking the Italian Lakes

MEDITERRANEAN
Jordan – Walks, Treks,
  Caves, Climbs and
  Canyons
The Ala Dag
The High Mountains
  of Crete
The Mountains of Greece
Treks and Climbs in Wadi
  Rum, Jordan
Walking in Malta
Western Crete

NORTH AMERICA
British Columbia
The Grand Canyon
The John Muir Trail
The Pacific Crest Trail

SOUTH AMERICA
Aconcagua and the
  Southern Andes
Hiking and Biking Peru's
  Inca Trails
Torres del Paine

SCANDINAVIA
Walking in Norway

SLOVENIA, CROATIA AND MONTENEGRO
The Julian Alps of Slovenia
The Mountains of
  Montenegro
Trekking in Slovenia
Walking in Croatia
Walking in Slovenia: The
  Karavanke

SPAIN AND PORTUGAL
Costa Blanca: West
Mountain Walking in
  Southern Catalunya
The Mountains of Central
  Spain
The Northern Caminos
Trekking through Mallorca
Walking in Madeira
Walking in Mallorca
Walking in the Algarve
Walking in the Cordillera
  Cantabrica
Walking in the Sierra
  Nevada
Walking on La Gomera and
  El Hierro
Walking on La Palma
Walking on Tenerife
Walking the GR7 in
  Andalucia
Walks and Climbs in the
  Picos de Europa

SWITZERLAND
Alpine Pass Route
Canyoning in the Alps
Central Switzerland
The Bernese Alps
The Swiss Alps
Tour of the Jungfrau Region
Walking in the Valais
Walking in Ticino
Walks in the Engadine

TECHNIQUES
Geocaching in the UK
Indoor Climbing
Lightweight Camping
Map and Compass
Mountain Weather
Moveable Feasts
Outdoor Photography
Polar Exploration
Rock Climbing
Sport Climbing
The Book of the Bivvy
The Hillwalker's Guide to
  Mountaineering
The Hillwalker's Manual

MINI GUIDES
Avalanche!
Navigating with a GPS
Navigation
Pocket First Aid and
  Wilderness Medicine
Snow

For full information
on all our guides, and
to order books and
eBooks online, visit
our website:
www.cicerone.co.uk.

Walking – Trekking – Mountaineering – Climbing – Cycling

Over 40 years, Cicerone have built up an outstanding collection of 300 guides, inspiring all sorts of amazing adventures.

 Every guide comes from extensive exploration and research by our expert authors, all with a passion for their subjects. They are frequently praised, endorsed and used by clubs, instructors and outdoor organisations.

All our titles can now be bought as **e-books** and many as iPad and Kindle files and we will continue to make all our guides available for these and many other devices.

Our website shows any **new information** we've received since a book was published. Please do let us know if you find anything has changed, so that we can pass on the latest details. On our **website** you'll also find some great ideas and lots of information, including sample chapters, contents lists, reviews, articles and a photo gallery.

It's easy to keep in touch with what's going on at Cicerone, by getting our monthly **free e-newsletter**, which is full of offers, competitions, up-to-date information and topical articles. You can subscribe on our home page and also follow us on **Facebook** and **Twitter**, as well as our **blog**.

Cicerone – the very best guides for exploring the world.

CICERONE

2 Police Square Milnthorpe Cumbria LA7 7PY
Tel: 015395 62069 info@cicerone.co.uk
www.cicerone.co.uk